AF147444

The March To Magdala

by

G. A. Henty

The March To Magdala
by G. A. Henty

ISBN: 978-93-59952-35-2

Published by

DOUBLE 9 BOOKS

2/13-B, Ansari Road
Daryaganj, New Delhi – 110002
info@double9books.com
www.double9books.com
Tel. 011-40042856

ABOUT THE AUTHOR

English author and war correspondent George Alfred Henty lived from 8 December 1832 to 16 November 1902. He is most well-known for his historical fiction and adventure books, including The Dragon & The Raven (1886), For The Temple (1888), Under Drake's Flag (1883), and in Freedom's Cause (1883). (1885). He was a British journalist who served as G. A. Henty's war correspondent. He was raised in Cambridge and finished his education there at Gonville and Caius College. He continued to cover important wars that followed, such as the Italian and Austro-Italian Wars. He wrote 122 books, most of which were geared toward young readers. He also wrote non-fiction, adult fiction, and short tales. In Henty's stories, the main character is a boy or young man who is going through a challenging situation. His characters are consistently low-key, astute, courageous, truthful, and resourceful with a lot of "pluck." The date was put at the bottom of the title page of each of Henty's 122 historical fiction works in their first printings.

CONTENTS

PREFACE

In submitting to the public in a collected form the Letters which have already appeared in the daily press, a Special Correspondent has the option of one of two courses. The one course is, to publish the Letters as nearly as possible as they originally stood, as a journal written from day to day, and from week to week; the other, to recast the whole, to rewrite the Letters, and to give a continuous narrative of the expedition as of a past event. The second of these courses has the advantage of unity of purpose; it will contain fewer errors, fewer mistaken predictions of the probable course of events, and, above all, less of the repetitions which must unavoidably occur in a series of letters. The style, too, will naturally be far smoother and more polished than in the original letters, written as they usually were in haste and under circumstances of great difficulty. But, on the other hand, such a narrative would lose much of the freshness which original letters possess, and it would be deficient in that interest which a knowledge of the hopes and fears, the doubts and anticipations, the plans destined to be frustrated, and the opinions constantly varying with the course of events, must give to a narrative. The present tense too is far more pleasant and less monotonous than the preterite. I have therefore determined, in submitting my Letters for republication, to adhere as closely as possible to the original form and matter; not hesitating, however, to make many additions, alterations, and excisions, where subsequent information or the course of events have proved my opinions or conclusions to have been erroneous.

The present work does not profess to be a scientific record of the expedition. It gives neither statistics, general orders, nor official documents. This will no doubt be hereafter done by some officer far better qualified for the task than I can be. It is merely the plain narrative of a looker-on, who accompanied the expedition from the commencement of December 1867, when affairs at Zulla were at their worst, to the closing scene at Magdala. At the same time, I have not shrunk from stating my own opinions as to the course of events. A great disaster like that of the complete break-down of the Transport-train at Zulla cannot occur without grievous blame attaching to somebody. I conceive it to be one of the first duties of a correspondent to state fearlessly the persons and the causes which, in his opinion, have brought on a great public disaster. Unpleasant, therefore, though it be to find fault, I have not hesitated to assign the blame where I consider it was due. This I did in the very first letter I wrote from Zulla after landing, before I had gone up to Senafe; and the opinion I then expressed, I now, after months have elapsed, and after hearing the matter discussed in every light, do not hesitate to reaffirm.

With the exceptions I have alluded to, the Letters are the same in form and substance as when they appeared in the columns of the *Standard*; and although, for the reasons I have given, I am convinced that it is the wisest course to leave them so, yet, remembering as I do the circumstances of haste, fatigue, and difficulty under which they were written, I cannot but feel extreme diffidence in submitting them to the public "with all their errors on their head."

G. A. H.

INTRODUCTORY CHAPTER

The Abyssinian expedition has, from the time it was first determined upon, attracted an amount of attention, not only in Great Britain but throughout the civilised world, altogether disproportionate to the strength of the army employed, or to the extent of the interests at stake. The total force engaged was under, rather than over, 10,000 men; not one-fifth the strength of an army which we might ourselves put into the field for a campaign in India; scarcely a fiftieth of the force at the command of either of the great Continental Powers. It was clearly not the magnitude of the expedition, then, which attracted attention: it was the extraordinary and novel circumstances under which it was undertaken; the almost insurmountable difficulties to be overcome; the unknown nature of the country to be traversed, and the romantic disinterestedness of the motives which led England to embark upon it, which has rendered it one of the most interesting and notable campaigns ever undertaken. Since the expedition of Pizarro and Cortes in the middle ages, no such novel and hazardous expedition is on record. The country itself was like that of the far-famed Prester John—everything about it smacked of the marvellous. It was more mountainous, more inaccessible, more war-loving, more wild than any other country in the world. The king with whom we waged war was a potentate who by his military talents had raised himself from a comparatively obscure position to the sovereignty of all Abyssinia: he was enlightened beyond his race; patronised strangers, encouraged manufactures, endeavoured in every way to improve the condition of his country, and was yet a bloodthirsty tyrant. The people themselves were a strange race, far more civilised than other African nations, Christians in the midst of a Mahometan and Pagan continent, a mixture of many races—African, Greek, Arab, and Jew. Altogether it was a land of romance. Nor had travellers done much to enlighten us as to the country. Some had described it as fertile in the extreme; others had spoken of it as a land of mountain and defile, where no sustenance could be hoped for for the army. They had united only in prophesying evil things—hunger and thirst, inaccessible mountain and pathless wastes, fever, cholera, small-pox, dysentery, the tetse-fly, tapeworm, and guinea-worm. We were to be consumed with fire; we were to be annihilated with stones rolled upon us when in ravines; we were to be cut off in detail upon our marches; we were to be harassed to death by repeated night and day attacks. All these and many other prophecies were freely uttered, and it really appeared as if our expedition was to partake strongly of the nature of a forlorn-hope. The friends of officers and men said good-bye to them as if they were going to certain death, and insurance-offices doubled and trebled the premium upon their lives. All this assisted to raise the public interest and anxiety to the highest point. It is needless now to say that almost the whole of the adverse predictions were entirely falsified, and that we have met with no difficulties whatever beyond mountain and ravine, the want of transport, and the scarcity of food.

Generally as the subject is known, it is yet necessary, before commencing the history of the campaign, to say a few words upon the events which preceded and caused it; and as the subject has been exhausted by Dr. Beke in his able work on the Abyssinian captives, I cannot do better than preface my story with a brief epitome of the facts recited in his volume. Dr. Beke was well-acquainted with Mr. Plowden, our late Consul there, and knew thoroughly the whole of the events which led to the captivity of the English party, and he was in intimate communication with their friends here. His statements are supported by numerous official documents; and this volume, in which he now sets forth the state of the case, may be apparently received with confidence as reliable in every particular.

The kingdom of Abyssinia is of extreme antiquity, and was once a great and flourishing empire. It has been ruled by a succession of monarchs claiming direct descent from Menilek, the son of King Solomon by the Queen of Sheba. For the last century the legitimate monarch has had very little power, the real authority being in the hands of the most powerful of the chiefs of the various tribes composing the empire, and who, as in turns they became dominant, assumed the title of ras or vizier, keeping the puppet emperor in a state of honourable captivity, administering affairs and carrying on wars without the slightest reference to his wishes and opinions. The kingdom of Abyssinia consists of an immense elevated plateau or table-land, of great fertility, and possessing a temperate and agreeable climate. At its north-eastern extremity it approaches very nearly to the sea, the port of Massowah at that point being its natural outlet. Towards the south the table-land trends away from the sea, being separated from it by a wide low-lying plain, inhabited by Mahometan tribes. The religion of the natives of Abyssinia itself has been from very early times Christian, and they possess a native version of the Scriptures which dates from the fourth century of the Christian era. The laws of this singular people are, like our own, founded upon the code of Justinian. The various tribes which form the empire, although acknowledging the supremacy of the emperor, are yet virtually independent, paying a mere nominal tribute, and making war upon and deposing him whenever they feel strong enough to do so. These tribes are very numerous, but the principal may be considered to be those inhabiting Tigre, which is the province nearest to Massowah, and therefore commanding the avenues of approach to the interior; Amhara, the capital, lying to the south of Tigre, Lasta in the centre, and Shoa, Godjam, and Kwara to the west. Of these Tigre is the representative of the ancient kingdom. It is almost entirely surrounded by the river Takkazye, which separates it from the rest of the empire; and its inhabitants speak the language of the ancient Ethiopic, in which is the early version of the Bible. Since the middle of the sixteenth century the Turks have claimed the entire seaboard, but have only occupied the Sawakin and Massowah.

In the year 1810 the English Government, alarmed at the attempts of the French to obtain a footing in Egypt, dispatched Mr. Salt, afterwards Consul-General in Egypt, to Abyssinia, to open friendly relations with that power; and that gentleman, being unable to penetrate beyond Tigre, the chief of which country was at the time the ras, or most powerful chief in the kingdom, delivered the letter from King George, and the accompanying presents, to that personage. Almost simultaneously, however, the power of the French in the Indian Ocean was annihilated, and a few years afterwards the fall of Napoleon relieving the British Government of all fear of French aggression in the East, the diplomatic relations between England and Tigre came to an end. A constant jealousy and struggle, however, appears to have been maintained between the Protestant and Roman Catholic missions, which were alternately fostered and expelled by the various sovereigns of the country.

In 1847 a British consulate was established, Mr. Plowden being selected for the post. He unfortunately committed the great error of entering into friendly relations with the potentate of Amhara, in place of the independent chief of Tigre, who, possessing the only outlet of communication, rendered an alliance with Amhara completely nugatory to both parties. Mr. Plowden himself, when too late, seems to have discovered that he had committed an error, and wrote to the Earl of Clarendon, who was then Foreign Secretary, that he feared that little commercial advantage could be obtained. His lordship replied that, having made the treaty and established the consulate, her Majesty's Government were reluctant to renounce all hope of benefit, and begged him to suggest some plan of establishing himself at Massowah or some other seaport, and of keeping up a communication with the interior.

Mr. Plowden in his report gave full details as to the country, and especially the northern portion, into which the Egyptians were constantly making plundering expeditions, carrying off the cattle and inhabitants, and selling the latter as slaves. Consul Plowden wrote strongly to the Egyptian authorities upon their conduct, and in consequence of his representations Lord Clarendon remonstrated energetically with the Viceroy of Egypt upon his aggressions against Abyssinia. While this was going on, a remarkable man had made his appearance. Dedjatj Kassai was chief of one of the Kawra tribes. A man of great ambition and talent, he conceived the design of making himself master of the whole of Abyssinia, and in turn attacked and defeated the neighbouring potentates, and speedily conquered the whole of the country, with the exception only of Tigre, and then assumed the title of the Emperor Theodore. Theodore is described in Mr. Plowden's despatches as a man of good impulses, and a desire to rule well and wisely, but of a violent temper, and an inordinate pride in his kingly dignity and position. With him Mr. Plowden entered into negotiations for a treaty with England, for the despatch of an embassy to this country, and for the establishment of the British consulate in Abyssinia, with power and jurisdiction in all cases in which a British subject might be interested.

The Emperor objected to the clause conferring jurisdiction on the Consul, but promised to give the matter his earnest attention when he should find time to do so, as he was most favourably disposed towards England. Lord Clarendon highly approved of the course Consul Plowden was pursuing, and stated that the Queen would have much pleasure in receiving, and treating with due honour, the ambassadors whom his Majesty might send to her Court. The ratification of this treaty and the sending the embassy were put off in consequence of the constant wars in which Theodore was engaged with rebellious tribes in various parts of his empire, but he always expressed himself as willing to carry out these engagements as soon as he could find leisure to enable him to do so. In March 1860, Consul Plowden was killed during his journey back to Massowah, from which he had been absent at the Court of Theodore for five years.

Mr. Layard most wrongfully accused Mr. Plowden, in a speech delivered in the House of Commons on June 30th, 1865, of breach of duty. He stated that Consul Plowden, "instead of attending to the object with which he was placed there, that of encouraging commercial intercourse between Great Britain and Abyssinia, plunged into local intrigues.... Her Majesty's Government at once sent out instructions for him to return to his post at Massowah, and no longer to interfere in their local differences." This accusation brought forth an indignant protest upon the part of Consul Plowden's brother. He showed that Mr. Plowden was accredited to Abyssinia, and not to Massowah, which is a Turkish port without trade, and with no British subjects or interests to protect, and only valuable as the means of entry into Abyssinia, and of communication with Europe, and obviously for that reason only made the head-quarters of the consulate. The duties of the Consul were to watch and counteract foreign intrigue, to keep peace between Abyssinia and Egypt, to put down the slave-trade, and to encourage commerce; duties which it is evident he could not perform if remaining at Massowah, separated from the seat of the empire by a hostile tribe. Mr. Plowden pointed out that his brother had commenced his consulship by going into the interior with letters and presents to the reigning potentate, and that he had during his whole term of office remained there with but few intermissions, his last visit there lasting for five years without a break. That during all this time he corresponded regularly with the Foreign Office, who were aware of his movements, and by whose instruction he was guided. Thus Mr. Plowden showed conclusively that the reckless attack which Mr. Layard so chivalrously made, five years after his death, upon an officer who had nobly performed most difficult duties, was altogether without foundation. Upon Consul Plowden's death Captain Cameron was gazetted "her Majesty's Consul in Abyssinia," but it was only on February 9th, 1862, that he arrived at Massowah. His instructions were rather vague, a good deal being necessarily left to his own discretion, but he was generally enjoined to carry on Consul Plowden's policy, to continue the negotiations for the treaty, and for the despatch of an embassy to England. Massowah was of course to be his head-quarters, but no injunctions were given him against going into the interior. On the contrary, he was furnished with letters and presents to the Emperor, to whom Earl Russell introduced him, and requested Theodore's protection and favour in his behalf. Captain Cameron, during the period which elapsed between his appointment and his departure for his post, had been thoroughly instructed in the progress which had been made in the negotiations by Consul Plowden, and had full authority to take them up at the point at which they were at that gentleman's death, and Mr. Stern, the missionary, was requested by Earl Russell himself to remain in London at that time in order to discuss with Captain Cameron the contemplated embassy and other matters. And yet, in the face of this, Mr. Layard ventured to say, in his place in Parliament, on October 31, 1865, when quoting Consul Cameron's despatch on the subject, "Now this was altogether contrary to the instruction he had received." Consul Cameron was received with great state and courtesy by the Emperor Theodore, who again expressed his desire to send an embassy to England. But a day or two after the Consul reached the Abyssinian Court the intelligence arrived that our Consul at Jerusalem, who had been always looked upon, and who had acted as the protector of the Abyssinian colony there, had received orders from the Foreign Secretary to withdraw that protection, and that consequently their convent had been plundered by the Armenians. This affair of the Jerusalem Abyssinians is told by Dr. Beke with great clearness, but space forbids me here to enter upon it; suffice it that Earl Russell without the smallest cause or pretext withdrew the protection, or rather good offices, which had been extended by Lord Malmesbury to the Abyssinian colony, and which had been one cause of the goodwill with which England was regarded in Abyssinia.

Upon the day after this the Emperor saw Captain Cameron, told him that he had well considered the subject of the treaty, about which there would be no difficulty, and he presented him with a letter which he had written to her Majesty. In this, after many expressions of regard and good wishes, the Emperor expresses his intention of attacking the Turks on account of their constant aggressions upon him, and requests her Majesty to arrange for the safe-conduct of the ambassadors, whom he is prepared to send at once to England. Upon receiving this letter Consul Cameron at once started for the sea-coast. He was, however, stopped upon his way by a rebel chief; but his letters were sent down by a native messenger, and arrived in London the 12th February 1863. Captain Cameron himself, accompanied by the Emperor's representative and a strong escort, proceeded to Bogos, to examine into the truth of the alleged inroads of the Turks or Egyptians, as they are indifferently called, into that province. Finding that these were still continued, Captain Cameron wrote to Consul-General Colquhoun at Alexandria, begging him to remonstrate with the Egyptian Government. He also wrote to Earl Russell from Bogos, and twice to the Emperor, acquainting him with the steps he was taking for the protection of his subjects, in these respects taking as guide the conduct of his predecessor, Consul Plowden, acting, as the advocate of the cause of the Christian Abyssinians against the Turks, in perfect accord with the representative and favourite of the Emperor, who was his companion. It is therefore clear that there is not the least foundation for Earl Russell's ill-advised allegation, "the chief cause of the Emperor's anger with Consul Cameron was this journey to Bogos." His proceedings, however, incurred the displeasure of both the Egyptian Government and the home authorities. In Mr. Plowden's time Egypt had been in a state of disorganisation, and therefore the British Government had, on receiving their Consul's account of the atrocities executed by the Egyptian troops upon the inhabitants of Bogos, addressed the energetic remonstrances of our Foreign Minister to the Viceroy; but now things were changed. Egypt was compact and strong, and Earl Russell would not for worlds offend so well regulated an ally; therefore a sharp reproof was sent off to Captain Cameron to mind his own business, and to return to Massowah. Such is the effect of a changed state of things, and poor Consul Cameron, by not reflecting on this, was blamed for doing precisely the same for which Consul Plowden had gained much credit.

When Captain Cameron returned to the Court in July, after his lengthened absence, his position was not a pleasant one, for he was still without an answer to the Emperor's letter to the Queen, which had been sent off October 31st of the previous year; he had not, indeed, received as yet an answer to his own despatch enclosing that letter; for owing to delays it had not, as has been said, reached England until February the 12th, and Earl Russell had not thought it of sufficient importance to answer it for more than two months afterwards, and then without making the slightest allusion to the Emperor's letter which it enclosed.

After the Consul had parted with the Emperor's representative at Bogos, he had made a visit into the Egyptian province of Soudan, in accordance with instructions he had received from the Foreign Office, to inquire into the prospects of cotton-growing there, as the subject of Egyptian cotton was then attracting great notice in England. This expedition added to the anger which the Emperor Theodore felt at not having received an answer to his letter to her Majesty. The following conversation took place at his first interview with Captain Cameron, and plainly enough testifies as to the real cause of the Emperor's anger:

"Where have you been since you parted from Samuel at Bogos?"

"Into the frontier provinces of Soudan."

"What for?"

"To see about cotton and trade, and so forth."

"Who told you to go there?"

"The British Government."

"Have you brought me an answer from the Queen of England?"

"No."

"Why not?"

"Because I have not received any communication from the Government upon the subject."

"Why, then, do you come to see me now?"

"I request permission to return to Massowah."

"What for?"

"Because I have been ordered by the Government to go there."

"So," exclaimed the exasperated monarch, "your Queen can give you orders to go and visit my enemies the Turks, and then to return to

Massowah; but she cannot send a civil answer to my letter to her. You shall not leave me till that answer comes."

Captain Cameron then, in July 1863, became a prisoner,—not in bonds, indeed, but a prisoner upon parole. In September the answer arrived from the Emperor Napoleon, to whom Theodore had despatched a letter at the same time as to the Queen. This answer gave great offence, as it was written by Marshal O'Neil, and not by the Emperor himself. Its contents, too, were singularly ill-judged, and the missive was torn to pieces before a council of the dignitaries by the Emperor, and trodden under foot. The French Consul and a companion were peremptorily ordered to quit the Abyssinian territory.

In October arrived Earl Russell's answer to Captain Cameron, but without the slightest allusion to Theodore's letter. Up to this time no cause of dispute whatever had arisen between Messrs. Stern and Rosenthal and the Emperor; but the fury which Theodore felt at the slight so wantonly passed upon him by the British Foreign Secretary now burst upon the heads of the whole of that nation. On October the 15th Captain Cameron's servant, or messenger, was seized and beaten; and in the evening of the same day Mr. Stern's two servants were seized and beaten so cruelly that they both died the same night. Mr. Stern himself, who was standing by at the time, happened, in his horror at the proceeding, to place his hand to his mouth. It was at once said he was biting his thumb at the Emperor, which is considered a threat of revenge; and he was accordingly seized and cruelly beaten, and his life was also for some time despaired of. For some time nothing further took place, and then the Emperor, who desired to justify in some way his fit of rage against a man with whom he had had no dispute or cause of complaint, had all Mr. Stern's and Mr. Rosenthal's books and papers examined and read, this office being performed by a Frenchman named Bardel, who appears throughout to have been a treacherous and bitter enemy of the English party. Enough criminatory matter was found here, in the shape of remarks in their diaries upon the conduct of the Emperor, and they were condemned to death; but this was commuted to imprisonment.

On Nov. 22d a young Irishman named Kearns arrived with another despatch from the Foreign Office,—probably the one of August 13th, but which contained no allusion whatever to the Emperor's letter. This naturally exasperated Theodore more than ever, and Captain Cameron was now ordered to be chained upon both hands. On the 4th of January Captain Cameron, his attendants, and the missionaries, were all put in fetters, and confined in the common prison. The cause of this fresh proof of the wrath of the King is reported by Mr. Steiger, a member of the Scottish mission, to have been the arrival of the head of the Abyssinian convent at Jerusalem with the news that the British Consul there had declined to interfere in their behalf. Is anything further necessary to establish the fact that the treatment of the unfortunate missionaries was a mere episode incidental to the main question, which was entirely between the Emperor Theodore and the British Government?

As to the long imprisonment, the torture and indignities inflicted upon the captives, they are already well known to the public. Let us now see what steps were taken by the late Government to procure their release.

The news of the imprisonment of Captain Cameron appeared in the Paris and London papers of the 15th of December; but no one could believe it, the favour in which the British Consul stood being a matter of notoriety. Lord Clarendon, however, stated in the House of Lords, in the debate on February 9, 1866, that the news had been received at the early date given of the Consul's detention; but it was only upon March 16, 1864, or three months after it was known at the Foreign Office, that the London Society for promoting Christianity among the Jews received and made public the sad intelligence. Mrs. Stern wrote a petition to the Queen, asking her to send a letter under the sign-manual, written by herself to the Emperor. Lord Shaftesbury handed this letter to Earl Russell, adding his own prayer to that of Mrs. Stern's, and requesting him to present the petition to the Queen. On the following day, May 7th, Earl Russell returned the petition, unpresented, to Lord Shaftesbury, saying that "after much deliberation he had come to the conclusion that he ought not to advise the Queen to write to the King of Abyssinia."

So matters might have remained to the present day had not a note which Captain Cameron had written during his captivity been received by his relatives, and by them most indiscreetly published in the papers. In this he said that there was no hope of his release unless an answer was sent to the Emperor's letter. Everyone was filled with indignation at the delay of fourteen months which had taken place in sending an answer to so important a document, and Earl Russell and his colleagues came to the conclusion that after all they ought to advise her Majesty to reply to the letter, which she accordingly did, and towards the end of June the letter was sent off. But so inefficiently was this done, that after it had reached Cairo it was sent back to England to have alterations made in it, and even then it was not perfect, for it was discovered many months afterwards that the royal signet had not been attached, and a fresh letter was accordingly sent out in February or March 1865. The person selected to carry out this delicate business was a Mr. Rassam, who had acted as paymaster to the men employed by Mr. Layard at Nineveh, and who was instructed to demand the release of Consul Cameron, but that as the other captives were not British subjects, he was not to speak too authoritatively in their behalf. But Mr. Rassam had, Dr. Beke affirms, another and far more delicate mission. "He was to make a good case for the British Government—to remove the blame from their shoulders, even if it were thrown on those of anyone else. It did not matter who might be the scapegoat as long as the Government were exonerated. This is said quite advisedly." Mr. Rassam went to Massowah, where he remained a year doing apparently nothing whatever. Dr. Beke thinks that all along, both in this and in his subsequent conduct, when he went into the interior and saw the Emperor, his conduct was not, to say the least of it, judicious. The release of the prisoners when Mr. Rassam did at last see the Emperor and present the Queen's letter, and their subsequent imprisonment, together with Mr. Rassam, are known to all.

Throughout all the numerous debates in the Houses of Parliament during this period, Earl Russell and Mr. Layard persistently endeavoured to burke all discussion by declaring that it would come to the ears of the Emperor; but when at last the House insisted upon being no longer put off with vague generalities, these two gentlemen, who had so deprecated anything being said which might hurt the feelings of the Emperor Theodore, were now guilty of applying the strongest and most offensive epithets to him, which, had they come to the knowledge of the Emperor, would have insured the instant execution of his captives. This was, to say the least of it, a strange and peculiar instance of inconsistency upon the part of these thoughtful statesmen. In consequence of these debates in the House, Earl Russell at length found that it was a matter which could no longer be tampered with, and he himself appointed Mr. Palgrave to start for Abyssinia to endeavour to effect the release of the Consul and his companions in captivity. Mr. Rassam, however, prevented anything being done by this gentleman. Nothing, indeed, if Dr. Beke is to be trusted, can be more extraordinary than the conduct of this person. He received the news of his recall while he was, as usual, waiting quietly at Massowah. Instantly he embarked in the steamer which brought the intelligence, steamed to Suez, and from there telegraphed to her Majesty's agent and Consul-General in Egypt that Consul Cameron had been released. This is proved to have been utterly without foundation, but it had the desired effect of putting a stop to Mr. Palgrave's progress, that gentleman having arrived at Cairo, and being upon the point of proceeding up the Nile. Mr. Rassam declined all fellowship with Mr. Palgrave, and refused to agree to the proposition that one should proceed up the Nile and the other viâ Massowah. Mr. Rassam then took the presents brought by Mr. Palgrave, and started back for Massowah, from whence he did what there is no apparent reason why he should not have done at first, started for the interior. Mr. Palgrave remained at Cairo to await the result of Mr. Rassam's mission. There he remained when the news came, in March 1866, that the captives were released, and were on their way to the coast; there he remained until Mr. Flad arrived in Egypt with the news of the detention of Mr. Rassam and the captives; and then, extraordinary to state, when it would seem that he might be of use, he started off by the first steamer to England.

As Dr. Beke says, the whole matter is an enigma which requires solution. This sudden passage of Mr. Rassam to Egypt upon the news of his recall being received by him, the untrue telegram which he sent off from thence, and which put a stop to Mr. Palgrave's expedition — in short, every incident connected with the conduct of Mr. Layard's ex-paymaster requires a most searching investigation.

Such is the account given by Dr. Beke; and as Mr. Layard, although openly attacked, has never disproved a single statement alleged against him, but has contented himself with vehement personal attacks upon Dr. Beke (probably upon the principle of the lawyer — "when you have no case, blackguard your opponent"), it must be assumed that in all material points Dr. Beke's statements are correct.

Such was the state of things when the Conservative Ministry came into power; and after another fruitless effort to ransom the prisoners, war was determined upon as the only resource remaining.

The announcement of the intention of Government was received with general satisfaction. It was not a war for which any enthusiasm was felt; there was no national glory to be gained, no national advantage; but a national stain was to be wiped off, and a party of our countrymen rescued from a position into which they had fallen by no fault whatever of their own, but by the disgraceful *lâches* of the Government they served; therefore it may be said that England in general, if it did not enter heartily into the war, and winced a little at the thought of the probable enormous expense, yet cordially acquiesced in its necessity. War once determined upon, the columns of the newspapers were inundated with suggestions from everyone who had ever been in Abyssinia, and from a vast number of persons who had not; and these, although they differed upon almost every point, yet agreed upon piling danger upon difficulty, and horror upon horror, until the very air, earth, and water of Abyssinia seemed to swarm with worms and other creeping things. In the mean time the preparations went steadily on. Officers were sent from England to Egypt, Spain, and various parts of the Mediterranean to purchase mules; Woolwich was busied with the preparation of mountain guns; transports were taken up, hospital-ships were fitted out, and large quantities of tents and other stores sent out from the Tower. This was nearly all which England was to contribute, for it was determined that the expedition should be entirely an Indian one, and that Bombay should have the honour as well as the responsibility of all the arrangements.

As soon as orders were received from England to fit out an expedition with all speed, Sir Seymour FitzGerald, the Governor of Bombay, and Sir Robert Napier, Commander-in-chief of the Bombay army, set to work in earnest. The greatest credit is undoubtedly due to the former for his untiring zeal and earnestness; he was indefatigable: but at the same time I doubt greatly the wisdom of committing the arrangements connected with a great expedition of this sort to a civilian, who necessarily must be unacquainted with the requirements of an army, and who must be entirely guided by the advice of his council. The consequence was that Sir Robert Napier was obliged to consult the Governor on every point, and the Governor again had to consult his own military adviser, an officer necessarily of far less standing than Sir Robert Napier, who was thus liable to be overruled, nominally by the Governor, but in reality by a subordinate officer. Thus, as one instance out of many, Sir Robert Napier's plan for a transport train, which was sent in to the Governor for sanction early in September, was entirely put aside, and the new scheme was not issued by the Governor for two months afterwards; thus Sir Robert, who when he once arrived in Abyssinia was solely responsible, was liable to have the whole of his arrangements destroyed by the break-down of a transport train, with the organisation of which he had nothing whatever to do.

As the present is merely a narrative of the march of the army to Magdala, I must pass cursorily over the preparations in Bombay. I will, however, give a few extracts from the memoranda issued by Sir Robert Napier, and which will be sufficient to show how accurately he estimated the difficulties of the work to be done, and how thoroughly he thought over every detail.

In his memorandum of August 8th, Sir Robert Napier estimates that he will require 12,000 men, for that 2000 must remain at the port, and at Post No. 1 upon the high land (Senafe); 2000 men at Antalo, or at some similar point in advance; and 2000 men to keep open communication with the advanced column, and to support it if necessary.

In minute of August 31st, he farther develops his plans. He there speaks of Post No. 1 as at Zulla, Post No. 2 as at Senafe, Post No. 3 as at Antalo, which, he says, "will be one of great importance, and should be very strong." "Post No. 4 will probably be not far from Socota, which will also be a very vital point. It is in a difficult and rugged country, and will be our last main base of supplies from which the operating force will be supported." Farther on he says: "It will be necessary to convey to our extreme base, which for convenience I will call Socota, for the force required to hold that mountainous country, and for the corps of operation (probably in all 7000 men), supplies for four months." In the same minute he says: "On advancing from Post No. 2 (Senafe) the leading division will move forward at once to Antalo, and the remainder of the advancing force will take post upon the road to cover the transit of supplies for five months from No. 2 to No. 3, being posted at stations where they may obtain water and forage, and then supplies will be passed on to the front for 9000 men. From Antalo the same process will be repeated until the supplies for 7000 men shall have been carried to Post No. 4 at Socota. From that point the operative column will act with supplies for one or two months as may be convenient."

These extracts are exceedingly interesting, as they show the original plans of the campaign as laid down by Sir Robert Napier. In the course of the narrative, it will be seen how entirely this plan had to be deviated from, owing to the scarcity of food and forage, and the partial break-down of the transport train; how Post No. 4, described as of "vital" importance, had to be altogether dispensed with; and how, in consequence, the army, when within five or six days of Magdala, were almost destitute of supplies, while their base at Antalo was two hundred miles distant.

On September 12th Sir Robert issued an excellent memorandum on the fitting-up of the ships and the appliances for landing animals, and making many suggestions for the health and comfort of the troops.

In regard to the selection of the troops to form the expedition, Sir Robert himself chose the various regiments. A considerable discussion arose between the different Presidencies, Madras and Bengal naturally wishing to contribute as large a quota as possible. Upon this subject the General wisely said, September 5th: "I consider it especially of advantage to have the native regiments, if possible, of one army, as they work in harmony with and rely upon each other; if they are of different Presidencies, feelings of great bitterness arise when one or other is left in the rear, and partialities are conjured up as the reason why one or other is not taken to the front."

Considerable correspondence took place in relation to the formation and constitution of the pioneer force, concerning which the General's opinion was overruled by that of his excellency the Governor. The following extract from memorandum of September 8th fully shows this: "I concluded that I should receive some formal and definite information of any change in his excellency's views or plans, and I was therefore not prepared to learn from Colonel Marriott, when the expedition was nearly ready to proceed, that his Excellency had decided to submit entirely to Colonel Merewether the responsible duty of determining finally the point of debarkation, and of converting the reconnoissance into an occupation of the coast by a body of about 1500 men. Of all the various circumstances which may have led his Excellency to this conclusion, I am not fully informed; but I entertain strong objections to the question being left entirely to Colonel Merewether's decision,—he being, in compliance with his Excellency's opinion (expressed in his Excellency's note to Colonel Marriott), in military command of the party,—because, while concurring entirely with his Excellency in his high estimation of that officer, it has seemed to me that Colonel Merewether has strong preconceived opinions in favour of a line of route which from the most recent reports, especially that of M. Munsinger, appears to me to be one that would be dangerous to the success of the expedition, and that his selection of a point of debarkation will be sensibly influenced by such very strong and sincere opinions." Sir Robert Napier's protest was attended to, and other officers were associated with Colonel Merewether; but this extract is sufficient to show how much was done by the Governor of Bombay without the concurrence or even consultation of Sir Robert Napier.

The general instructions to the pioneer force were precise: they were directed to select a place of landing, and then to inquire about the question of obtaining carriage and supplies from the natives (this last being Colonel Merewether's special duty); and to Colonel Wilkins, R.E., was assigned specially to determine the adaptability of the shore for landing, the erection of piers, floating wharves, and shelter of all kinds; he was also ordered to advise upon the military value of positions selected, and to assist in general reconnoissance. But the point upon which above all others General Napier laid stress was, that the pioneer force should on no account push forward into the high land; he knew that there could be no possible utility in their so doing, and that it would entail a great and unnecessary labour to provision them at a distance from the sea, especially up so difficult a country. Both upon Colonel Merewether and Colonel Phayre did he impress this point. In his letter of the 9th October to the former officer he said, "*It is not at all intended that this force shall take up a position on the high ground*, for which its strength and composition are unfitted." Farther on he says, "If news is satisfactory, Staveley's brigade will sail, and *upon its arrival* the advance may be made." To Colonel Phayre he was equally explicit. In a letter to him dated 9th October he says, "*It is not of course intended that Colonel Field should move to the high table-land* at Dexan, &c., but merely to take up such position as will cover the dépôt and protect the cattle." And again farther on, "You will understand that it is *not my desire to precipitate a lodgment upon the table-land*, which we should have to maintain too long before advancing."

How these officers carried out the instructions thus clearly and strongly laid down, we shall see hereafter.

It is needless now to enter into any detail of the preparations at Bombay, but it may be said that they were of the most extensive and complete character. Everything which could be thought of was provided for the health and comfort of the troops. Money was lavished like water; but, in the haste and bustle which prevailed, there is no question that the authorities were in many cases grossly imposed upon, and that stores were sent out of quality so utterly bad as to be perfectly useless. I may mention as an example the boots for the drivers of the transport train, which never lasted over a week, and very few of which attained even that comparatively respectable age. As with these, so with many other stores; but it is probable that cases of this sort are inseparable from a hastily-prepared expedition. The stores which were subsequently forwarded were very much better in quality.

After these introductory remarks, I begin my narrative from the date of my own sailing from Bombay.

THE MARCH TO MAGDALA

On board Transport General Havelock,
December 1st, 1867.

I am happy to say that, speaking personally, the Abyssinian expedition has begun. I am on my way to that cheerful and well-ordered country. Had I known on landing in Bombay that I should be detained there for a month, I should have made myself very comfortable, and should have enjoyed myself exceedingly. But I thought that, although the Commander-in-chief and the main body of the expedition were not sailing for two months, I should do better to push on at once. I accordingly applied for a passage, and was promised one as soon as possible. This phrase, "as soon as possible," in the mouth of an ordinary individual, means something. From an official it means just nothing. It is merely one of those vague ambiguities in which the official mind delights. It is a phrase which admits of no argument whatever.

Day after day passed, and nothing came of it. A steamer or two started, but although we expressed our willingness to sleep on deck, and put up with any accommodation whatever, no room could be found. One of our number, hopeless and disgusted, took passage in the last Peninsular and Oriental steamer, and is probably at the present moment wandering about Aden, praying for a passage across. I thought it better to wait here until I could be taken direct to our destination. At last came the intelligence that our horses could be put on board a sailing-ship. This was something done, and I felt really thankful when, after a long day's work, I left the ship's side, leaving the horses and their syces on board. Indeed, the servant question is one of the most serious of those which present themselves to the mind of an intending Abyssinian expeditionist. It is not difficult to get one. You only have to speak, to get half-a-dozen servants and syces. But you know, both by the warnings of your friends and by your own instincts, that so many applicants, so many rogues. It is at present the very best profession in Bombay to get hired to a master going to Abyssinia, and to disappear two days before he leaves with his purse and any other portable valuables which may come handy. My first servant, a mild Hindoo of engaging aspect, was seized with a pulmonary affection, while his brother, who was servant to a friend of mine, was at the last moment melted by the tears of an aged and despairing mother, and both left us; but not until some hours after their departure did we find that they had, of course accidentally, carried away with them a considerable amount of specie and small valuables. When at last a servant is obtained who really does mean to go to Abyssinia, there is no little trouble to be gone through with him. He must have a month's, or perhaps two months', pay in advance. He must have an arrangement made for the payment of the greater part of his wages to his family during his absence. He must be provided, at your expense, with warm clothes, boots, blankets, &c.; and all this with the strong chance of his bolting at the last moment. One of my syces alarmed me greatly by not turning up on the morning when the horses were to be embarked; but he finally appeared upon the landing-stage just as they were being slung into a lighter, three hours after the time named. Whether he or any of the syces finally accompanied the horses I am unable to say, as the ship, instead of sailing that afternoon as positively settled by the authorities, was detained three or four days; and it is very probable that during that time the syces slipped ashore with their warm clothes, advance of wages, &c. This painful question cannot be solved until the ship with the horses arrives at Annesley Bay. Another four or five days passed, and then came the welcome order to go at once on board the General Havelock, which was to start the next day at noon. On board we accordingly went, but found, as we anticipated, that there was no chance of her starting for that day at any rate. The usual conflict of departments was taking place. Some department had ordered a force of twenty European soldiers and fifty Sepoys belonging to the transport train to come on board. This they did. Then came a committee of some other department, and questioned whether the Havelock was fit to carry this force, and whether they had not better be transferred to some other ship. Finding that the men's things were all below, it was determined to leave them as they were. Then the same committee, with a view, I suppose, of making the vessel more comfortable, determined to send three and a half tons of gunpowder on board, and with this intent sent a carpenter in the course of the afternoon, who took down the only available bath, and prepared to convert the same into a powder-magazine. The next morning the same carpenter came on board and brought some more tools, and then returned to shore. In the afternoon he fetched the tools away. In the mean time one department had sent the water-lighter alongside; but another department had sent no tanks on board to receive it. Presently that department sent some tanks, but as it had not occurred to it to measure the hatchways, the tanks were considerably larger than the opening down which they had to go, so they had to be taken away and a fresh set of tanks brought on board. Then, long after dusk, the water-ship again came alongside, and we took in our water. In the mean time we went ashore to the department which had sent us on board, to ask when it was probable that the Havelock would really sail. We were assured by that department that she had already started, and we had great difficulty in persuading it that she was still at anchor, and likely to remain so. The next morning, the powder not having arrived, and nothing more having been heard either of it or of the carpenter, our captain got up steam and started; and it is by no means improbable that the powder, with one or two committees of departments, are at present cruising about Bombay harbour looking for the Havelock. And yet ours is an absolutely favourable example, for a steamer last week was detained six days after the date of the embarkation of its passengers. And if this confusion exists now, when only one or two vessels are starting a-week, what a scene of confusion will it be when the main body of the force sails! It always is so, and always will be so, as long as our army is managed by a set of independent departments, who have no concert whatever between them. We have here the quartermaster-general's department, the commissariat, the land-transport, the marine, the adjutant-general's department, the ordnance, and so on *ad infinitum*. Military men are the first and loudest to complain of this multiplication of offices without union or concert, which work together well enough in quiet times, but which in emergencies paralyse each other's efforts, and cause a confusion in exact proportion to their own number. It needs some military reformer of an iron will, and an assured parliamentary support, to put an end to all this, to do away with the independence of the various departments of the service, and to make them all subordinate branches of the adjutant-general's office; so that a general upon service may give his orders to his adjutant-general only, and the latter may instruct the officers of the departments under him as to what should be done. All indents and orders should be given to him alone, and he should be responsible for the working of the several branches. In some respects it turned out to be as well that we had not started at the time named, for at night, when the rations were served out to the troops, it was found that both the porter and arrack, which form a somewhat important part of a soldier's rations, had not been sent on board by the commissariat. Great was the consternation. However, fortunately next day, while departments were skirmishing over water and water-tanks, and the carpenter was going and coming with his tools, there was time to send to the commissariat, and for them to repair their error.

The General Havelock is a steamer of about 250 tons, and the object of her builders appears to have been to combine the maximum of rolling qualities with the minimum of speed. In calm weather she can steam six and a half knots an hour; in a slight swell she can roll to an angle of thirty-five degrees. Having said this, I have said all that can be said in dispraise of the vessel. She has capital accommodation for a ship of her size, a snug little poop-deck, extremely comfortable seats and chairs, a perfect absence of any smell from the engine-room, and one of the jolliest skippers in existence. So we are very comfortable. We are five in number; three officers of the Land Transport Corps, and two "specials;" and as we get under the awnings on the poop-deck, while a fair breeze is helping us along at the rate of eight knots an hour, we agree that we have all the advantages of keeping a steam-yacht without the expense. The charge Government makes to officers while on board is eight rupees a-day, which is handed over to the captain of the ship, who has to supply everything for that sum. I do not think that the captain of the Havelock will be a gainer by this transaction. We all sleep on deck, not from necessity, for there are plenty of berths below, but partly because the nights on deck are charming, although a little cold, and partly from horror of a species of monster, which appears to me to be as large as cats—but this may be the effect of imagination and extreme terror—and to run much faster. They have many legs, and horns resembling bullocks'. They are fearless of man, and indeed attack him with ferocity. I call them vampires—their ordinary name is cockroaches. This sleeping on deck is attended with occasional drawbacks. Last night I was awakened by a splash of water on my face. Thinking it was spray, I pulled my rug over my face, but only for an instant, for a rush of water came down upon me as if emptied from a bucket. In an instant everyone was upon his feet, and began dragging his bed over to the leeward side of the ship. But it was no use. The rain tore across the deck as if pumped by a hundred steam fire-engines, and nothing remained for us but to beat a retreat down through the cabin staylight, for to go outside the awning by the ordinary poop-ladder was out of the question. Our first amazement and consternation over, we had a great laugh as we gained the cabin-floor, drenched through, and with our silk sleeping-dresses clinging to us in the most uncomfortable manner. By the time we had changed these the storm was over as suddenly as it had begun, and taking fresh rugs we soon regained our beds, which, turned over, were dry enough on the lower side for all practical purposes.

Over the engine-room is a large bridge-deck, and here are the quarters of the European soldiers, twenty-five in number, while the sepoys occupy the main deck. Both the Europeans and sepoys are volunteers from various regiments into the Land Transport Train. This is a newly-organised corps, and is only formed for the purposes of the expedition, both officers and men returning at its conclusion to their regiments. It is commanded by Major Warden, and consists of fourteen divisions, each containing two thousand baggage-animals. To look after each of these divisions are a captain and two subalterns, together with thirty-eight men—Europeans and sepoys, who are divided into four classes. When it is remembered that among the two thousand animals are oxen, horses, mules, camels, and elephants, and that there will be an attendant to each two animals, it will be seen that the post of officer in a division of the Land Transport Corps will be by no means a sinecure. His difficulties, too, will be heightened by the fact that the drivers will be men of innumerable nationalities and races—Spaniards and Italians with the mules, Greeks from Smyrna and Beyrout, Egyptians and Nubians, Arabs and Affghans, together with men from all the varied tribes of India. The sepoys who are with us do not appear to me at all the sort of men for the service. They belong entirely to infantry regiments, and are quite unaccustomed to horses. The Hindoo is not naturally a horseman; and to take a number of infantry sepoys and put them on horses, and set them at once to severe work, is an absurdity, which will be speedily demonstrated to be such by the men being knocked up and in hospital by the end of the first week. Only men belonging to the native cavalry should have been allowed to volunteer. It is true that many of the Europeans also belong to line regiments, but the same objection does not hold good to them, for most Englishmen are more or less accustomed to horses, and if not they soon fall into it.

Annesley Bay, December 4th.

Our voyage has not terminated so uneventfully as it began, and I am no longer writing on board the General Havelock, but on the Salsette, a very fine Peninsular and Oriental steamer, having a portion of the 33d regiment from Kurrachee on board, and having the Indian Chief, with another portion of the same regiment, in tow. This Red-Sea navigation is a most intricate and dangerous business, and this western shore is in particular completely studded with islands and coral-reefs. These islands differ entirely in their character—some are bold rocks rising perpendicularly from the water with rugged peaks and fantastic outlines, and attaining an elevation of two or three hundred feet; others, far more dangerous, are long flat islets, rising only two or three feet above the sea, and imperceptible on a dark night at a distance of fifty yards. Still others, again, most dangerous of all, have not yet attained the dignity even of islets, although millions of little insects work night and day to bring them up to the surface. These are the coral-reefs, which, rising from a depth of many fathoms to within a few feet of the surface, form so many pitfalls to the unsuspecting mariner. The General Havelock was running along the coast with a favourable breeze, and we had been all the morning watching the low shore, with its stunted bushes and the strangely-conical hills which rise from it, bearing a fantastic resemblance to haycocks, and barns, and saddles, and with a mighty range of mountains in the distance. These mountains had a strange interest to us, for among and over them we have to go. They were our first sight of Abyssinia, and were by no means encouraging as a beginning. In this way we spent the morning, and after lunch were about to resume doing nothing, when we were startled by hearing the man who was standing in the chains heaving the lead, shout out, "Five fathoms!" His call two minutes before had been ten fathoms. The captain shouted "Stop her!" "Turn her astern!" and the chief engineer leapt below to see the order carried out. In the momentary pause of the beat of the screw, the leadman's voice called out "Two fathoms!" The screw was reversed, and a rush of yellow foaming water past the side of the ship told us at once that it was at work, and that the sandy bottom was close to her keel. Very gradually we stopped, and were congratulating ourselves on the near shave we had had, when, looking over her side, we saw that, vigorously as the screw was working astern, the ship remained just where she was. The General Havelock was palpably ashore. At first we were disposed to make light of the affair, for, grounding as she did imperceptibly, we imagined that she would get off with little difficulty. Accordingly we first worked ahead, then astern, but with an equal absence of result. The head and stern both swung round, but she was fast amidships, and only moved as on a pivot. The troops were now ordered on deck, and were massed, first aft and then forward; but the General Havelock gave no sign. Then it was resolved to roll her, the men running in a body from side to side. Then we tried to jump her off. The whole of the Europeans and sepoys were set to jump in time—first on one side, and then on the other. A funnier sight, eighty men, black and white, leaping up and down, and then going from side to side, could not be conceived. Everyone laughed except those who swore when their naked feet were jumped upon by the thick ammunition-boots of some English soldier. Presently the laughter abated, for everyone was getting too hot even to laugh. The scene was strangest at this time, and reminded me, with the leaping figures, the swarthy skins, and the long hair, more of a New Zealand war-dance than anything I had ever seen. Hours passed in experiments of this sort, but still the General Havelock remained immovable, only when the sun went down and the wind rose she rolled almost as heavily as if afloat, and lifted on the waves and fell into her bed with a heavy bump which was very unpleasant. Boats were now lowered and soundings taken, and it was found that the water was deeper on nearly every side than at the exact spot upon which we had struck. Hawsers were got out and the men set to work at the capstan; but the anchors only drew home through the sandy bottom, and brought up branches of white coral. Part of the crew were all this time occupied in shifting the cargo. But in spite of every effort the ship remained perfectly fast. It was evident that she would not move until a portion at least of her cargo was removed from her. While we were debating how this was to be done, for the shore on either side was a good mile distant, the wind fresh, and the boats small, an Arab dhow, which we had observed running down, anchored about a hundred yards off. The Sheik came on board, and after immense talk agreed to come alongside for three or four hours to take a portion of the cargo and the troops on board, and so to lighten our ship. When the bargain was closed, and the sum to be paid agreed upon, he discovered that there was not water enough for his boat to float alongside. The negotiations thus came to an end, and the Sheik returned to his own craft. Soon after another and larger dhow came up and anchored at a short distance. We sent off to see if he could help us, but it seemed that he had no less than seventy-two camels on board bound for Annesley Bay. How the poor brutes could have been stowed in a boat which did not look large enough to hold twenty at the very most, I cannot imagine, and they had come in that state all the way from Aden. About an hour after we had got ashore, a large steamer, which we knew by her number to be the Salsette, with a ship in tow, had passed at a distance of about three miles, and to her we signalled for assistance. She, however, passed on, and anchored with her consort under the lee of an island, and about six miles off. We had given up all hopes of aid from her, and had begun as a last resource to throw our coal overboard, when at nine o'clock in the evening we saw a boat approaching with a lug-sail. When she came alongside she turned out to belong to the Salsette, which had most fortunately orders to anchor at the spot where we had seen her. We found, on conversation with the officer who had come on board, that, loaded with troops as she was, it would not be safe for her to come within towing distance of us, and therefore that she must leave us to our fate, especially as we did not appear to be in any immediate danger. They kindly offered, however, to take my fellow-correspondent and myself on board, an offer which we gratefully accepted, as it was quite possible that we might not be off for another week. When we arrived on board the Salsette we were received with the greatest kindness, and before starting in the morning had the satisfaction of seeing the signal flying from the Havelock of "We are afloat."

Relieved from all anxiety on account of our late shipmates, our servants, and our luggage, we enjoyed the run to Annesley Bay exceedingly. It is an immense bay, and, indeed, a finer harbour, once in, could hardly be imagined. The entrance, however, is intricate and dangerous. Long shoals extend for miles near its mouth, and there are several islands within the bay itself. All eyes, or rather all telescopes, were directed towards the spot which was to be our destination. My glass, one by Salomans, is a wonderful instrument for its size, and is indeed far better than any I have tried it against since I left England. My first impressions of our landing-place are, I confess, anything but pleasing. A mist hangs over the land, which excludes a view of the hills, or, indeed, of anything except the foreshore. This is a dead flat, covered with low bushes. The town consists of about fifty tents and marbuees, a large skeleton of a wooden storehouse, piles of hay and grain-bags, hundreds of baggage-animals, with a throng of natives wandering about. There is but one pier, and this is still in course of construction. In the harbour are anchored a dozen or so of transports and a few native dhows. Some of these dhows are occupied in transporting forage and stores from the ships to shore; and as they cannot themselves approach within a distance of a couple of hundred yards of the shore, long lines of natives transport the goods upon their heads to land. One ship is unloading mules; this she accomplishes by lowering them on to a raft, upon which they are towed with ropes to within a short distance of the shore, when the horses are pushed or persuaded to alight and walk. The Havelock came in just before sunset, about two hours after ourselves. I have not yet been ashore. The Beloochees, who arrived yesterday in the Asia and the Peckforten Castle, are landing to-day.

Annesley Bay, December 6th.

I had not intended to write again until the time of the departure of the next mail, as my last letter went off only yesterday morning; but two companies of the 33d regiment are to land this afternoon and to start at midnight, and as this is the first body of European troops who have landed, I think it as well to accompany them to Senafe, sixty miles distant, where Colonels Merewether and Phayre have gone up with the pioneer force. They will not advance beyond this point for some time, and I shall therefore, when I have seen the passes, return, after a few days' stay there, to this place, which is at present the main point of interest. I should not move from it, indeed, were it not that there is some doubt whether the King of Tigré will permit us to pass. He is at present stationed near the head of the pass with a body of 7000 men, but I fancy his only object in this is to make us buy his friendship at as high a rate as possible. If he really means mischief it will be a very serious matter indeed; for, although we should of course scatter his forces easily enough, it would give us such an enormous line of march to be guarded that it would be impossible to move a step until we had completely subdued Tigré. I sincerely hope that this will not be the case. But another week or two will show; and in the mean time, as I shall have plenty of opportunities of writing on the subject, I must return to my present topic, which is the state of things at the landing-place here. It is not, as I said in my last, a cheerful place to look at from on board ship, but it is very far worse on landing. The pier is nearly finished, and is a very creditable piece of work indeed. It is of stone, and about 300 yards long, and is wide enough for a double line of rails. One line is already laid down, and saves an immensity of labour; for the goods are landed from the native boats, which bring them from the ship's side, are put on to the trucks, and are run straight into the commissariat yard, which is fifty yards only from the end of the pier. Before this pier was finished everything had to be carried on shore upon the heads of the natives; and as a boat cannot approach within 300 yards of shore, owing to the shallow water, it may be imagined how slowly the work of debarcation went on. The pier is ridiculously insufficient for the purpose. Even now the ships are lying in the harbour for days, waiting for means of landing their goods, although lines of natives still supplement the pier, and pass bales of goods through the water on their heads. When the whole expedition is here there will be a complete dead-lock, unless a very great increase of landing accommodation is afforded. The commissariat yard is piled with enormous quantities of pressed hay, Indian and English, grain, rice, &c. They are well arranged, and in such weather as we have at present there is no fear of their taking damage from being exposed to the air, especially as the precaution has been taken to have trusses of pressed hay laid down as a foundation for the piles of grain-bags. The commissariat yard is distinguished by the fact that here only do we see women—bright-coloured, picturesquely-clad creatures, a hundred of whom have been sent across from India to serve as grinders of corn. Beside the commissariat tents are a few others belonging to the other departments, and these, with a large unfinished wooden storehouse, at which a dozen Chinese carpenters are at work, constitute the camp at the landing-place. But this is only a small portion of the whole, the main camp being a mile and a half inland; and, indeed, there are half-a-dozen small camps, a cluster of tents scattered within the circle of a mile.

The reason why the main camp was fixed at such an inconvenient distance from the landing-place was, that water was at first obtainable from wells sunk there. But this supply has ceased some time, and it would be better to concentrate the offices of the departments near the landing-place, and that every soul whose presence down here is not an absolute necessity should be sent up to Koomaylo, which is fourteen miles inland, and which is the first place at which water can be obtained. As it is, all living things, man and beast, have to depend for their supply of water upon the ships. Every steamer in harbour is at work night and day condensing water, the average expense being twopence-halfpenny a gallon for the coal only. The result is of course an enormous expense to the public, and very great suffering among the animals.

Leaving the camp, I proceeded to the watering-place, and here my senses of sight and smell were offended as they have not been since the days of the Crimea. Dead mules and camels and oxen lay everywhere upon the shore, and within a short distance of it. Here and there were heaps of ashes and charred bones, where an attempt had been made to burn the carcasses. Others, more lately dead, were surrounded by vultures, who, gorged with flesh, hardly made an effort to rise as we approached. One ox had fallen only a few minutes before we reached it, and several vultures were already eying it, walking round at a respectful distance, and evidently not quite assured that the animal was dead. Here and there half-starved mules wandered about, their heads down, their ears drooping, and their eyes glazing with approaching death. Some would stagger down to the sea-side, and taste again and again the salt water; many of them, half-maddened by thirst, would drink copiously, and either drop dead where they stood, or crawl away to die in the low scrub.

More miserable still was the appearance of the camels. Several native boats were unloading them at a distance of two or three hundred yards from shore. The water was not more than three or four feet deep; but when the poor beasts were turned into it most of them lay down, with only their heads above water, and positively refused to make an effort to walk to land. Some never were able to make the effort, and their bodies drifted here and there in the smooth water. Some of the camels had got within fifty yards of shore, and then had lain down, looking, with their short bodies and long necks, like gigantic water-fowl. Those who had been driven ashore were in little better plight. Their bones seemed on the very point of starting through their skin, and they lay as if dead upon the sand, uttering feebly the almost human moaning and complainings peculiar to the camel. Others had recovered a little. These were endeavouring to browse the scanty leaves on the bushes around. Some of these camels have been twenty days on the voyage, and during this time have been crowded together like sheep in a pen, with next to nothing either to eat or drink during the whole time. The wonder is that any of them survived it. Government suffers no loss by the death of these unfortunates, as a contractor agreed to deliver them here in a fair condition, and only those who survive the voyage, and recover something of their former strength, are accepted and paid for. At least, this is one version of the story. The other is, that they are consigned to the Land Transport Corps. That body, however, receive no intimation of their coming, and boatload after boatload of camels arrive, and wander away from the beach to die for want of the water within their reach. At a mile from the landing-place the scene is painful in the extreme. Camels and mules wander about in hundreds without masters, without anything. Here they strive for a few days' existence by plucking scanty shoots; here they sicken and die. The scenes were frightful everywhere, but were worst of all at the watering-troughs. These were miserably-contrived things. Only ten or a dozen animals could approach at once; they were so unevenly placed, that when one end was full to overflowing there was not an inch of water at the other; and beside this, at a time when water was worth its weight in gold, they leaked badly. They were only supplied with water for an hour or so in the morning, and for a similar time in the evening; and in consequence the scene was painful in the extreme. There was a guard to preserve order, but order could not have been kept by ten times as many men. There were hundreds of transport animals, with one driver to each five or six of them. What could one driver do with six half-mad animals? They struggled, they bit, they kicked, they fought like wild-beasts for a drink of the precious water for which they were dying. Besides these led animals were numerous stragglers, which, having broken their head-ropes, had gone out into the plain to seek a living on their own account. For these there was no water; they had no requisition pinned to their ears, and as they failed thus scandalously to comply with the regulations laid down by the authorities, the authorities determined that they should have no water. They were beaten off. Most of them, after a repulse or two, went away with drooping heads to die; but some fought for their dear lives, cleared a way to the trough with heels and teeth, and drank despite the blows which were showered upon them. I inquired of the Land Transport Corps why these scattered mules are not collected and fed. I am told that nearly the whole of these mule- and camel-drivers have deserted and gone to Massowah. And so it is. The mules and camels are dying of thirst and neglect; the advanced brigade cannot be supplied with food; the harbour is becoming full of transports, because there are no means of taking the men inland, although there are plenty of animals; and all this because the land transport men desert. The officers of that corps work like slaves; they are up early and late, they saddle mules with their own hands, and yet everything goes wrong. Why is all this? One reason undoubtedly is, that the animals have been sent on before the men. A few officers and a comparatively small body of native followers are sent out, and to them arrive thousands of bullocks, thousands of mules, thousands of camels. The Arab followers, appalled by the amount of work accumulating upon them, desert to a man, the officers are left helpless. Had a fair number of officers and followers been sent on to receive the animals as they came, all might have gone well. It was simply a miscalculation. And so it is, I regret to say, in some other departments. You apply for a tent, and are told there are no bell-tents whatever arrived. You ask for a pack-saddle, and are told by the quartermaster-general that there is not a single pack-saddle in hand, and that hundreds of mules are standing idle for want of them. You ask for rations, and are informed that only native rations have yet arrived, and that no rations for Europeans have been sent, with the exception of the sixty days' provisions the 33d regiment have brought with them. Why is this? There are scores of transports lying in Bombay harbour doing nothing. Why, in the name of common sense, are they not sent on? The nation is paying a very fair sum for them, and there they lie, while the departments are pottering with their petty jealousies and their petty squabbles.

The fact is, we want a head here. Colonels Merewether and Phayre have gone five days' march away, taking with them all the available transport. Brigadier-General Collings only arrived yesterday, and of course has not as yet been able to set things in order. I am happy to say that General Staveley arrived last night, and I believe that he will soon bring some order into this chaos. The fact is, that in our army we leave the most important branch of the service to shift for itself. Unless the Land Transport Train is able to perform its duty, nothing can possibly go right; but the Land Transport Corps has no authority and no power. It is nobody's child. The commissariat owns it not, the quartermaster and adjutant-general know nothing whatever of it. It may shift for itself. All the *lâches* of all the departments are thrown upon its shoulders, and the captains who are doing the work may slave night and day; but unaided and unassisted they can do nothing. The land transport should be a mere subordinate branch of the commissariat; that department should be bound to supply food at any required point. Now, all they have to do is to join the other departments in drawing indents for conveyance upon the unhappy land transport, and then sitting down and thanking their gods that they have done everything which could be expected of them. General Staveley is an energetic officer, and will, I believe, lose no time in putting things straight. Even to-day things look more hopeful, for General Collings yesterday afternoon put the services of 200 Madras dhoolie-bearers at the disposition of the Transport Corps to supply the place of the mule- and camel-drivers who have deserted. I have therefore every hope that in another week I shall have a very different story to tell. In addition, however, to the mortality caused by the voyage, by hardships, and by bad food and insufficient water, there is a great mortality among the horses and mules from an epidemic disease which bears a strong resemblance to the cattle-plague. Ten or twelve of the mules die a day from it, and the 3d Native Cavalry lost ninety horses from it while they were here. The district is famous, or rather infamous, for this epidemic; and the tribes from inland, when they come down into the plain, always leave their horses on the plateau, and come down on foot. The Soumalis and other native tribes along this shore are a quarrelsome lot, and fights are constantly occurring among the native workmen, who inflict serious, and sometimes fatal, injuries upon each other with short, heavy clubs resembling Australian waddies. The washing, at least such washing as is done, is sent up to Koomaylo. Yesterday two dhoolies, or washermen, were bringing a quantity of clothes down to the camp, when they were set upon by some natives, who killed one and knocked the other about terribly, and then went off with the clothes.

Some of the ships have brought down the horses in magnificent condition. The Yorick, which has carried the horses of the officers of the 33d, is a model of what a horse-ship should be. The animals are ranged in stalls along the whole length of her main-deck, and the width is so great that there is room for a wide passage on either side of the mast. These passages were laid down with cocoa-nut matting, and the animals were taken out every day—except once when the vessel rolled too much—and walked round and round for exercise. In consequence they arrived in just as good condition as they were in upon the day of starting. While I am writing, the Great Victoria is signalled as in sight. This vessel contains, it is said, the Snider rifles, the warm clothing, the tents, and many other important necessaries. Her arrival, therefore, will greatly smooth difficulties and enable the troops to advance.

At the time that the above letter was written I had only been a few hours upon shore, and was of course unable to look deeper than the mere surface. I could therefore only assign the most apparent reason for the complete break-down of the transport train. The disaster has now become historical, and rivalled, if it did not surpass, that of the worst days of the Crimea; and as for a time it paralysed the expedition, and exercised throughout a most disastrous influence, it is as well, before we proceed up the country, that we should examine thoroughly into its causes.

After a searching inquiry into all that had taken place prior to my arrival, I do not hesitate to ascribe the break-down of the transport train to four causes, and in this opinion I may say that I am thoroughly borne out by ninety-nine out of every hundred officers who were there. The first cause was the inherent weakness of the organisation of the transport train, the ridiculous paucity of officers, both commissioned and noncommissioned, the want of experienced drivers, and the ignorance of everyone as to the working of a mule-train. The second cause was the mismanagement of the Bombay authorities in sending animals in one ship, drivers in another, and equipments scattered throughout a whole fleet of transports, instead of sending each shipload of animals complete with their complement of drivers and equipments, as was done by the Bengal authorities. The third cause was the grossly-overcoloured reports of the officers of the pioneer force as to the state of water and forage, and which induced the Bombay authorities to hurry forward men and animals, to find only a bare and waterless desert. The fourth reason was the conduct of the above-mentioned officers in marching with all the troops to Senafe, in direct disobedience of the orders they had received. This last cause was the most fatal of all. In spite of the first three causes all might, and I believe would, have gone tolerably well, had it not been for the fourth.

At Koomaylo and at Hadoda, each thirteen miles distant from Zulla, there was water in abundance, together with bushes and browsing-ground for the camels. Had the animals upon landing been taken at once to these places, and there allowed to remain until the time approached for a general forward movement of the whole army, as Sir Robert Napier had directed, everything would have gone well. The officers would have had plenty of time to have effected a thorough and perfect organisation; the men would have learnt their new duties, and would have acquired some sort of discipline; the camels could have gone to Zulla and brought out forage for the mules; not an animal need have remained at Zulla, not one have suffered from thirst; and the immense expense of condensing water for them would have been avoided, besides the saving of life of many thousands of animals. But what happened? As I have shown in the previous chapter, General Napier had said to Colonel Merewether, in his parting instructions, "It is not at all intended that this force shall take up a position upon the high land, for which its strength and composition are not fitted;" and again, he had written at the end of October, "that if the news were satisfactory, Staveley's Brigade would sail, and *upon its arrival* the advance may be made." To Colonel Phayre he had written October 9th: "It is not of course intended that Colonel Field should move to the high table-land at Dexan, &c., but shall merely take up such position as will cover the dépôt and protect the cattle;" and again, in the same letter: "You will understand that it is not my desire to precipitate a lodgment upon the table-land, which we should have to retain too long before advancing." General Napier, then, had been as explicit as it was possible for a man to be in his orders that no advance should take place; and he had specially said, in his memorandum of 7th September, the subject of the transport train, that "great care should be taken to prevent their being overworked." And yet, in spite of these orders, Colonels Merewether and Phayre, together with Colonel Wilkins,—to whom the making of piers, &c., had been specially assigned by the General in his instructions to the pioneer force,—with Colonel Field and the whole of the troops, start up to Senafe on or about the 1st of December! And this at a time when two or three large transports might be expected to arrive daily! The consequences which might have been expected ensued. The unfortunate animals, the instant they arrived, were saddled, loaded, and hurried off without a day to recover from the fatigue of the voyage. The muleteers were in like way despatched, without a single hour to acquire a notion of their duties.

Senafe is five days' march from Zulla, up a ravine of almost unparalleled difficulty.

Up and down this ravine the wretched animals stumbled and toiled, starving when in the pass, and dying of thirst during their brief pauses at Zulla; the fortunate ones dying in scores upon the way, and the less happy ones incurring disease of the lungs, which, after a few painful weeks, brought them to the welcome grave. And all this to feed Colonels Merewether and Phayre and the troops at Senafe. *Cui bono?* No one can answer. No one to this day has been able to offer the slightest explanation of the extraordinary course adopted by these officers. If Colonel Merewether had felt it his duty to go to Senafe in order to enter into political relations with the chiefs in the neighbourhood, and to arrange for the purchase of animals and food, a small escort would have enabled him to do so. Not only was their absence disastrous to the mule-train, but it was productive of the greatest confusion at Zulla. There no one was left in command. Astounding as it may appear to every military man, here, at a port at which an amount of work scarcely, if ever, equalled, had to be got through, with troops, animals, and stores arriving daily in vast quantities, there was at the time of my arrival absolutely no "officer commanding,"—not even a nominal head. Each head of department did his best; but, like Hal o' the Wynd, he fought for his own hand. The confusion which resulted may be imagined but cannot be described. Having thus briefly adverted to the causes which led to the breakdown of the transport train, I continue my journal.

Koomaylo, December 9th.

I mentioned in my letter of two days since, that the news from the front was, that the King of Tigré, with an army of 7000 men, was inclined to make himself unpleasant. Our last "shave," that of yesterday, goes into the opposite extreme, and tells us that the Kings of Shoa and Lasta have both sent to Colonel Merewether, and have offered to attack Theodore. The hostilities and the alliances of the kings of these tribes are, of course, matters of importance; but as these native potentates seldom know their own minds for many hours together, and change from a state of friendship to one of hostility at a moment's notice, or for a fancied affront, I do not attach much importance to any of them, with the exception of the King of Tigré, through whose dominions we have to pass. If he allows us to pass to and fro without interference, we can do very well without the alliance of Shoa or of Lasta. We are strong enough to conquer Theodore, even if he were backed by the three kings named; and now we have got everything ready, the difference of expense between a war of a few weeks' duration and one of twice as many months, will be comparatively trifling. As for the troops, nothing would cause such disgust as to return without doing anything, after all the preparations which have been made. I do not think, however, that it would make much difference in our movements now, even if the prisoners are given up. Of course, had they been released a year ago, in consequence of our entreaties or in exchange for our presents, we should have been contented; but now we must demand something more than a mere delivery of the prisoners. There is compensation to be made for their long and painful sufferings, and an attempt at any rate made to obtain some sort of payment for our enormous expenses. I attach, therefore, little importance to what is doing at Senafe, but consider the state of the preparations at the landing-place at Annesley Bay to be the central point of interest. For the last two days much has been done towards getting things in order. Pack-saddles in abundance have been landed. Sir Charles Staveley has disembarked, and is hard at work; and in the Land Transport Corps, in particular, great things have been done. Captain Twentyman, who is in command, laid a number of suggestions before the general, which he at once sanctioned. Fodder was strewed near the watering-place, and as the starving animals strayed down they were captured. One hundred and fifty of them were handed over to the Beloochee regiment, whose men cheerfully volunteered to look after them. Tubs were obtained from the commissariat to supplement the absurdly-insufficient troughs at the watering-place, and which were only kept full of water at certain times of the day. The 200 Madras dhoolie bearers, who have been transferred to the transport, are doing good work, and there is every hope that in another week things will be straight, and the wretched stragglers who at present shock one with their sufferings be again safely hobbled in line with other animals.

The work which the officers of this corps get through is prodigious. Captains Twentyman, Warren, and Hodges, and Lieutenant Daniels, are beginning to forget what a bed is like, for they are at work and about for more than twenty hours out of the twenty-four. Indeed, I must say that I never saw a greater devotion to duty than is shown by the officers of the various departments. The quartermaster's department, the commissariat, and others, vie with each other in the energy which they exhibit, and the only thing to be wished is that there were a little more unanimity in their efforts. Each works for himself. Whereas if they were only branches of an *intendance générale*, the heads of the departments might meet each other and their chief of an evening, each state their wants and their wishes, concert together as to the work to be performed next day, and then act with a perfect knowledge of what was to be got through. However, this is a Utopia which it is vain to sigh for. Probably till the end of time we shall have separate departments and divided responsibilities; and between the stools the British soldier will continue to fall, and that very heavily, to the ground.

On the afternoon of the 7th the first two companies of the 33d regiment were to land; and this spectacle was particularly interesting, as they were the first European regiment to land upon the shores of Abyssinia. A large flat, towed by a steam-barge, came alongside, and the men, with their kit-bags and beds, embarked on board them. As they did so, the regimental band struck up, the men and their comrades on board ship cheering heartily. It was very exciting, and made one's blood dance in one's veins; but to me there is always something saddening in these spectacles. This is the third "*Partant pour la Syrie*" that I have seen. I witnessed the Guards parade before Buckingham Palace. I saw them cheer wildly as the band played and the Queen waved her handkerchief to them; and six months afterwards I saw them, a shattered relic of a regiment, in the Crimea. Last year I described a scene in Piacenza, on the eve of the march of the Italian army into the Quadrilateral. There, too, were patriotic songs and hearty cheerings, there were high hopes and brave hearts. A week after I saw them hurled back again from the land they had invaded, defeated by a foe they almost despised. Fortunately, in the present case I have no similar catastrophe to anticipate. As far as fighting goes, her Majesty's 33d regiment need fear nothing they will meet in Abyssinia, or, indeed, in any part of the world. It is a regiment of veterans; it won no slight glory in the Crimea, and a few months later it was hurried off to aid in crushing the Indian mutiny. In India they have been ever since, and are as fine and soldierlike a set of men as could be found in the British army. We were to have landed at two o'clock, but a few of the little things which always are found to be done at the last moment delayed us half an hour; and that delay of half an hour completely changed the whole plans of the day. It had been intended that, after landing, the men should remain quiet until five o'clock, by which time the heat of the day would be over; that they should then pack the baggage upon the camels, which were to start at once with a guard, that the men should lie down and sleep till midnight, and that they should then march, so as to arrive at Koomaylo at five o'clock in the morning. All these arrangements, admirable in their way, were defeated by this little half-hour's delay. There was not a breath of wind when we left the ship, but in the quarter of an hour the passage occupied the sea-breeze rushed down, and when we reached the pier the waves were already breaking heavily. Time after time the man-of-war's boats came to us as we lay thirty yards off, and took off a load each time; once, too, we drifted so close to the end of the pier that the men were able to leap off upon the rough stones. In this way all the troops got off except the baggage-guard. But by this time the surf had increased so much, that the boats could no longer get alongside; accordingly the tug had to tow the barge a couple of hundred yards out, and there to remain until the sea-breeze dropped. In consequence it was nine in the evening before the baggage got ashore, and nearly one in the morning before the camels had their loads; and even then some of the men's beds had to be left behind. Considering the extreme lateness of the hour, and the fact that the moon would soon be down, I thought it best to get a sleep until daylight. Under the shelter of a friendly tent I lay down upon the sand until five o'clock, and then, after the slight toilet of a shake to get rid of loose sand, I started.

The road from Annesley Bay to Koomaylo can hardly be termed either interesting or strongly defined. It at first goes straight across the sand, and, as the sand is trampled everywhere, it is simply impossible to follow it. We were told that the route lay due west, but that just where the jungle began there was a sign-post. Compass in hand, we steered west, and entered the low thorny scrub which constitutes the jungle. No sign-post. We rode on for a mile, when, looking back at the rising sun, I saw something like a sign-post in the extreme distance. Riding back to it, it proved to be the desired guide, and the road from here is by daylight distinct enough. For the first six miles it runs across a dead-level of sand, covered with a shrub with very small and very scanty leaves, and very large and extremely-abundant thorns. Bustards, grouse, deer, and other game are said to be very abundant here, but we saw none of them. A sort of large hawk was very numerous, but these were the only birds we saw. At about six miles from the sea the ground rises abruptly for about ten feet in height, and this rise ran north and south as far as the eye could reach. It marked unquestionably the level of the sea at some not very remote period. From this point the plain continued flat, sandy, and bushy as before for two miles; but after that a rocky crag rose, rather to our right, and the sand became interspersed with stones and boulders. Our path lay round behind the hill, and then we could see, at about four miles' distance, a white tent or two, at the mouth of an opening in the mountain before us. These white tents were the camp at Koomaylo. About three miles from Koomaylo we came upon a very curious burial-place. It was in a low flat, close to a gully, and covered a space of perhaps fifty yards square. The graves were placed very close together, and consisted of square piles of stones, not thrown together, but built up, about three feet square and as much high. They were crowned by a rough pyramid of stones, the top one being generally white. Underneath these stone piles was a sort of vault. From this point the ground rose more steeply than it had yet done.

Koomaylo is situated at the mouth of the pass which takes its name from it. The valley here is about half-a-mile wide. It is rather over thirteen miles from the sea, and is said to be 415 feet above the sea-level; but it does not appear to be nearly so high. At any rate, its height does not make it any cooler; for, hot as it is at Annesley Bay, it is at least as hot here. The greatest nuisance I have at present met with in Abyssinia are the flies, which are as numerous and irritating as they are in Egypt. Fortunately they go to sleep when the sun goes down; and as there are no mosquitoes to take their place, one is able to sleep in tranquillity. We found on arriving at Koomaylo that the troops had not been in very long. They had got scattered in the night, owing to some of the camels breaking down; had lost their guides, lost each other, and lost the way. Finally, however, all the troops came in in a body under their officers at about eight o'clock. The animals were not quite so unanimous in their movements; for a number of them took quite the wrong road, and went to Hadoda, a place about six miles from here, to the north, and twelve miles from Zulla. There are wells there, so they got a drink, and came on in the course of the day. A few, however, have not yet turned up, and one of these missing animals bore a portion of my own luggage and stores. The others will perhaps arrive; but I have a moral conviction that that animal will never again make his appearance. As the men were too tired upon their arrival to pitch their tents, many of which indeed had not yet arrived, they were allowed to take possession of a number of tents which had been pitched for head-quarters. When we arrived they were all shaken down; the men were asleep in the tents, and the camels had gone down to water. The first step was to go down to water our horses and mules, the next to draw rations for ourselves, our followers, and beasts. The watering-place is a quarter of a mile from this camp, which is on rather rising ground. The wells are, of course, in the bed of what in the rainy season must be a mighty torrent fifty yards wide.

I have seen many singular scenes, but I do not know that I ever saw a stranger one than these wells presented. They are six in number, are twelve or fourteen feet across, and about twelve feet deep. They are dug through the mass of stones and boulders which forms the bed of the stream, and three of the six have a sort of wooden platform, upon which men stand to lower the buckets to the water by ropes. The other wells have sloping sides, and upon them stand sets of natives, who pass buckets from hand to hand, and empty them into earth troughs, or rather mud basins, from which the animals drink. The natives while so engaged keep up the perpetual chant without which they seem to be unable to do any work. The words of this chant vary infinitely, and they consist almost always of two words of four or five syllables in all; which are repeated by the next set of men, with the variation of one of the syllables, and in a tone two notes lower than that used by the first set. Round these wells are congregated a vast crowd of animals—flocks of goats and small sheep, hundreds in number, strings of draught-bullocks, mules, ponies, horses, and camels, hundreds of natives, with their scanty attire, their spears, their swords exactly resembling reaping-hooks, and their heavy clubs. Here are their wives and sisters, some of them in the ordinary draped calico, others very picturesquely attired in leathern petticoats, and a body-dress of a sort of sheet of leather, going over one shoulder and under the other arm, covering the bust, and very prettily ornamented with stars and other devices, formed of white shells. Round their necks·they wear necklaces of red seeds and shells. Some of them are really very good-looking, with remarkably intelligent faces. The scene round the wells is very exciting, for the animals press forward most eagerly, and their attendants have the greatest difficulty in preserving order, especially among the mules and camels. The supply, however, is equal to the demand, and by the end of the day the wells are nearly deserted, except by the soldiers, who like to go down and draw their water fresh from the wells. The upper wells, where buckets with ropes only are used, are really very fair water; those for the animals are not clear, but are still drinkable. All have a taste somewhat resembling the water from peat-bogs. Natives are employed digging more wells, which can be done, for the quantity which is drawn appears to make little or no difference in the level of the water in the present wells. Some of the camels occasionally get quite furious; to-day I saw one, whose saddle had slipped round under its belly, begin to jump and plunge most wildly, with its head in the air, and uttering the most uncouth cries. There was a general stampede, especially among the mules, many of whom have, I fancy, never seen a camel before. It was some minutes before the animal could be caught and forced down upon its knees by its driver, and by that time he had quite cleared the ground in his neighbourhood. The camels are kept as much as possible kneeling, and there were a hundred or two near him at the time he commenced his evolutions. When one camel rises, all in his neighbourhood always endeavour to do the same; and the efforts of these beasts to rise, the shouts of their drivers, and the stampede of the mules, made up a most laughable scene. Near the wells is another large graveyard; the tombs here are rather more ornate than those I have already described, some of them being round, and almost all having courses of white quartz stones. Upon the top of many of these tombs are two or three flat stones, placed on end, and somewhat resembling small head- and foot-stones. As there is no inscription upon them it would be curious to find out the object with which the natives erect them.

Having finished watering our horses, we proceeded to the commissariat tent. Here an immense quantity of work is got through, all the animals and men drawing their rations daily; and I have heard no complaint of any sort, except that some Parsees, while I was getting my rations, came up and complained bitterly because there was no mutton, and it was contrary to their religion to eat beef. The commissariat officer regretted the circumstance, but pointed out that at present no sheep had been landed, and that the little things of the country are mere skin and bone, and quite unfitted for the troops. The Parsees, who were, I believe, clerks to one of the departments, went off highly discontented. The moral of this evidently is that Parsees should not go to war in a country where mutton is scarce. As for the Hindoos, I cannot even guess how they will preserve their caste intact. It is a pity that their priests could not give them a dispensation to put aside all their caste observances for the time they may be out of India. As it is, I foresee we shall have very great difficulty with them.

Koomaylo, December 12th.

When I wrote two days ago I hardly expected to have dated another letter from Koomaylo. I had prepared to start for Senafe, leaving my baggage behind me, and returning in ten days or so. The great objection to this plan was that neither at Zulla nor here are there any huts or stores where things can be left. The only thing to be done, therefore, was to leave them in the tent of some friend; but as he, too, might get the route at any moment, it would have been, to say the least of it, a very hazardous proceeding. The night before last, however, I received the joyful and long-expected news that the ship which had left Bombay with my horses six days before I started myself was at last in harbour. My course was now clear; I should go down, get my horses, and then go up to Senafe, carrying my whole baggage with me. Vessels and troops are arriving every day, and the accumulations of arrears of work are increasing in even more rapid proportion. Major Baigrie, the quartermaster-general, is indefatigable, but he cannot unload thirty large vessels at one little jetty, at whose extremity there is only a depth of five feet of water. Unless something is done, and that rapidly, and upon an extensive scale, we shall break down altogether. It is evident that a jetty, at which at most three of these country boats can lie alongside to unload, is only sufficient to afford accommodation for one large ship, and that it would take several days to discharge her cargo of say one thousand tons, using the greatest despatch possible. How, then, can it be hoped that the vessels in the harbour, whose number is increasing at the rate of two or three a-day, are to be unloaded? In the Crimea great distress was caused because the ships in Balaclava harbour could not manage to discharge their stores. But Balaclava harbour offered facilities for unloading which were enormous compared to this place. There was a wharf a quarter of a mile long, with deep water alongside, so that goods could be rolled down planks or gangways to the shore from the vessels. The harbour was land-locked, and the work of unloading never interrupted. Compare that with the present state of things. A boat-jetty running out into five-foot water, and only approachable for half the day owing to the surf, and, as I hear, for months not approachable at all. It can be mathematically proved that the quantity of provision and forage which can be landed from these boats, always alongside for so many hours a-day, would not supply the fifth of the wants of twenty-five thousand men and as many animals. Everything depends upon what the state of the interior of the country is. If we find sufficient forage for the animals and food for the men—which the most sanguine man does not anticipate—well and good. If not, we must break down. It is simply out of the question to land the stores with the present arrangements in Annesley Bay, or with anything like them. The pier-accommodation must be greatly increased, and must be made practical in all weather, that is to say, practical all day in ordinary weather. To do this the pier should be run out another fifty yards, and should then have a cross-pier erected at its extremity. The native boats could lie under the lee of this and unload in all weathers, and there would be sufficient depth of water for the smaller transports to lie alongside on the outside in calm weather, and to unload direct on to the pier. I know that this would be an expensive business, that stone has to be brought from a distance, &c. But it is a necessity, and therefore expense is no object. I consider that the railway which is to be laid between the landing-place and this point will be of immense utility to the expedition; but I believe it to be a work of quite inferior importance in comparison with this question of increased pier-accommodation. There is no doubt that in spite of the troops and animals arriving from Bombay before things were ready for them here, things would have gone on far better than they have done, had there been any head to direct operations here. But the officers of the various departments have been working night and day without any head whatever to give unity and object to their efforts. I understand that General Staveley was astonished to find that before the arrival of General Collings, two days previous to himself, there had been no head to the expedition.

Sir Robert Napier was fully alive to the extreme importance of this question of wharfage, for in his memorandum of September 12th he recommended that planking, tressles, piles, and materials to construct wharves should be forwarded with the 1st Brigade. "There cannot," he proceeded, "be too many landing-places to facilitate debarkation, and on such convenience will depend the boats being quickly cleared, and the stores removed from them dry. It would be advisable that a considerable number of empty casks should be forwarded to be used as rafts, or to form floating-wharves for use at low water, particularly should the shores shelve gently.

Spars to form floating shears should also be forwarded." Thus Sir Robert Napier, himself an engineer, had long before foreseen the extreme importance of providing the greatest possible amount of landing accommodation; and yet three months after this memorandum was written, and two months after the arrival of the pioneer force at Zulla, an unfinished pier was all that had been effected, and Colonel Wilkins, the officer to whom this most important work had been specially intrusted, was quietly staying up at Senafe with Colonels Merewether, Phayre, and Field. A second pier was not completed until the end of February, and consequently many vessels remained for months in harbour before their cargoes could be unloaded, at an expense and loss to the public service which can hardly be over-estimated.

We had quite a small excitement here this afternoon. I was writing quietly, and thinking what a hot day it was, when I heard a number of the soldiers running and shouting. I rushed to the door of my tent and saw a troop of very large monkeys trotting along, pursued by the men, who were throwing stones at them. Visions of monkey-skins flashed across my mind, and in a moment, snatching up revolvers and sun-helmets, three or four of us joined the chase. We knew from the first that it was perfectly hopeless, for the animals were safe in the hills, which extended for miles. However, the men scattered over the hills, shouting and laughing, and so we went on also, and for a couple of hours climbed steadily on, scratching ourselves terribly with the thorn-bushes which grow everywhere—and to which an English quickset-hedge is as nothing—and losing many pounds in weight from the effect of our exertions. Hot as it was, I think that the climb did us all good. Indeed, the state of the health of everyone out here is most excellent, and the terrible fevers and all the nameless horrors with which the army was threatened in its march across the low ground, turn out to be the effect of the imagination only of the well-intentioned but mischievous busybodies who have for the last six months filled the press with their most dismal predictions. I have heard many a hearty laugh since I have been here at all the evils we were threatened would assail us in the thirteen miles between Annesley Bay and this place. We were to die of fever, malaria, sunstroke, tetse-fly, Guinea-worm, tapeworm, and many other maladies. It is now nearly three months since the first man landed, and upon this very plain there are at present thousands of men, including the Beloochee regiment and other natives, hundreds, taking Europeans only, of officers, staff and departmental, with the conductors, inspectors, and men of the transport, commissariat, and other departments. From the day of the first landing to the present time there has not been one death, or even an illness of any consequence, among all these men upon this plain of death. As for the two companies of the 33d, their surgeon tells me that the general state of their health is better than in India, for that there has not been a single case of fever or indisposition of any kind in the five days since they landed, whereas in India there were always a proportion of men in hospital with slight attacks of fever. All this is most gratifying, and I believe that all the other dangers and difficulties will, when confronted, prove to have been equally exaggerated. The difficulties of the pass to the first plateau, 7000 feet above the sea, have already proved to be insignificant. There are only four miles of at all difficult ground, and this has already been greatly obviated by the efforts of the Bombay Sappers. The December rains have not yet begun, but yesterday and to-day we have heavy clouds hanging over the tops of the mountains. The rain would be a very great boon, and would quite alter the whole aspect of the country. The whole country, indeed, when not trampled upon, is covered with dry, burnt-up herbage, presenting exactly the colour of the sand, but which only needs a few hours' rain to convert it into a green plain of grass, sufficient for the forage of all the baggage-animals in the camp.

While I have been writing this the Beloochees and a company of Bombay Sappers and Miners have marched into camp, with their baggage and camels. The Beloochees are a splendid regiment—tall, active, serviceable-looking men as ever I saw. Their dress is a dark-green tunic, with scarlet facings and frogs, trousers of a lighter green, a scarlet cap, with a large black turban around it; altogether a very picturesque dress. The Sappers and Miners are in British uniform. Both these corps go on early to-morrow morning to Upper Sooro. I have not decided yet whether I shall accompany them, or go on by myself this evening.

A letter has just come down from Colonel Merewether saying that all is going on well at Senafe. The King of Tigré has sent in his adhesion, and numbers of petty chiefs came in riding on mules, and followed by half-a-dozen ragged followers on foot, to make their "salaam." I do not know that these petty chiefs, who are subjects of the King of Tigré, are of much importance one way or another, but their friendship would be useful if they would bring in a few hundred head of bullocks and a few flocks of sheep. It is, I understand, very cold up there, and the troops will have need of all their warm clothing.

Upper Sooro, December 13th.

I must begin my letter by retracting an opinion I expressed in my last, namely, that the defile would probably turn out a complete bugbear, as the fevers, guinea-worm, and tetse flies have done. My acquaintance with most of the passes of the Alps and Tyrol is of an extensive kind, but I confess that it in no way prepared me for the passage of an Abyssinian defile. I can now quite understand travellers warning us that many of these places were impracticable for a single horseman, much less for an army with its baggage-animals. Had not Colonel Merewether stated in his report that the first time he explored the pass he met laden bullocks coming down it, I should not have conceived it possible that any beast of burden could have scrambled over the terrible obstacles. Even now, when the Bombay Sappers have been at work for three weeks upon it, it is the roughest piece of road I ever saw, and only practicable for a single animal at once. It is in all twelve miles; at least, so it is said by the engineers, and we took, working hard, seven hours to do it; and I found that this was a very fair average time. A single horseman will, of course, do it in a very much shorter time, because there are miles together where a horse might gallop without danger. I remained at Koomaylo until the afternoon, as it was too hot to start till the sun was low. Nothing happened during the day, except the arrival of the Beloochees and Bombay Engineers. The soldiers had two or three more chases after the monkeys, of which there are extra ordinary numbers. I need hardly say that they did not catch any of them: a dog, however, belonging to one of the soldiers seized one for a moment, but was attacked with such fury by his companions that it had to leave its hold and beat a precipitate retreat. I have just been watching a flock or herd—I do not know which is the correct term—of these animals, two or three hundred in number, who have passed along the rocks behind my tent, at perhaps thirty yards' distance. They have not the slightest fear of man, and even all the noise and bustle of a camp seem to amuse rather than alarm them. They are of all sizes, from the full-grown, which are as large as a large dog, down to tiny things which keep close to their mothers, and cling round their necks at the least alarm. The old ones make no noise, but step deliberately from rock to rock, sitting down frequently to inspect the camp, and indulge in the pleasure of a slight scratch. These full-sized fellows have extremely long hair over the head and upper part of the body, but are bare, disagreeably so, towards the caudal extremity. The small ones scamper along, chattering and screaming; they have no mane or long hair on the head. The old monkeys, when they do make a sound, bark just like a large dog. In the afternoon an enormous number of locusts came down the pass, and afforded amusement and diet to flocks of birds, who were, I observed, rather epicures in their way, for on picking up many of the dead bodies of the locusts, I found that in every case it was only the head and upper part of the thorax which had been eaten. I shall accept this as a hint; and in case of the starvation days with which this expedition is threatened—in addition to innumerable other evils—really coming on, I shall, when we are driven to feed on locusts, eat only the parts which the birds have pointed out to me as the tit-bits. I am happy to say that there is no probability of our being driven to that resource at present; for on our way here yesterday I passed considerable quantities of native cattle, and any quantity is procurable here, and as for goats they are innumerable. We bought one this morning for our servants for the sum of a rupee. The commissariat have made up their minds that all servants and followers must be Hindoos, and therefore abstainers from meat, and so issue no meat whatever in their rations—nothing, indeed, except rice, grain, a little flour, and a little ghee. Now, the fact is that the followers are generally not Hindoos. Many of the body-servants are Portuguese, Goa men; and the horse-keepers are frequently Mussulmans, or come from the north-west provinces, where they are not particular. Even the mule-drivers are Arabs, Egyptians, and Patans, all of whom eat flesh. It thus happens that the whole of our five servants are meat-eaters, and it is fortunate that we are able to buy meat from the natives for them, especially as they have really hard work to do; and in the cold climate we shall enter in another day or two meat is doubly necessary.

We had intended to start at three o'clock, but it was four before our baggage was fairly disposed upon the backs of the four baggage-animals— two strong mules and two ponies—and we were in the saddles of our riding-horses. Our route, after leaving the wells, ran, with of course various turnings and windings, in a south-westerly direction. The way lay along the bottom of the valley, a road being marked out by the loose stones being removed to a certain extent, and laid along both sides of the track. The valley for the first seven or eight miles was very regular, of a width of from 200 to 300 yards. Its bottom, though really rising gradually, appeared to the eye a perfect flat of sand, scattered with boulders and stones, and covered with the thorny jungle I have spoken of in a previous letter. This scrub had been cleared away along the line of road, or there would have been very little flesh, to say nothing of clothes, left upon our bones by the time we came to our journey's end. Backward and forward, across the sandy plain, as the spurs of the hills turned its course, wound the bed of the torrent—I should think that we crossed it fifty times. It is probable that on occasions of great floods the whole valley is under water. To our left the hills, though rocky and steep, sloped somewhat gradually, and were everywhere sprinkled with bushes. On the right the mountain was much more lofty, and rose in many places very precipitously. Sometimes the valley widened somewhat, at other times the mountains closed in, and we seemed to have arrived at the end of our journey, until on rounding some projecting spur the valley would appear stretching away at its accustomed width. Altogether, the scenery reminded me very much of the Tyrol, except that the hills at our side were not equal in height to those which generally border the valleys there.

At half-past six it had become so dark that we could no longer follow the track, and the animals were continually stumbling over the loose stones, and we were obliged to halt for half-an-hour, by which time the moon had risen over the plain; and although it was some time longer before she was high enough to look down over the hill-tops into our valley, yet there was quite light enough for us to pursue our way. In another three-quarters of an hour we came upon a sight which has not greeted my eyes since I left England, excepting, of course, in my journey through France—it was running water. We all knelt down and had a drink, but, curiously enough, although our animals had been travelling for nearly four hours enveloped in a cloud of light dust, they one and all refused to drink; indeed, I question if they had ever seen running water before, and had an idea it was something uncanny. This place we knew was Lower Sooro, not that there was any village—indeed, I begin to question the existence of villages in this part of the world, for I have not yet seen a single native permanent hut, only bowers constructed of the boughs of trees and bushes. But in Abyssinia it is not villages which bear names; it is wells. Zulla, and Koomaylo, the Upper and Lower Sooro, are not villages, but wells. Natives come and go, and build their bowers, but they do not live there. I fancy that when there is a native name, and no well, it is a graveyard which gives the name. We passed two or three of these between Koomaylo and Sooro, all similar to those I have already described. From Lower to Upper Sooro is a distance of four miles. It is in this portion of the road that the real difficulties of the pass are situated, and I never passed through a succession of such narrow and precipitous gorges as it contains. The sides of these gorges are in many places perfectly perpendicular, and the scenery, although not very lofty, is yet wild and grand in the extreme, and seen, as we saw it, with the bright light and deep shadows thrown by the full moon, it was one of the most impressive pieces of scenery I ever saw. The difficulty of the pass consists not in its steepness, for the rise is little over three hundred feet in a mile, but in the mass of huge boulders which strew its bottom. Throughout its length, indeed, the path winds its way in and out and over a chaos of immense stones, which look as if they had but just fallen from the almost overhanging sides of the ravine. Some of these masses are as large as a good-sized house, with barely room between them for a mule to pass with his burden. In many places, indeed, there was not room at all until the Bombay Sappers, who are encamped about half-way up the pass, set to work to make it practicable by blasting away projecting edges, and in some slight way smoothing the path among the smaller rocks. In some places great dams have been formed right across the ravine, owing to two or three monster boulders having blocked the course of the stream, and from the accumulated rocks which the winter torrents have swept down upon them. Upon these great obstacles nothing less than an army of sappers could make any impression, and here the engineers have contented themselves by building a road up to the top of the dam and down again the other side. We were three hours making this four-mile passage, and the labour, the shouting, and the difficulties of the way, must be imagined. Of course we had dismounted, and had given our horses to their grooms to lead. Constantly the baggage was shifting, and required a pause and a readjustment. Now our tin pails would bang with a clash against a rock one side; now our case of brandy—taken for purely medicinal purposes— would bump against a projection on the other. Now one of the ponies would stumble, and the other nearly come upon him; now one of the mules, in quickening his pace to charge a steep ascent, would nearly pull the one which was following, and attached to him, off his feet; then there would be a fresh alarm that the ponies' baggage was coming off. All this was repeated over and over again. There were shouts in English, Hindostanee, Arabic, and in other and unknown tongues. Altogether it was the most fatiguing four miles I have ever passed, and we were all regularly done when we got to the top. I should say that the water had all this time tossed and fretted between the rocks, sometimes hidden beneath them for a hundred yards, then crossing and recrossing our path, or running directly under our feet, until we were within a few hundred yards of Upper Sooro, when the ravine widening out, and the bottom being sandy, the stream no longer runs above the surface. Altogether it was a ride to be long remembered, through that lonely valley by moonlight in an utterly unknown and somewhat hostile country, as several attempts at robbery have been made by the natives lately upon small parties; and although in no case have they attacked a European, yet everyone rides with his loaded revolver in his holster. A deep silence seemed to hang over everything, broken only by our own voices, except by the occasional thrill of a cicada among the bushes, the call of a night-bird, or by the whining of a jackal, or the hoarse bark of a monkey on the hills above.

It was just eleven o'clock when we arrived at Upper Sooro. An officer at once came to the door of his tent, and with that hospitality which is universal, asked us to come in and sit while our tent was being pitched. We accepted, and he opened for us a bottle of beer, cool, and in excellent condition. Imagine our feelings. Brandy-and-water would have been true hospitality, but beer, where beer is so scarce and so precious as it is here, was a deed which deserves to be recorded in letters of gold. I forbear to name our benefactor. The Samaritan's name has not descended to us; the widow who bestowed the mite is nameless. Let it be so in the present case. But I shall never cease to think of that bottle of beer with gratitude.

My tent was now pitched; my servant procured some hot water and made some tea; and having taken that and some biscuit, and having seen that the horses were fed, I slightly undressed, lay down upon my water-proof sheet, and lighted a final cigar, when to my horror I observed many creeping things advancing over the sheet towards me. Upon examination they turned out to be of two species—the one a large red ant, the other a sort of tick, which I found on inquiring in the morning are camel-ticks. They are a lead colour, and about the size of sheep-ticks, but they do not run so fast. This was, indeed, a calamity, but there was nothing to be done. I was far too tired to get up and have my tent pitched in another place; besides, another place might have been just as bad. I therefore wrapped myself as tightly as I could in my rug, in hopes that they would not find their way in, and so went to sleep. In the morning I rejoiced greatly to find that I had not been bitten; for they bite horses and men, raising a bump as big as a man's fist upon the former, and causing great pain and swelling to the latter.

I describe thus minutely the events of every day, because the life of most officers and men greatly resembles my own, and by relating my own experience I give a far more accurate idea of the sort of life we are leading in Abyssinia than I could do by any general statements.

Upper Sooro is a large commissariat dépôt, exceedingly well managed by Conductor Crow. It is a new basin of five hundred yards long by two hundred across, a widening out of the pass. It is selected for that reason, as it is the only place along the line near water where a regiment could encamp. Owing to its elevation above the sea the temperature is very pleasant, except for two or three hours in the middle of the day. Another agreeable change is that the thorny bushes have disappeared, and a tree without prickles, and which attains a considerable size, has taken their place.

At seven o'clock this morning the Beloochees began to arrive, having started at midnight. The advanced guard were therefore exactly the same time doing the distance that we were. Their baggage, however, has been dropping in all day, for it was loaded on camels, and most of these animals stuck fast in the narrow passages of the pass, and had to be unloaded to enable them to get through; and this happened again and again. The pass, in fact, is not, as yet, practicable for camels; mules can manage it, but it is a very close fit for them, and it will be some time yet before camels can pass with their burdens. I suppose after to-day's experience camels will not be again employed this side of Koomaylo until the pass has been widened. Some of the poor animals were stuck fast for a couple of hours before they could be extricated. There are now a hundred of them lying down within fifty yards of my tent. I consider the camel to be the most ridiculously-overpraised animal under the sun. I do not deny that he has his virtues. He is moderately strong—not very strong for his size, for he will not carry so much as a couple of good mules; still he is fairly strong, and he can go a long time without water—a very useful quality in the desert, or on the sea-shore of Abyssinia. But patient! Heaven save the mark! He is without exception the most cantankerous animal under the sun. When he is wanted to stand up, he lies down; when he is wanted to lie down, he will not do it on any consideration; and once down he jumps up again the moment his driver's back is turned. He grumbles, and growls, and roars at any order he receives, whether to stand up or lie down; whether to be loaded or to have his packs taken off. When he is once loaded and in motion he goes on quietly enough; but so does a horse, or a donkey, or any other animal. After having made himself as disagreeable as possible, there is small praise to him that he goes on when he cannot help it. I consider the mule, which people have most wrongfully named obstinate, to be a superior animal in every respect—except that he wants his drink—to the much-bepraised camel.

A messenger passed through here yesterday from Abyssinia. He was bringing letters from Mr. Rassam to Colonel Merewether. He reports that Theodore is continuing his cruelties, and killing his soldiers in numbers. Under these circumstances one can hardly feel surprised at the news that, in spite of his efforts, he is unable to increase his army beyond seven or eight thousand men. He is still at Debra Tabor.

Camp, Senafe, December 16th.

I arrived here only half-an-hour since, and find that the post is on the point of starting. I therefore have only time to write a few lines to supplement my last letter, which was sent from Sooro. All description of the pass between that resting-place and Senafe I must postpone to my next letter, and only write to say that there is no particular news here. The messenger from Mr. Rassam arrived in the camp yesterday. He states that the King of Shoa's men are between Theodore and Magdala, and that there is every hope that they will take the latter place, and liberate the prisoners. The reports about the King of Tigré are, to a certain extent, founded on fact. He has professed the greatest friendship, but there are sinister reports that he really means mischief, and for two or three days the pickets have been doubled. It is not thought that there is any foundation for the report of his intention to attack us. The situation of this camp is very pleasant—upon a lofty table-land, seven thousand feet above the sea, and with a delightfully bracing wind blowing over it, and reminding one of Brighton Downs in the month of May. At night I am told that the thermometer goes down below freezing-point. The camp is situated in a slight hollow or valley in the plain; through its centre flows a stream, which when the camp was first formed was knee-deep, but has greatly fallen off since, so much so that reservoirs are being formed and wells sunk in case the supply should cease. Short as the time is before the post goes, I might have sent you more intelligence were it not that Colonels Merewether and Phayre are both absent upon some expedition in the surrounding country, and I am therefore unable to draw any news from any official source. The health of everyone up here is excellent, and the horses are suffering less from the disease which has almost decimated them in the lower ground. There are plenty of cattle brought in for sale, but unfortunately the authorities have no money to buy them with.

Senafe, December 19th.

I wrote a few lines, upon my arrival here two days ago; but as the post was upon the point of starting, I could not do more than state that the rumours which had reached us down below respecting the King of Tigré were untrue, and that that monarch was at present pursuing a course of masterly inactivity. I will now, therefore, resume my letter at the point where my last regular communication ended—namely, at the station of Sooro, in the pass leading to this place. I do not apologise for making my description of this pass very detailed, for at present the whole interest of the expedition centres in the passage of the troops and baggage from Zulla to this point, and I feel sure that any particulars which may enable the public to picture to themselves the country through which our soldiers are marching will be read with keen interest. From Sooro to Rayray Guddy, the next regular station, is, according to the official report, twenty-eight miles; but I am convinced, and in this opinion I am borne out by every officer I have spoken to, that thirty-three would be much nearer the fact. Indeed, in every march up here the official distances are a good deal under the truth. But, indeed, the officers of the exploring force appear to have seen everything through rose-coloured spectacles. At Zulla they reported plenty of water, and they found, a short way further, an abundance of forage, which no one else has been able to discover before or since. It was on the strength of these reports of forage and water that the baggage-animals were hurried forward. I am not blaming the officers who made the reports. They simply acted as it is the nature of explorers to act. Every father thinks his own child a prodigy. Every discoverer believes that the country, or river, or lake which he has been the first to report on, is a country, river, or lake such as no man ever saw before. Over and over again this has happened, and disastrous consequences have ere now arisen from the persistent use by explorers of these rose-coloured spectacles. It is not more than four or five years—to give one example out of a thousand—since Dr. Livingstone reported that he had discovered a magnificent navigable river in Eastern Africa, with rice, cotton, and corn abounding upon its banks, and a climate beyond reproach. In consequence of this report the "Universities Mission" was organised, and a band of missionaries, headed by their bishop, Mackenzie, started. After months of struggle they arrived at the place of disembarkation, having already discovered that their noble stream was, at a good average time of year, about three feet deep. There they set up their mission; there, one by one, these noble fellows died of want and of fever, victims of an explorer's rose-coloured spectacles. After that we must not grudge the few hundred mules that have fallen a sacrifice to the want of springs and forage which could be seen only through the glasses of the chiefs of the exploring party.

From Sooro to Rayray Guddy is too far a march to be made in one day along such a road as there is at present, and accordingly it is generally broken at a spot called Guinea-fowl Plain, where there is a well yielding a small supply of water, the colour of pea-soup. We had had quite sufficient of night-marching previously, and, having passed one day at Sooro, we started at ten o'clock the following morning. We had intended to have started an hour earlier; but making a start here is a very different thing from sending for a cab at an appointed time to catch a train. In the first place there are the trunks, which have been opened the night before, to close; there is the tent to strike and pack up. Then at the last moment you discover that your servants have not washed up the breakfast-things, and that your mule-wallah has not yet taken his animals to water. At last, when all is ready, comes the important operation of loading the four baggage-animals. Each load has to be adjusted with the nicest precision, or the very first piece of rough ground you arrive at, round goes the saddle, and your belongings come to the ground with a crash. With our two mules we have the "Otago saddle," which is excellent. Indeed, in the opinion of almost everyone here, it is by far the best of the rival saddles. Upon these saddles we pack our own baggage, and once fairly adjusted this is pretty safe for the day. Not so the other animals, for which we have common mule-saddles. Upon these is piled a multifarious collection of bundles. Our servants' five kits, our animals' rugs and ropes, our tents, two sacks containing cooking-utensils and numerous etceteras, and a water-skin for use upon the road. The actual weight that these animals have to carry is not so great as that borne by the others; but the trouble of adjusting and fastening on is at least ten times as great. The loads have frequently to be taken off three or four times, and then when we think all is right, and get fairly into motion, we have not gone twenty yards before there is a gradual descending motion observed on one side of an animal, and a corresponding rise of the opposite burden, and we are obliged to stop and readjust everything, or in another minute or two the whole would have toppled over. These things ruffle the temper somewhat, and our equanimity is not improved by the intense stupidity which our native servants always manifest upon these occasions. They seem to have no eye. They heap bundles on the side which was before palpably the heaviest; they twist cords where cords can be of no earthly use: altogether they are horribly aggravating. However, by this time I am getting accustomed to these things, and take matters into my own hands, and insist on things being done exactly as I direct them. At ten o'clock, then, we were fairly off, and I do not know that I ever rode through a more monotonous valley than that between Sooro and Guinea-fowl Plain. It was the counterpart of that I described in my last letter as extending between Koomaylo and Lower Sooro. A dead flat of two or three hundred yards across, with the torrent's bed winding across it, and spur after spur of mountain turning it every quarter of a mile. Some of the mountain views which we saw up the ravines were certainly very fine, but it became monotonous in the extreme after six hours' march at the rate of little over two miles an hour. The vegetation, however, had changed since the preceding day. The thorny bush no longer covered everything, but a variety of shrubs now bordered the path, and the diversity of their foliage was a relief to the eye. Immense quantities of locusts were everywhere met with, making the ground yellow where they lay, and rising with a rustling noise, which was very discomposing to the horses at our approach. They did not eat all the shrubs, but the species upon which they fed were absolutely covered with them, and most of their favourite plants were stripped completely bare. Monkeys, or rather baboons, still abounded: we saw numerous large troops of them, which must have been over a hundred strong. It was about five o'clock when we reached Guinea-fowl Plain, which may have guinea-fowls, although we saw none; but which is most certainly not a plain, for at the place where the well is the valley is narrower than it had been for miles previously. Here we found some really large trees, and under them we pitched our tent. It was not long before our servants had fires lighted and dinner in a forward state. There were two or three other parties who had arrived before us, and, as it got dusk, all lighted fires; and, as each party, with their cooking and grooms' fires, had at least three bonfires going, it made quite a picturesque scene. The night was raw and cold, and we had a few drops of rain. It was fortunate that we had brought water with us for cooking purposes, for the water in the well was perfectly undrinkable.

The next morning we were again off early for our longest journey, that on to Rayray Guddy, where food would be procurable for horse and man, neither one nor the other being obtainable at Guinea-fowl Plain, where there is no commissariat station. We had carried our own food, and a small portion of grain for the horses; but they would have fared very badly had we not met some natives in the pass with a bundle of hay, and done a little barter with them for rice. The valley for the first twelve or fourteen miles from Guinea-fowl Plain greatly resembled in its general features that we had passed the day previously, but the vegetation became more varied and interesting every mile. We now had great trees of ivy, we had the evergreen oak, and occasionally gigantic tulip-trees. We had great numbers of a tree, or rather large shrub, of the name of which I am ignorant; its leaves more resembled the sprays of the asparagus when it has run far to seed than any other foliage I know, but the growth of the shrub was more like a yew. Upon its branches were vast quantities of a parasite resembling the mistletoe, whose dark-green leaves afforded a fine contrast to the rather bluish tint of the tree. Climbing everywhere over the trees, and sometimes almost hiding them, were creepers of various kinds; on the ground grew vast quantities of the aloe. There were, too, numerous cacti of various kinds, some thick and bulky, others no thicker than a lady's little finger, and growing like a creeper over the trees. But, strangest of all, upon the hill-sides grew an immense plant, or rather tree, of the cactus tribe, which I had never seen before. It started by a straight stem fifteen or twenty feet high, and thicker than a man's body. This branched out into a great number of arms, which all grew upwards, and to just the same height, giving it a strange and formal appearance, exactly resembling a gigantic cauliflower. I believe its name is *Euphorbia candalabriensis*, but do not at all vouch for this. Some of the mountain slopes were quite covered with this strange tree, but as a general thing it grew singly or in pairs. The tulip-trees were superb; they grew generally in rocky places, and with their huge twisted trunks, and glossy green leaves, and limbs more than a hundred feet long, they were studies for a painter.

At about three miles from Rayray Guddy the valley narrowed to a ravine, and we came upon running water. The pass from here to the station is steep and difficult, but nothing to that at Sooro. Having drawn our rations, and received the unwelcome intelligence that there was no hay, and only the scantiest possible amount of grain for our animals, we established our camp and went up to look at the land transport division, about a quarter of a mile higher up the valley. There were four or five hundred mules and ponies here, in good order, but hardly good condition; in fact, the work has been hard and forage scant. How hard the work has been, our journey of the two preceding days had testified. All along the line of march we had come across the carcasses of dead animals, from which great vultures rose lazily at our approach. As we approached Rayray Guddy the remains of the victims occurred much more frequently, and the air was everywhere impregnated with the fœtid odour. This was only to be expected, as the poor animals had been obliged to endeavour to accomplish the march of thirty miles from Sooro without food, and in most cases without water. No time should be lost in forming a small commissariat dépôt at Guinea-fowl Plain, where a ration of hay and grain could be served out to the animals as they pass through. The work these baggage-animals have to go through is extremely severe, and their half-starved appearance testifies that they have not sufficient food served out to them, and to expect them to do two days' work on their one day's scanty rations is a little too much even from mules. We found our friends who had started before us from Guinea-fowl Plain encamped up there with Captain Mortimer of the transport train. It was proposed that we should throw in our mess with them. We accordingly returned to our own encampment, took our meat and rum, our plates and knives and forks, and marched back again. In an hour dinner was ready, and in the mean time I was glad of an opportunity of inquiring how this advanced division of the transport train had got on. I found that they had, like the one down at Zulla, had the greatest trouble with their drivers. The officer complained bitterly of the class of men who had been sent out—Greeks, Italians, Frenchmen, Spaniards, the mere sweepings of Alexandria, Cairo, Beyrout, and Smyrna. The Hindoo drivers, he said, upon the whole, worked steadily, and were more reliable than the others, but were greatly wanting in physical strength. The Persians, on the contrary, were very strong and powerful men, and could load three mules while a Hindoo could load one; but they had at first given very great trouble, had mutinied and threatened to desert in a body, but, upon the application of the lash to two or three of the ringleaders, things had gone on more smoothly. The Arab drivers had almost all deserted. Even up here the mules still suffer from the disease which prevailed down upon the plain, and which carried off a hundred horses of the 3d Native Cavalry. It is very sudden in its action, and is in nearly every case fatal. The animals seem seized with some internal pain, arch their backs, and become rigid. In a short time the tongue grows black, a discharge takes place from the nostrils, and in a few hours, sometimes not more than one, from the time he is attacked, the animal is dead. At present, as with our cattle-disease, all remedies are ineffectual. Animals in good condition are more liable to be attacked than are the poorer ones. After dinner we returned to our tent, where, however, we did not pass a remarkably-pleasant night. In the first place, it was bitterly cold—the temperature of Rayray Guddy is indeed colder than it is here; and in the second, a mule had broken loose from its head-ropes, and came down to our encampment. Five or six times it nearly upset our tent by tumbling over the tent-ropes, in addition to which it made our horses so savage by going up among them, that we were afraid of their breaking loose. Four or five times, therefore, did we have to get up and go out in the cold to drive the beast away with stones. The grooms were sleeping at their horses' heads, but were so wrapped up in their rugs that they heard nothing of it. The next morning it was so cold that we were really glad to be up and moving, and were on our way at a little before eight. The first six miles of the road is narrow and winding, and is as lovely a road as I ever passed. With the exception only of the narrow pathway, the gorge was one mass of foliage. In addition to all the plants I have mentioned as occurring below, we had now the wild fig, the laburnum, various sorts of acacia, and many others, One plant in particular, I believe a species of acacia, was in seed; the seed-pods were a reddish-brown, but were very thin and transparent, and when the sun shone upon them were of the colour of the clearest carmine. As these shrubs were in great abundance, and completely covered with seed-pods, their appearance was very brilliant. Among all these plants fluttered numerous humming-birds of the most lovely colours. Other birds of larger size and gorgeous plumage perched among the trees at a short distance from the path. Brilliant butterflies flitted here and there among the flowers.

At last we came to an end of this charming ride, and prepared for a work of a very different nature. We turned from the ravine which we had now followed for sixty miles, and prepared boldly to ascend the hill-side. As soon as we left the ravine all the semi-tropical vegetation was at an end; we were climbing a steep hill covered with boulders, between which stunted pines thrust their gnarled branches and dark foliage. We had gone at one leap from a tropical ravine to a highland mountain-side. The ascent was, I should say, at the least a thousand feet, and a worse thousand-feet climb I never had before and never wish to have again. It is a mere track which zigzags up among the rocks and trees, and which was made by the 10th Native Infantry and the Sappers, as the pioneer force rested below and had breakfast. The men effected marvels considering that it was the work of two hours only; but it is at best a mere track. Sometimes the mules mount a place as steep as a flight of stairs; then they have to step over a rock three feet high. In fact, it is one long struggle up to the top, and in no place wide enough for two mules to pass. One mule falling puts a stop to a whole train, and this was exemplified in our case, for we were following a long line of mules when they suddenly came to a stop. For half-an-hour we waited patiently, and then, climbing up the rocks and through the trees at the side of the stationary mules, we finally came to the cause of detention—one of the mules had fallen. The drivers had taken no efforts to remove his pack or his saddle, but were sitting by his side quietly smoking their pipes. After a little strong language we took off his saddle, got things right, and the train proceeded again. This is the great want of the transport corps—a strong body of inspectors, as they are called, volunteers from European regiments. There ought to be one of these to every ten or fifteen drivers, who, as in the present case, if not looked after by a European, will shirk work in every possible way. But this is a subject upon which I shall have much more to say at a future time. This road or path is really not practicable for the passage of mules, for, although singly they can go up well enough, if one party going up were to meet another going down, it is probable that, if no European came up to make one party or other retrace their steps, they would remain there until the last animal died of starvation. Three companies of the Beloochee regiment arrived yesterday at the bottom of the hill, and have set to work to widen and improve it; and as a party of sappers and miners have begun to work downwards from the top, the road will soon be made passable. For this hill-side is not like the pass of Sooro, which would require an incredible amount of labour to render it a decent road. There are no natural obstacles here beyond trees to be cut down and stones to be rolled away; so that by the time the main body of the army arrives I have no doubt that they will find a fair road up to the plateau.

Senafe, December 20th.

I closed my letter in great haste yesterday afternoon, for the authorities suddenly arrived at the conclusion that it was the last day for the English mail. I was obliged to break off abruptly in my description of the road, being at the point where we had just arrived upon the plateau. Looking backwards, we could see peak after peak extending behind us, which when we had been winding among their bases had looked so high above us, but which now were little above the level of the spot where we were standing. A few of the peaks around us might have been a thousand or fifteen hundred feet higher than the plateau, and we were standing nearly on the summit of that high range of hills we had seen from the sea. We are now seven thousand four hundred feet above Zulla, and by my description of the pass it will be seen that it is no child's-play to attain this height. It is not that the ascent is so steep; on the contrary, taking the distance at seventy miles, the rise is only one in a hundred, an easy gradient for a railway; but more than half the rise takes place in three short steep ascents, namely, the Sooro pass, a rise of one thousand five hundred feet in four miles; the Rayray Guddy pass, a rise of one thousand feet in three miles; and the last climb on to the plateau, a rise of one thousand five hundred feet in two miles. Thus four thousand feet, or more than half the rise, takes place in nine miles, and over the remaining distance the rise is only one foot in every two hundred. The difficulties of the journey are the general roughness of the road, the long distances the animals have to go without water, and the ascent of the Sooro pass, for there is no doubt that the final rise to the plateau will soon be made a good road by the exertions of the Beloochees and Sappers. Turning our horses' heads we proceeded onward. The change to an open plain and a fresh wind in place of the long valley and oppressive stillness was charming. One would have thought oneself on the top of a Welsh hill. The ground was a black peaty soil, with a short dried-up grass. Here and there were small patches of cultivated ground, and clumps of rock cropped up everywhere. Looking forward, we could see that the general character of the ground was that of a plain; but enormous masses of rock, of seven or eight hundred feet in height, rose perpendicularly in fantastic shapes sheer up from the plain. Here and there were ranges of mountains, some of considerable altitude. Far in the distance we could see hills rising between hills, but never attaining any great height. Everywhere over the plain were little groups of cattle and sheep grazing. We were evidently in a thickly-populated country.

After about two miles' ride we turned the corner of a slight rise, and there before us lay the camp. It is prettily situated on the side of a little valley, and faces the north. The 10th Native Infantry are encamped on the right wing; the Mountain Train occupy the centre; and the 3d Cavalry camp lies on the left. Behind the rise a plain stretches away, and upon this the troops will be encamped as they arrive. The soil of the valley-side and of the plain beyond is a mere sand, covered with grass and bushes, but in the hollow of the valley, where the stream runs, or rather used to run, it is a deep black peat. Wells are now being sunk in this peat, and these rapidly fill with water. There are still deep pools where the stream formerly ran, and dams have been formed, which will keep back a considerable supply of water. The troops are not, therefore, likely to fall short for some time, and if they should, there is plenty at a stream two or three miles farther on. The health of the troops is pretty good, but both officers and men are subject to slight attacks of fever, much more so than they were when encamped on the plain by the sea. This is singular, for except that the nights are rather cold, this feels the very perfection of climate. The horses and mules are doing much better up here, and although some died at first, it is probable that they had brought the seeds of the disease with them from the pass below. As it is, the cavalry have suffered terribly. The 5th Cavalry, out of five hundred horses, have lost one hundred and seventy, and the officers' horses of the infantry and Mountain Train have been nearly exterminated.

Things are very tranquil here. The King of Tigré, after first being friendly, and then blustering a little, has just at present, influenced probably by the reports of the increasing force of the expedition, determined upon the prudent policy of friendship, at any rate until he sees a better opportunity of plunder than he does at present. Yesterday afternoon an ambassador arrived from him, saying magnanimously, "Why should we not be friends? My foes are your foes; my interests your interests. Take therefore my forage, and my blessing." Colonel Merewether is greatly delighted at this message, and sees, through those rose-coloured spectacles of his, an early end to the expedition. Everyone else is perfectly indifferent. The King of Tigré's army of 7000 men could be scattered like chaff by a battalion of Europeans; and if he ever sees a chance of falling upon our rear, it is more than probable that his friendly professions will go for nothing. I do not think that the smallest reliance can be placed in the friendship of these semi-savage chiefs.

We gave his ambassador a lesson this morning, which will, I have no doubt, have its effect. It was a brigade field-day, and Colonel Merewether took the ambassador out to witness it. It is a great pity that the artillery and the infantry had not a few rounds of blank cartridge, which would have given his ambassadorship a much more lively idea of what the real thing would be like, and would have given him such a tale to bear to his king and master as would have opened his Majesty's eyes to what the consequences of a war with us would probably be. But even as it was, it no doubt had a very salutary effect. The enemy were supposed to be holding a steep rise at the mouth of a long valley. The infantry threw forward skirmishers, and the mountain guns took up a position upon a neighbouring hill, and were supposed to open a heavy fire. Presently the infantry advanced in line, and made a rush up the steep rise. As they reached the top they lowered bayonets to the charge, and with a loud cheer rushed upon the defenders. An instant afterwards the word "Charge!" was given to cavalry, and away they went down the valley, sweeping the enemy's supports and the fugitives from the hill before them for half a mile, and then scattering in pursuit. It was very well done, and, as I have said, no doubt had its effect, especially when the ambassador was made to understand that the force he saw before him was only one-tenth of our advancing army. The movements of the troops were fairly performed, and did great credit to their respective commanding-officers. Their remaining horses are in excellent condition, and are very strong serviceable animals. Their uniform is a very effective one, light-blue and silver, with white covers to their forage caps. The infantry, whose uniform is precisely similar to our own, also wear white cap-covers. Going out to the parade-ground, which is about two miles distant from here, we passed several native villages, and a great number of them can be seen scattered all over the plains. The country, indeed, is very thickly populated; very much more so than a rural district in England of the same extent. The people possess goats, sheep, and cattle in abundance, together with ponies, donkeys, and mules. They are ready to sell all these animals to us, but demand very high prices, which has been to a certain extent encouraged by the prices Colonel Merewether has ordered to be paid at the bazaar for them. Thus, he has fixed the price of a goat at a dollar and a half, that is six and ninepence, whereas I paid down in the pass only two shillings for a goat, and could have bought any number at that price. It is probable, too, that the current price for goats, or indeed for any animals, is considerably less here than in the valley, for there forage is extremely scarce, and must be sought at long distances; whereas here it is abundant, the plains being covered with it. Of course, this price having been once fixed, the natives will not take less, that is, in specie. They would take a shilling's worth of rice for a goat; but of course we have no rice to give them. It may make but little difference to Colonel Merewether whether he pays seven shillings or two shillings for a goat; but the subalterns naturally grumble at having to pay three times the real value for their food. Not, indeed, that the officers here have to buy much, for their guns supplement their rations to a very considerable extent. Guinea-fowls, partridges, ducks, and geese abound, and a large number are daily shot by the sportsmen of the camp. The ration allowance of one pound of meat, including bone, a pound of biscuit, two ounces of preserved vegetables, and a quarter of a pound of rice, is quite insufficient for one's wants in a bracing atmosphere like this. The meat issued contains an enormous proportion of bone, so that there is little if at all more than half a pound of clear meat in a ration. I am sure that I consume at least three times my daily allowance of meat.

The natives completely swarm about our camp. The men do not do much, but loiter about with their swords and spears, and shields made of elephant-hide. These spears are really formidable weapons. They are from six to ten feet long, and weighted at both ends, and the natives are able to throw them with great force and considerable accuracy for a distance of over thirty yards. These would be ugly weapons in a hand-to-hand fight in a bush, but as it is, against a disciplined force armed with firearms, they are simply absurd, and I have seen no offensive weapons—such as bows or arrows—which could be used with effect against us during the passage of a defile, in their possession, since my arrival in the country. The women appear to do all the work. They come into the camp in hundreds laden with firewood, and keep up a perpetual cry of "Lockaree, lockaree!" — which is the Hindoostanee for wood, they having picked up that word, — and "Parnè!" water. Even the children bring their bundles of wood. The women are not nearly so pretty as some of them I saw down the pass, nor are they so neatly clad. They are dressed in cotton and leather; but neither are these so tastefully arranged, or so fancifully ornamented with shells, as were those I described in a previous letter. They are very thin, many of the children painfully so, which is surprising when one sees the abundance of their flocks and herds. The villages, too, are well built. The houses are low and flat-roofed. They are in many cases built of stone, and some of them have inner courts, with a sort of veranda formed of boughs to sit under. They have, like the Arab villages I saw at Alexandria, and which they strongly resemble, no windows; but as the native's life is entirely passed in the open air, I suppose that matters but little. The natives seem to feel the cold much, and go shivering about in the early morning and evening in a pitiful way. They bring in honey for sale in pots, weighing about ten pounds, and for which they charge two dollars. Their own drink is made of this honey, fermented with the juice of a plant which grows abundantly upon the plain. The honey, as they bring it into camp, is very impure, and needs refining before using. The commissariat officer rode out yesterday to one of the villages, and bought a quantity of chillies, which will prove a great addition to our fare when they begin to issue them, for we have had no pepper served out since we landed; and a course of mutton, unrelieved by condiment of any kind, is apt to pall upon the stomach.

All praise must be given to the commissariat for the way in which they have performed the service from Zulla to this place. Not one day have the troops been without their rations; and the animals, although they have not always received their full supply, have yet always had something to eat at the end of the day's work. No commissariat officer accompanied the pioneer force in their march up; but the whole arrangements were made by Conductor Darcey, to whom the greatest credit is due. During the whole march he did not lose a single animal, or a single bag of grain. A commissariat officer has arrived within the last two days; but honour should be given where it is due, and certainly the greatest credit is due to those noncommissioned officers for the manner in which, alone and unaided, they have carried out the difficult duties intrusted to them. Two prisoners were brought in yesterday. They are part of the gang who have been infesting the pass, robbing every convoy without a guard of Europeans. They were captured by a friendly chief, who, with his men, came upon the whole gang. The rest fled, throwing away their weapons, of which quite a bundle was brought into camp. The prisoners, being old men, were unable to escape, and were brought in triumph by their captors into Rayray Guddy, whence they were forwarded to Colonel Merewether. Their preliminary examination by the interpreter took place in the open air. The prisoners and their accusers squatted in a circle, and a number of natives gathered round. These last were evidently greatly amused and surprised at the formality of the proceedings,—as the guilt of the accused was undoubted, articles of European manufacture, such as portions of harness, being found in their possession,—and the idea being evidently prevalent that we should hang them at once. They were removed to the guard-tent, and will, I suppose, be regularly tried, and well flogged, in a day or two.

This expectation was not verified; the prisoners were let off, with an admonition to behave better in future; and this happened again and again. The absurd course pursued by our political officer towards native offenders produced, as might have been expected, very disastrous consequences afterwards. The natives learnt that our baggage could be plundered with impunity, and that even when taken red-handed in the act, the chances were that no punishment whatever would be inflicted. They naturally ascribed this conduct on our part to fear—for in Abyssinia the punishment for theft is very severe, the culprit frequently having his hand cut off—and were encouraged to plunder accordingly. A moderate share of energy, one grain of common sense among the authorities at Senafe at this time, so that the first two or three offenders caught plundering our convoys in open day should have been flogged to within an inch of their lives, and plundering would have been put a stop to at once and for ever; and a very great many lives, both of our own muleteers and of the natives themselves, would have been eventually saved.

It is a great satisfaction to know that in the course of a short time we shall be able to purchase for the use of the army any number of bullocks and sheep. We have not been able to do so heretofore, for the absurd reason that we have had no money. Will it be believed that a body of troops marching on into a country where it is supposed they would be able to purchase any quantity of animals for themselves and the army which is to follow them, should have come up with the military chest totally unprovided with money? It is almost too preposterous, but it is perfectly true. A chest of two thousand pounds arrived yesterday under a guard. But what are two thousand pounds when we want three or four thousand bullocks alone, and when Colonel Merewether has fixed the price of each at six dollars and a half—that is, as nearly as possible, thirty shillings?

I shall be able to send you but little news from here. Colonel Merewether proceeds to-morrow morning forty miles into the interior. He takes with him a troop of cavalry, a large stock of mules, &c., but he declines positively to allow a *confrère* and myself to accompany him. He is civil, but firm. "The addition of two persons would probably break down the whole party. Starvation might ensue, and he could not guarantee that we should be fed." These are actually word for word the reasons he gives for declining to allow the only two special correspondents here from accompanying his force. He can victual himself, Colonel Phayre, three or four other staff-officers, and a troop of cavalry; but two correspondents were too much for the resources of the commissariat. We called upon him twice; we urged upon him that it was a matter of great interest to the public that we should go forward. We said that we would put him to no trouble, but would bring our own mules, with ten days' provisions, if necessary. He declined positively to allow us to go. He would, when he returned, give us details, and that was all he would do. The public, in fact, might read his official report and be thankful; for none other, says he, shall they receive. Had we arrived here as two unaccredited strangers, his conduct was perfectly explicable; but provided as we were by the courtesy of the India Office with letters to Sir Robert Napier, and furnished by him, in consequence, with a circular letter, requesting all officers of the army to forward our wishes in every way, we certainly had not expected to have been refused the chance of availing ourselves of the very first opportunity which has fallen in our way of sending you something really new from Abyssinia.

Camp, Senafe, December 23d.

At the time I closed my last letter I had no idea that my next communication would be dated Senafe. Colonel Merewether's unaccountable refusal to allow my fellow-correspondent and myself to accompany him upon his expedition had rendered our further stay here useless.

Accordingly, an hour or two after the expedition had started from camp, I packed up a light kit and started for the sea-shore. The road, as far as the top of the first descent, is now so free from stone that it might be used as a race-course, but we found that nothing had yet been done with the zigzag down the face of the hill. However, as we met no mules upon our way it was an easy descent enough; indeed the whole pass, from end to end, although it has its difficulties, still presents no real obstacle to a single traveller. It is only when viewed in the light of a highway for an army, as the only line of communication up which the stores of 20,000 men must come, that one considers it to be a really terrible business. No forage is procurable for the baggage-animals between the sea and Senafe, seventy miles. A large proportion, therefore, of the mules is occupied in carrying food for themselves and their companions. The stages, too, for heavily-burdened animals across an exceedingly-rough road are distressingly long. Twelve miles a-day, with a pause for an hour to feed and water in the middle of the day, could be done by heavily-loaded mules without deterioration of their quality. But here all the stages, except the last, considerably exceed that distance; and from Sooro to Rayray Guddy, over thirty miles, is practically without food or water. This is what makes the Koomaylo Pass so difficult as the highway of an army—want of forage the whole distance, and long intervals between the watering-places; to which may be added the disease which infects the pass and decimates the animals as they go up and down. The mule, although one of the most enduring of creatures, and capable of sustaining great privations, is yet a delicate animal. Feed him well, keep him supplied with water and hay, and he will do wonders; but without regular and abundant food he falls away rapidly. During the last campaign in Italy there were thousands of mules engaged transporting provisions up the Tyrol to Garibaldi. They had great fatigue and long marches, but they were well fed and had plenty of water; and consequently throughout the campaign I never saw a dead mule, and hardly one out of condition. Here it is just the reverse; the mules are greatly fallen off, and although they are now much better fed, they will be a very long time before they regain their lost strength. In respect to food a great improvement has been effected in the last few days. Captain Sewell has been here about a week. He is in charge of the commissariat, and has purchased considerable quantities of hay, which is now served out to the mules here, and to their even worse-off brethren down at Rayray Guddy; for here, at least, in their intervals of labour the mules were able to graze, while in the valley there is not a blade of grass to be had. Captain Mortimer, indeed, who is in charge of the transport division there, only kept his animals alive by compelling their drivers to go up to the summit of the hills, either before their day's work is begun or after it was over, and to cut and bring down a certain weight of hay. It is very fortunate that vultures are so abundant in this country. Were it not for them the pass would be unbearable from the taint of dead animals. Between the top of the pass and Rayray Guddy, a distance of eight miles, we passed more than that number of dead mules and ponies, most of which had been only dead three days at most; and everyone of these had been partially eaten by the vultures, who keep wheeling and circling in the air overhead, and scarcely is life out of an animal before these scavengers swoop down upon it. I have seen as many as seven or eight of these great birds eating and fighting over the carcass of a single horse. The ride from the bottom of the steep incline to Rayray Guddy I have already described, and it is certainly the most beautiful ride of seven miles I ever traversed, the brilliancy and variety of the foliage, the number and beauty of the humming-birds and butterflies, all being in addition to the ordinary scenery of a mountain pass. I find that the great trees I described as tulip-trees are not really tulip-trees, although their foliage strangely resembles that tree. Authorities differ as to what they really are; some affirming that they are banyan-trees, while others say that no banyan-tree was ever seen without the long pendulous roots from its branches, of which there are here no trace.

Upon reaching Rayray Guddy we found that Sir Charles Staveley had arrived there two hours previously from Sooro. He had not heard of the departure of Colonels Merewether, Phayre, and Wilkins, and as the principal object of his journey had been to see them, he was of course much disappointed. However, he determined now he had come so far, to go on to Senafe, and we decided upon returning with him, as we had now no motive for going down, and, indeed, it was possible that he might either ride out himself to the point whither Colonel Merewether had gone, or might send an aide-de-camp to request him to return, in either of which cases we knew that he would grant us permission to go. General Staveley was the more disappointed at the absence of Colonel Merewether because he had taken the precaution of writing two days previously to announce his coming. The letter, of course, had not arrived, for the general had performed the distance in three days from Zulla to Senafe, and the post would take at least two days longer. Nothing, indeed, can possibly be worse than the postal arrangements, or rather want of arrangement. Relays of men on foot carry the letters, and even these do not travel at night. But the great question which everyone is asking is, "What becomes of the letters?" I have not received a single letter or newspaper of a later date than November 4th. Some few people have been more fortunate, and occasionally get a letter or paper; but they are exceptions. One feels as absolutely cut off from England as if a great gulf had opened between us. I did hear this morning from someone who had had the luck to receive an odd newspaper that the amount for the Abyssinian war had been voted, and we had a hearty laugh over the news that the expenses were laid at four millions. I only hope that the post down is a little better regulated than that up, for if not, instead of getting my letters regularly once a-week, they will probably arrive in a mass about the end of next June. The general came up here on the 22d. He will, I believe, start on his return journey to-morrow, whether Colonel Merewether and his party come into camp or not, as his presence is absolutely necessary on the sea-shore. It will be unfortunate if he should miss them after his long journey up here, especially as he had made certain of seeing them; for the committee of exploration, which consisted of Colonels Merewether, Phayre, and Wilkins, was dissolved by an order of General Napier, which was published ten days since, and of which these gentlemen of course received a copy. General Napier thanked them warmly for their efforts to carry out their duty, and for the success which had attended them, but stated that General Sir Charles

Staveley had gone to Zulla to take the command until he himself arrived, and that therefore there was no longer any occasion for the existence of the committee. In the face of this order General Staveley could hardly have expected that these gentlemen would have proceeded on an expedition forty miles into the interior without any consultation or reference to himself.

An important messenger came into the camp on the afternoon of the 22d. He stated that he was the servant of Mr. Flad, and, indeed, was identified as being so by several people in camp. He stated that he had started with a letter from Mr. Flad, and with one from King Theodore, but that he had been robbed of them upon the way. He brought, however, one piece of important and very disagreeable news, namely, that Theodore had marched from Debra Tabor to Magdala; had raised the siege of that place by the King of Shoa, and had taken the whole of the captives back with him to Debra Tabor. This is the most unfortunate occurrence which could possibly have taken place. As long as the captives were separated from him by his enemies they were safe; and if, as will in all probability be the case, the army of Theodore should disband at our approach, and he himself rule safely in the fortresses of the mountains, where search for him would be out of the question, we should have marched to Magdala and effected the release of the prisoners. Now we have no such hope. We may toil on across mountain and ravine, but we know that our hands are shackled, and that the tyrant we war against can at any moment purchase peace upon his own terms. Theodore can laugh our efforts to scorn; he knows that he need not disquiet himself. He can let the expedition approach him. He can chuckle over the enormous waste of treasure and effort, even if not of human life; and he knows that at the last moment he can arrest us with the ultimatum—"Return at once, and I will release my prisoners; move one step forward, and I will sacrifice every one." This is very disheartening, and takes away from the expedition that zest and buoyancy which the thought of a possible skirmish at the end of the toilsome journey would give it. Nothing could be more unfortunate than the loss of Theodore's letter by Mr. Flad's servant. It may be that in it Theodore offered to restore the captives at once upon the agreement that we would advance no farther. It may be that he held out the threat that the prisoners would be put to death did we not at once agree to his terms. Altogether it is most unfortunate. It is to be hoped that Theodore will see the manifest likelihood of his messenger being stopped upon the way, and will send his letter in duplicate by some other hand. There is a rumour current among the natives this morning that Theodore has released the captives, and that they are upon their way down. There is, of course, no finding out the origin of this report, but it is most unlikely that he would deliver them up until, at any rate, he had obtained a promise that we in return would abandon all idea of advancing upon him.

The disease among the horses still continues. Those who have been the longest up here appear comparatively safe, but it would seem to require some time to get the disease out of the blood. Every morning three or four mules are dragged out of the camp to the foot of the hills, a mile off, there to be eaten by the vultures. Yesterday afternoon my groom came to me with the unpleasant intelligence, "Sahib, your baggage-pony ill." I went out and found him lying down. Upon the veterinary surgeon arriving he shook his head, and, pointing to the swollen tongue, said that it was the disease, and that in a couple of hours it would be dead. We tried brandy-and-water in the vain hope of reviving him, but it was quite useless, and in a little over the two hours the pony died, having been apparently unconscious for an hour and a half previously. Yesterday, too, the horse of Dr. Lamb, chief veterinary surgeon of the transport corps, died. Dr. Lamb came up with us a week since. After spending three days here inspecting the animals he returned, but as he did not wish his horse to run the risk of again going down into the pass, he left it here in perfect health, and rode down again upon a baggage-pony. Yesterday the poor animal died, after the usual three hours' illness. Dr. Lamb strongly recommended that all animals which can be spared should be at once sent up here. Unfortunately none of the baggage-animals, except those which work the last stage from Rayray Guddy here, can be spared. They must remain below to carry up provisions and baggage whatever the mortality may be. General Staveley has ordered that in future 10 per cent of spare animals shall accompany every train of loaded mules, to take the baggage off those who give in on the way. He has also ordered that the artillery-horses shall be instantly sent up here with their native attendants. The soldiers cannot accompany them, as their warm clothing has not yet arrived. He has also ordered that the cavalry regiments shall be sent on the instant they land. The general has taken particular interest in the transport train since he arrived at Zulla, and it is due to the order he gave and to the assistance with which he supplied them from the 33d and Beloochee regiments, that the train down at Zulla has been enabled to make head against the tremendous difficulties they have sustained owing to the wholesale desertion among the drivers, and to the uselessness of a great portion of those who remain. He has divided the baggage-animals which are in the country into regular squadrons, stationing a number at each station proportioned to the length and hardship of the journey. General Staveley, indeed, is the very man for an expedition of this sort. Whatever he sees is necessary, he takes upon himself the responsibility of ordering to be done. I consider his arrival at Zulla to have been most providential. Everything was going wrong, disorder ruled supreme. All this is now at an end. General Staveley has taken the command, and unity of action is once more introduced. Whether Colonel Phayre, now that his committee of exploration is dissolved, may determine to go down to Zulla or to remain here, is now of little importance, as Major Baigrie, the deputy-quartermaster-general, is fully capable of carrying on the duties, supported as he is by the weight of General Staveley's authority.

This morning the 10th Native Infantry were engaged in clearing a large space of ground of stones, in order to make it suitable for a parade-ground. It was wonderful to see how fast they got through the work, and how much more they accomplished than an equal number of Europeans would have done in the same time. And this because squatting is the normal attitude of an Oriental. In this attitude they can remain for hours; therefore the work of collecting the stones into heaps, which in turn were carried away in empty rice-bags by another party, was the easiest affair possible. It is very amusing looking on at these native fatigue-parties, the varieties of costume are so great. The 10th Native Infantry, like the Beloochees, is recruited from all parts of India, and contain Mussulmans, Punjaubees, Sikhs, Patans, Hill-men, and, in fact, specimens of most of the native races, the Hindostanee proper being greatly in the minority. To a certain extent these men cling to their own costume, consequently in a party of a hundred of them on fatigue-duty the variety is astonishing. Men in red turbans and white turbans, in red, white, or violet nightcaps—these articles having been served out to these men as part of their warm clothing—some in coloured jackets, white underclothing, and long drawers, others with nothing on but the cumberband, or loincloth, some entirely in white, with their legs covered to the knee. Many are the shades of colour too, from nearly jet black down to the rich bronze of the Sikhs. Almost all are fine, well-built men, and all appear to work with good temper and with a will. The parade is to take place upon the new ground to-morrow evening. It is not settled yet upon what day General Staveley will leave, but his present intention is, in case Colonel Merewether returns on the morning of the 25th, to start the same afternoon.

Camp, Senafe, December 26th.

When I wrote on the 23d instant I had not made up my mind whether I should spend Christmas here or on the road downwards. But circumstances finally compelled me to wait here until to-day; and I am glad for several reasons that I did so. The first and most important was in reference to the story brought by Mr. Flad's servant, namely, that Theodore had marched to

Magdala, had raised the siege of that fortress by the rebels, and had taken all the captives back with him to Debra Tabor. As this news was brought by a man who was recognised by some in camp as being what he claimed—Mr. Flad's servant—his statement was received without suspicion, and the event was justly considered to be most unfortunate. When, however, the exploring-party returned, Dr. Krapf, the chief interpreter, examined the man, cross-questioned him as to time and dates, and found that these were quite incompatible with the truth, as the man described them as having taken place in the latter part of October, whereas our last news from Mr. Flad himself was to November 7th, at which time none of these movements had taken place. Finding himself thus caught, the man confessed that his whole statement was a lie. I need not say that this contradiction of the false news gave the greatest satisfaction to everyone, but the general feeling was that six dozen, well laid on, would be of enormous benefit to the man who thus invented false news, apparently merely for the pleasure of gratuitous lying. Of course he will not be punished, for the policy pursued with respect to the natives is mild in the extreme. By all means conciliate natives, by all means pay for all you take, do no wrong to anyone; but at the same time make them respect you by the firmness with which you administer justice upon thieves and plunderers, and do not encourage the people to cheat you by ordering a price at least six or eight times above their former prices for every animal or article you buy. The men who were taken in the act almost of robbery down the pass, and whose preliminary examination I described a week since, have not been flogged, or, as far as I am aware, in any way punished, nor have three other ruffians who were captured the following day. The natives put this forbearance down to timidity on our part. They cannot comprehend that any other feeling could prevent our punishing these men, who have been robbing our convoys, now that we have them in our power. It may be a course of Christian forbearance, but officers whose kits have been plundered are very sore that fellows of this kind are not summarily punished upon the spot.

The exploring-party went forward to Attegrat, a place of some size, about thirty-five miles from here. They went by one route and returned by another. One line was rather more mountainous than the other, but both are, I hear, quite practicable, and water, forage, and wood were found in abundance. At Attegrat a large fair was going on, and very large quantities of cattle, sheep, goats, ponies, and mules, together with grain, chillies, honey, &c., were exposed for sale. The appearance of the escort of cavalry excited the greatest curiosity, and the party were almost mobbed as they walked through the fair. On parts of the route they passed through enormous flights of locusts, which the people were endeavouring to frighten away from their fields by beating drums and pieces of metal together, and by lighting great fires. The locusts abound everywhere here; not a bush which has not half-a-dozen of these insects, hardly a rock without one or two crawling over it. The natives say they have not had so many for years, and that the crops have been very greatly damaged by them. The only things which benefit by them are the monkeys and birds, both of which feed upon them. The natives themselves also eat them to a certain extent. The method of preparation is as follows: A large hole is made in the ground. This is lined smoothly with clay. A large fire is lighted in this, and when this has burnt down the ashes are scraped out, the hole is filled with locusts, and covered up with clay. When the insects are sufficiently baked they are taken out and pounded into a fine powder, which is eaten mixed with rice or flour. At Attegrat the expedition found blocks of salt used as the medium of exchange: we have not seen any in this part of the country. In the fair they also saw some really warm cloths of native manufacture. This is important, as, if the supply turns out to be abundant, it will save the expense of bringing warm clothing for the native troops from England. Indeed, warm clothes appear to me to be a most unnecessary portion of our enormous baggage. The weather by day, even at this the coldest time of year, and upon one of the most elevated parts of our journey, is never cold enough for warm clothing. At night men require an extra blanket for warmth, and this they might wrap round them over their greatcoat upon unusually cold nights. On Christmas-eve the general inspected the troops, who performed several manœuvres. He left on Christmas-day at three o'clock, four hours after the return of the expeditionary force, and having had a conversation of some length with Colonels Merewether and Phayre. One good result among the many brought about by the general's visit here will be, that we shall now have some little attention paid to health. A medical officer had been appointed as sanitary officer, but his appointment, for any good it did, might as well have never been made. It was not that this officer failed in his duty, or that there was no need for his services; on the contrary, the state of the watering arrangements was disgraceful, the native troops washing, &c. in the pools above those from which the drinking-water was taken. The water certainly has to filter through the peat before it reaches the other pools, but that is little satisfaction. It is true that this was against orders, but the number of sentries posted was quite insufficient, or else they winked at the proceedings of their fellow-soldiers. I myself rode past half-a-dozen times, and never without seeing native soldiers washing on the edge of the pool. The latrine arrangements connected with the 10th Native Infantry hospital were also simply scandalous. But worst of all was the state of the pass, dotted with dead baggage-animals in every stage of decomposition, and the stench from which was almost overpowering. The sanitary officer had pointed out these evils, and had applied for power to take on a few natives to burn the carcasses in the pass. This suggestion, however, had been passed over as absurd, and he might as well have been in Bombay. Nothing whatever was done. General Staveley, however, restored this officer to his proper place, and gave him authority to take on the natives and burn the dead animals, which, had nothing been done, were offensive enough to have created the worst epidemic among the advancing troops. Other medical officers have been appointed to take bands of coolies and clear the different stages of this pass. The horse-disease still continues very bad. Of the six horses brought up by the general and the members of his staff, four were taken ill the day after his arrival here. They do not, however, appear to have taken it in a virulent form, and will, I hope, get over it. Yesterday being Christmas-day was of course kept with all honour; that is to say, with such honours as could be paid. It was hard to believe it was Christmas-day, especially among native troops; to them, of course, it was no festival. The day was fine and hot—the thermometer 75° in the shade, but very hot where there was no shelter. I fastened a large bunch of fir and of a plant somewhat resembling myrtle to my tent-pole, and two or three of the other tents were similarly decorated. One of the engineer officers had quite a triumphal arch of green erected before his tent. Large circular arbours were built up by the 10th Native Infantry and by the 3d Cavalry, to serve as shelter from the wind while they sat round the fire after dinner. I was invited by the 3d Native Cavalry to take my Christmas dinner with them, and a capital dinner it was under the circumstances. Two huge bunches of fir were fastened to the tent-poles, the table was formed of the lids of packing-cases, and we sat round upon boxes and chairs of every height and make. Here was a man on a seat so low that his chin hardly appeared above the table; next to him one perched up so high that his knees were on a level with his plate. Nor were the fittings of the table less various. It was the camp rule that everyone should bring his own plates, knives, forks, and glasses. Some of us therefore fed off tin, some off crockery, some off enamelled iron. Some drank from glasses, some from pewter-pots. The only uniformity was in the bottle of champagne placed before each diner. Most of us would, I think, have preferred beer; but there was not a bottle left in the camp, and the champagne before us had been hoarded for this sacred occasion. The dinner was various. Mutton and guinea-fowl; spur-fowl and venison; but, whatever we ate, everyone present religiously took a piece of the joint of roast beef. It was the only reminder of the occasion. I need not say how heartily each joined in the toast of "All friends at home."

I start this afternoon on my way down the pass again to Zulla, and shall carry this letter down to post there, as the ridiculous arrangements to which

I have before alluded still prevail. A native still creeps up and down the pass with a bag on his back, and takes his four or five days to do the seventy miles, whereas two relays of men on mules or ponies would bring the bag down in fifteen hours easily. As it is, no one knows whether they will be in time to catch a post or not. In fact, it is a pure haphazard proceeding.

Zulla, Annesley Bay, January 2d, 1868.

I have been now three days back in Zulla, which is literally crowded with troops. In respect to the pass, nothing could be more surprising than the change which has taken place in the road during the fortnight which has elapsed since I first passed up. This is due to the way in which the sappers and miners, under officers of the Royal Engineers, and the advanced companies of the Beloochees, under Major Hogg, have worked. The latter are at work in the valley below the Rayray Guddy pass, and here they make very nearly a mile of road a day, along which artillery might be taken without difficulty. It is wonderful to see the change which they have effected, and the hearty way in which they work. Not less surprising is the change which the sappers and miners have effected in the Sooro Gorge. When I last rode up it, it was, as I described it, all but impracticable for loaded animals. One had to clamber over a huge boulder here, to scramble through between two others there. It was a really difficult proceeding, and loaded camels were unable to get through the narrow places. Now all this is changed. A path winds here and there among the rocks, down which I was able to ride my horse without the smallest difficulty. The worst part of the journey was the passage of the thirty-three miles between Rayray Guddy and Sooro, without water, except a bucket of pea-soup-coloured stuff at Guinea-fowl Plain for the animals. It is proposed to sink more wells at this point, to put up some pumps, and to establish a small commissariat dépôt, in order that troops may break their march there. As we rode down this dry parched valley for thirty miles, occasionally meeting detachments of weary men, who asked us pitifully how far it was to water, we could not help thinking of one of Colonel Phayre's reports, in which he stated, "From Sooro to Senafe, about thirty miles more, water never fails." The fact being, not one single drop is to be found in the thirty miles above Sooro, save at one muddy well.

At Koomaylo I found an astonishing change. The thorn-trees which had lined the bottom of the valley had been all cut down; a large space had been cleared as a camping-ground for troops as they march through; fresh wells have been sunk, and there are some of the American pumps at work, discharging a stream of clear water, which, flowing through a succession of tubs, enables the animals to be watered in one quarter the time formerly occupied. These pumps, which are called "the Douglas pitcher-spout pump," are certainly admirable machines. When I had first heard of their arrival, and of the principle of their construction, I had not thought it possible that they could be used in such ground as this. They consist of a number of thin iron tubes like gas-pipes, screwing into each other, the lowest one terminating in a sharp spike of slightly bulbous form, so that, being thicker than the rod itself, it only touches the soil through which it is driven at that point, thus greatly diminishing the friction and resistance. On to the pipe, at about four feet from its upper end, is screwed a block of iron, which can be shifted as the rod gradually descends. A heavy weight of iron, with a hole through it, is put on the rod above this block, and to this weight ropes are attached working through pulleys placed on the top of the rod four feet higher. Two men pull these ropes, and the weight rises, and then falls, acting as a rammer upon the anvil of iron below. In this manner the whole rod is driven down, fresh lengths being added as required, and then a pump is established without the labour of sinking a well. The whole thing is simple in the extreme, and admirably adapted for clay or gravel soils. It could, however, hardly be expected to be successful in the bed of a torrent, where the gravel is mixed with blocks of stone of every size, as it is evident that a hollow pipe could not be driven through solid rock. The tube, however, in nine cases out of ten, pushes any obstacle aside, and reaches the required depth. It is intended to arrange a series of troughs, so that the animals may be enabled to drink upon their arrival without the weary hour of waiting which they have now to go through. Indeed, it is a wonder that serious accidents have not occurred owing to the eagerness with which the maddened animals struggle and fight to get to the water. At Koomaylo we found two companies of the 33d regiment. They have since been joined by another, and the three marched last night on their way to Sooro. Three other companies of the same regiment marched from here this morning, and will at once follow their advanced wing, while the head-quarters and remaining companies go on to-morrow. There is also a battery of the Royal Artillery at Koomaylo, that is, the guns, and a portion of the men are there, the horses and drivers having been sent up to Senafe to be clear of the disease. I met them at Sooro, and the animals were then all in splendid condition, and not a single horse or baggage-animal was as yet affected. Great as I had found the changes at other points along the line, the alterations were as nothing to those which had taken place at Zulla. The harbour contained more than double the number of vessels that were here before. It is probable that hardly a great commercial port in the world contains such a fine fleet of steamers and sailing-transports as are now lying off this place, of which no one had ever heard six months ago. The camp, too, was so altered that I had the greatest difficulty in finding the tent I was in search of, although it stood precisely where I left it three weeks since. But the place, which then contained under twenty tents, can now count ten times that number. The 33d are encamped to the right of the landing-place, at a quarter of a mile distant. General Staveley and his staff have moved their tents from the spot where they before stood, in the very centre of the dust and din of the place, to a little beyond the 33d lines, where General Napier's tents are also pitched. The harbour is full of troops, who are clamouring for carriage to enable them to get on. The Scinde Horse are landing, as are the 3d Native Infantry. The 25th Native Infantry and her Majesty's 4th Foot are there, as are artillery batteries and mountain trains, as are mules and horses innumerable, and a bewildering amount of stores. Very large quantities of these latter are now being forwarded to the front, and 3000 of the little cattle and donkeys of the natives have been engaged upon the service. The price paid is two and a quarter dollars per bag, and each bullock carries two bags, some of the smaller donkeys taking one each. The natives are responsible for any loss of stores, but up to the time I left Senafe not one single bag had gone astray. These animals are rather a nuisance to meet going down the pass. Our own mules go in strings, one tied behind the other, and the drivers, if one meets them, endeavour, as far as possible, to make room for an officer to pass. The natives, on the contrary, drive their animals in a herd before them, occupy the whole width of the track, and make no effort whatever to get their cattle out of the way. It is in vain shouting and being angry. The Shohos regard one with placid indifference, and you must push your horse into a thorn-thicket or up a rock to get out of their way. If you happen to overtake one of these native herds in rather a narrow place, it is still more provoking, for there is nothing to do for it but to follow patiently in their train for perhaps half-a-mile, half smothered in the dust they raise, until the valley opens, and you are able to leave the path, and get past them among the stones and scrub. These oxen are very small, but extremely hardy. There is nothing for them in the way of forage all the way up. All they have to eat are a few leaves from the bushes, and such handfuls of grass as their masters may get for them by climbing the sides of the hills, and yet they arrive at Senafe in good condition and without signs of distress, with their skin smooth, and their eyes bright. This accession of stores at Senafe is a great assistance. It is an addition to our stock there, and it is a great relief to the transport corps to be able to continue their regular work of forwarding regiments, and stores for present consumption of man and beast. The transport train is now doing its work very much better; but I shall have more remarks to make upon them in my next. Brigadier-general Collings started yesterday to take the command at Senafe, and I expect to find that very material changes have, in consequence, taken place there. Brigadier-general Schneider has arrived here, and will take the command at this landing-place.

The great event of to-day is the arrival of Sir Robert Napier, whose ship, her Majesty's steam-ship Octavia, Captain Colin Campbell, was signalled as about to enter the harbour early this morning. The anchor was dropped at about half-past ten, and General Staveley and the heads of departments went off at once to see him. He is to disembark this evening. As it is war-time, there was no salute or demonstration upon the arrival of the ship.

Zulla, Jan. 6th.

It is only after a ride or two round camp that one sees how very great are the changes which have taken place in the last three weeks. I do not know that anywhere in the world could more objects of various interest, more life and movement and bustle, be found than in a couple of hours' ride through this camp. Start we from the head of the *bunder*—in England called pier; but here everything has its Indian name. The *bunder* has, since I last wrote, been lengthened a few yards, and has been widened at the end to a width of fifteen or twenty yards. On one side, too, wooden piles have been driven down, so that the great landing barges can lie safely alongside and discharge. It will be a great thing when it is finished in the same way all round the pier-head. Not very pleasant are one's first steps upon Abyssinian soil, for the pier is made of great rough pieces of rock and pumice-stone, painful to walk upon, and utterly destructive to boots. In spite of this the pier-head is crowded. The hour at which we start upon our ride is daybreak, and from daybreak until eight o'clock bathing is allowed from the pier, as also from five to seven in the evening. Here we have a number of figures, some dressing, some undressing, some picking their way painfully over the stones to their clothes, others in the act of plunging into the water, which is at high tide seven feet deep. Around, the sea is dotted with heads, many of which we recognise and address. Here is a quartermaster-general, there a colonel of infantry, next to whom is a drummer-boy, and beyond a dozen privates. There is no distinction of rank here. Everyone picks out the softest stone he can find to sit upon, and cares nothing whether his next neighbour be a general officer or a full private. We pick our way as well as we can across this bit of rough ground and through the groups of bathers, and then at ten yards from the head of the pier we come upon smoother ground. Here is a line of rails, and the surface has been smoothed by spreading sand over it, an improvement which has only been completed two or three days since. Before, a walk down the bunder was certain destruction to any but the most iron-shod pair of boots. By the side of the bunder, where the rail commences, a large barge is lying. She has just come alongside, and fifty or sixty mules and ponies, her cargo, are looking over her rail with excited eyes and restless inquiring ears at the bustle on the quay, and at this land, which, although they know it not, is destined to be the grave of many of them. On the pier, awaiting their arrival, is one of the indefatigable officers of the transport train. He has with him a couple of men. A long gangway is laid from the barge, which is much higher than the pier, down on to the stones; on this are thrown some gunny-bags, and then the animals, some coming readily enough, others resisting strenuously, snorting and struggling, are led down. As they reach the land their head-ropes are tied together in fours, and they are sent off with their drivers to wait at the end of the bunder until all are landed. It is not a long operation. Ten minutes or so, and then an inspector takes them off, first to the watering-troughs and then to the lines. Opposite the landing-barge, on a vacant spot on the pier, a distilling apparatus is at work. This machine, I believe, partly supplies the sailing-ships, and also the wants of the fatigue-parties at work on the pier. Next to the barge lie two native boats discharging stores, which a fatigue-party are loading into the trucks, under the direction of the officers of the quartermaster's or commissariat departments. As soon as the trucks are loaded, a party of Soumalis seize them and push them along the track to the yard, shouting their universal chorus as they do so. Next to the native craft unloading are a number of boats belonging to the ships in harbour, and which are either supplied to one of the departments, or are waiting while their skippers are on shore. On the opposite side of the pier the water is more shallow, and boats never come in here, but it is by no means empty at present, for there are a couple of hundred men bathing all along—less adventurous spirits, who do not care for the plunge into deep water, or for walking over pumice-stones with naked feet.

When we get to the end of the bunder we mount our horses, which our gorrawallahs have been holding, and we follow the line of rails. As soon as we are fairly ashore, we find great piles of stores lying by the rails. These belong to the land transport stores. Hundreds of great cases, each containing four Otago mule-saddles. Piles of Bombay pads and of camel-saddles. Their other stores are sent up to their own lines, a quarter of a mile farther; but the heavy saddles have not been sent there, as the line has only been opened to that point during the last two days, and it is much easier to bring the mules down and to saddle them here than it is to take the heavy cases on farther. There is a saddling-party at work now. It consists of a fatigue-party of artillery, directed by an officer of the transport corps. A Chinese carpenter opens the cases. Two of the men lift the contents out, and cut the lashings which secure each separate article of the fittings together. Others stand round and fit the saddles together—no easy task, for they are extremely complicated. This, however, is not of so much consequence as it would otherwise be, for, once put together, they do not require much subsequent unstrapping. Others then put the saddles and bridles on to the mules, some of which object most strongly to the operation, pull back violently, turn round and round as fast as the man with the saddle approaches, and lash out with a steady power which, exerted in any other way, would be highly satisfactory. In vain the soldiers try to keep them steady. In vain pat, coax, strike, and swear. In vain they strap up one of the fore-legs. Some of the beasts are quite unmanageable, and are only subdued by strapping up a leg, and then keeping them going round and round upon the other three until quite exhausted. The cases of the saddlery are broken up, and spread out upon the ground to pile bags of rice or grain upon—no unnecessary precaution, for a high tide the other night wetted an immense quantity of hay, and the stores have been since shifted farther inland. The engineers had constructed a sort of sand-wall to prevent the recurrence of such an event; but they calculated without their host. They fortified against the enemy in front, but made no account of him in the rear. The consequence was that in the heavy rain of Saturday night the water came rushing down from behind, and being prevented flowing into the sea by this dam, again created a small flood, but this time of fresh water, in the commissariat yard. The commissariat yard when I was last here stood where the transport yard now stands, but it is now shifted more to the left. The reason of this was that the commissariat stores, the bundles of compressed hay and the bags of rice and grain, are not too heavy to be carried ashore by the natives, while the heavy cases of the transport corps necessarily were put in the cars. The commissariat stores are therefore principally landed in native boats, which come into three-foot water, and from which lines of wading Soumalis bear them to land. The heavier stores, such as barrels of rum and ghee, are of course landed on the bunder and brought up on the trucks. Everywhere about the end of the pier is bustle. Here are a party of Madras coolies moving stores. There are a hundred mules just starting with provisions for the front. Here come a detachment of one of the regiments to take charge of some of their baggage just being landed. Everywhere an energetic officer of the various departments directing the operations. We now ride on. Leaving the line of rails we turn to the right, bearing gradually away from the sea. The first group of tents we come upon are those of the officers of the land transport. They will not be there long, however, for they have orders to shift over to the other side, where the lines of their animals are five minutes' walk away, and at the extreme right of the camp. Did these officers' duties lie principally at their lines, there would be some reason for this; but as it is, they are either on the bunder landing horses, or else saddling down by the shore. The duties of looking after the animals in their lines have of course to be generally supervised by an officer from each division, but are under the charge of English inspectors, who are sergeants in cavalry or line regiments. The lines, being to leeward of the camp, are constantly enveloped in a cloud of blinding dust, so thick that one cannot see fifty yards. To live in such an atmosphere is next to impossible, especially when delicately scented by the odour of the three or four thousand mules, ponies, and oxen, to say nothing of the native attendants close at hand. The former spot where they were encamped was only five minutes' walk distant, and to insist upon these officers living and working close by their lines is about as reasonable as an order would be for the officers of the Life Guards to sleep in their stables. I am convinced that General Schneider will have to revoke his order, for it will be simply impossible to keep books or accounts in a dust which would be two inches thick in five minutes upon everything; and although an officer's comfort or health may be a very trifling matter, anything which might be an obstacle to his returning the necessary number of reports and statements will be certain to be considered.1 Riding through the transport officers' lines, we come upon a line of tents occupied by the medical staff. Then comes a gap, and then we enter the lines of the European regiments, at present occupied by portions of the 33d and 4th infantry and artillery. Its appearance bears little resemblance to that presented by a regiment under canvas at home. The tents are of an entirely different shape; they are single-poled tents, and are perhaps fifteen feet square. They have canvas walls of nearly six feet high, so that one can stand upright anywhere. Above the tent itself is a cover, which extends over it and projects three feet beyond the walls, making the tent double over the roof, and forming an awning around it. About eight inches is left between the two roofs for the circulation of air. These tents are in their way perfect, but they are extremely heavy, and will be left here, and the troops will take up with them tents known as native "routies" —I do not guarantee the spelling of this or any other native word—which I shall describe hereafter. Not less than the tents do the men differ from the European standard. The gray suits of karkee—a sort of stout jean—and the ugly helmets of the same material, look like anything rather than the garb of the British soldier. Then, too, the arrangement of the camp looks unfamiliar, for the tents are placed far asunder. This is necessitated by the great length of the ropes of the tent. Here, too—strange sight in an English camp—interspersed among the tents are queer bowers of shrubs, covered with gunny-bags, old sacks, and other odds and ends. Round these bowers squat swarthy figures scantily clothed. These are the camp-followers, the attendants on the British soldier; these their abodes. These men draw his water, pitch his tents, sweep out his camp—in fact, perform all the work which a soldier in England does for himself. In India the soldier is a valuable animal. He is valued at one hundred pounds, and is too costly to be risked by doing hard work in the sun. He is kept for fighting only, and it is very right that it should be so. It has been questioned whether it would not have been better to have brought soldiers direct from England, who are accustomed to rough it for themselves. There is much to be said upon the subject, to which I shall some day revert, but at present I am inclined to think that in this respect the authorities have judged rightly, for judging by the 102° which the thermometer marked here in the shade on New Year's-day, we shall have a more than Indian heat—that is, those down upon this plain will—in the middle of summer, and although the heat in the interior will probably be nothing to what it will be here, there can be no doubt that the less men are exposed to it the better. But we must continue our ride.

Just behind the European lines, that is, between them and the sea, is a line of tents, some of which are of large size, and by the side of one of these the British ensign is flying. These are the tents of the head-quarters staff. We turn our backs on this and gallop across the European lines, that is, inland. There is an unoccupied space of perhaps four hundred yards, and then we come upon a camp of quite different aspect from the last. Here the tents are ranged in two lines, and are placed quite close together, that is, with not more than three or four yards between them. The neat and orderly appearance of these lines of tents shows to all the greater advantage after the straggling look of the European lines. These tents are routies. They are large double-poled tents, single, but lined with blue bunting. The tents, like the English bell-tents, reach nearly to the ground, with only a wall of about eighteen inches in height. The opening is at one end, and extends from the pole downwards. This is, for a climate like the present, a great drawback, for the opening is very large and cannot be closed. In a hot climate this would matter but little; but for a country with heavy dews and cold nights in winter, and with heavy downpours in the rainy season, it is a very serious disadvantage. Opposite the long line of the routies are the mess and officers' tents. There are two regiments camped in these lines, or, more properly, portions of two regiments. The men on duty look more like England than the European troops had done, for they are all in their scarlet tunics and black trousers. It is only the headgear which is different. The 3d Native Infantry have blue puggaries round their forage-caps. The 25th Native Infantry have green. The 10th Native Infantry wear white puggaries, and the Sappers and Miners black, and this acts as an easily-distinguished mark between the various native regiments. They all wear the regulation tunic and trousers, but vary the puggary or cap-cover according to the taste of their commander. When I say they all wear the British uniform, I mean that the old sepoy regiments do so. Some of those who have only been admitted among the regular Indian army of late years, such as the Beloochees, wear quite different uniforms. I have omitted to state that in our ride between the 33d and Native Infantry camps, we passed through some artillery; but these, as well as the sappers and miners, and the ordnance commissary tents— which, with the telegraph, railway, and other departments, are pitched near the line of railway—I must reserve for another letter. We are only making a tour of the outside of the camp upon the present occasion. Riding on through the native infantry lines, and crossing a few hundred yards of open ground, we come to the bazaar, which is on the main road to Koomaylo. The bazaar is certainly not much to look at. Two or three dozen tents, composed of rough poles covered with matting, constitute it. As there are no windows to any of these establishments, it is unnecessary to state that there is no display of goods. There is an open doorway through which any intending purchaser enters, and asks for anything he desires. If it is kept there a box is opened and the article produced, if not he goes into the next shop. There is a guard of European soldiers at the entrance to the bazaar to keep order, and their services are not unfrequently called into requisition. During the last part of our ride we have fairly got into the dust, which hangs over Zulla in a sort of lurid cloud, and entirely shuts off all the view, even the nearest hills from the harbour. This dust is terrible. It fills the eyes, mouth, and nostrils, and equals the dust on the Champ de Mars in Paris, which I had hitherto considered unrivalled in the world. Sometimes the wind blows steadily, and then there is one great uniform swoop of dust; at other times it seems to lull for a while, and then from three or four spots a straight column ascends, such as burning piles of green wood upon a calm day might produce. These columns will remain stationary for three or four minutes, and then move rapidly along, and woe to the unfortunate tents over which they may pass, for they will make a clean sweep of every light object, and will leave three inches deep of sand on everything. In camp phraseology, these little whirlwinds are called devils. Passing from the bazaar, still moving as before in the arc of a circle, we come upon the railroad. The railroad has made far less progress in the last month than anything else here has done; at this rate it will not be near Koomaylo by next Christmas. I do not hesitate to say that ten English navvies would have done very much more in the same time; and as for the Army Works Corps, which we had in the Crimea, they would have half-finished it to Koomaylo. But this delay is due to no want of zeal on the part of those who have the direction of it, but simply a want of method, and of materials, which are, no doubt, somewhere on board ship, but cannot be got at. Just at this part we pass under some poles with a fine copper wire extending between them. This is the telegraph, which in a very short time will be open to Koomaylo, and thence will be pushed on in a week or so, for the wire is at all the stations along the line of march; and it would have been completed to Senafe by this time were it not that the poles have not come to hand, from some reason or other.

We now are approaching the lines of the transport animals. This is the most interesting sight in the whole camp. Here are long lines of ponies, just arrived from Suez. Next to them are hundreds of mules of all nations and breeds. Here are the cart-mules, and 200 light carts, to be drawn by one or two animals, are ranged near them. Beyond them are the baggage-mules, 600 in number. All of them have arrived during the last two or three days; many of them have not yet been saddled, for the unpacking and fitting together of the saddles is a long and tedious operation. Many of the mules are not even branded. Beyond them, again, come the draught-oxen, with their carts. They are the same beautiful white Brahmin cattle which I saw at Bombay—enormous animals, as strong as camels and quiet and docile as sheep. Near them are ranged their carts, which are of altogether different construction from those for the mules. On the ground under the feet of all these animals is scattered a thick layer of chopped straw and hay, and their condition and state afford as strong a contrast as can possibly be conceived to that of the famished, dying animals I described in the letter I wrote upon landing a month since. This extraordinary improvement must be assigned to the immense efforts which all the officers of the Transport Corps have made, and especially to those of Captain Twentyman, of the 18th Hussars, who during that period has been in command. But even the exertion of all these officers would have been in vain had it not been for the strong and cordial assistance which General Staveley has given to Captain Twentyman. Every suggestion made by the latter has been indorsed and ordered to be carried out by the general, who is fully alive to the fact that the Transport Corps is the all-important branch of the expedition. The animals are all picketed by their head-ropes to long lines of picket-rope, but no heel-ropes are used. Certainly the use of heel-ropes adds greatly to the uniformity of the appearance of picketed animals, as they all retain the same distance from each other and from the ropes, and there is also the advantage that they cannot kick each other or any passer-by. On the other hand, it may be said that mules seldom or never do set to and kick when picketed. I have seen no instance of their so doing; and I understand from the transport officer that there have been no cases of mules being injured by kicks received when picketed. The advantages of their not having foot-ropes are that they have much greater freedom of position. They can lie down, get up, and move across the rope, and, in fact, stretch their tired limbs far better than they can when they are confined by foot-ropes; and, lastly, the mules are not accustomed to the ropes, and frequently get sore fetlocks from their use. The balance of advantages is, then, in favour of allowing them to remain picketed only by their head-ropes, especially as the fastening by the heel-rope involves driving in pegs and loss of time in roping—matters of importance when a train arrives late at night with drivers and animals alike jaded and fatigued. The whole of the animals are now in fair working condition, with the exception only of about 200 camels, which are out at Hadoda, where they were sent to recruit, having arrived in too bad a condition to be set to work. There were more sent out, but some have returned to work, others have died—many of pure starvation, although there were stores of grain lying at Weir, within two or three miles, literally rotting. But the custom is not to give camels grain, but allow them to get their livelihood by plucking a few leaves from the shrubs. It is not to be wondered at, then, that the poor beasts gained no strength. This will now be remedied, for Dr. Lamb, one of the veterinary surgeons of the Transport Corps, has reported that they are dying of pure starvation; and I understand that General Staveley at once ordered that grain should be issued to them.

In my next letter I shall describe the organisation of the Transport Corps; but at present we must continue our ride, which is now nearly over, for we have almost completed our circle, and are again approaching the sea-shore. We pass on our way some strange bower-like structures, whose progress I have watched for the last few days with some curiosity. I first saw three or four long lines of sand, which were carefully levelled, and were four or five yards wide, and perhaps fifty yards long. By each side of these lines of sand coolies were engaged sticking rods, about the same length, but thinner, than hop-poles. I could not even guess the object of these lines. Next day I found that poles had been stuck in across the ends, and that at distances of four yards across partitions had been made. Riding close, I saw that in the side row a gap was left as a doorway to each of these partitions. The next day I found that thinner rods were being fastened to the tops of the others—along which horizontal pieces had been tied—and that these were being bent over and twined in the centre, so as to form a bower. The mystery was now explained. These long rows of poles were the framework for rows of huts; bushes are to be entwined between them, and the whole, when finished, will accommodate, or rather hold, five hundred of the commissariat coolies, for whom they are destined. We now trot on to the watering-place. The last time I was here it was one of the most painful sights I ever witnessed to see the animals watered. They were formed in lines near the miserable little troughs, and were with the greatest difficulty kept back until these were full. Half maddened with thirst as they were, it was a service of real danger to restrain them, and when they were allowed to rush forward it was too often to find that there was scarcely a mouthful of water each. It was no wonder that they screamed and struggled and fought.

It was a battle for life, in which the victors moved off unsatisfied, but with sufficient water to enable them to live until the next scanty supply was issued, while the vanquished dragged themselves away to die. Thank God this is over now. There is plenty of water for all. I do not think an animal in this camp has an insufficiency of water. The trough is long and wide, and the animals advance on each side and drink as much as they desire. The times for watering them is from six to eight in the morning, and from four to six of an evening. A strong fatigue-party are present to pump the water from the tank into the trough, and to keep order. They are ordered to leave the trough full when they cease pumping, so that any animal which may arrive late may not be deprived of its drink.

We have now only to ride along the shore for another 300 yards to arrive at the commissariat stores on the left of the bunder, from which we started. Here everything is excellently arranged and managed. The great piles of stores are covered with tarpaulins and old sails to keep off the rain; and as it was impossible to procure stones to form a foundation for the sacks, and to keep them clear of the damp, broken-up packing-cases were laid down first on the sand, then empty sacks, and then bales of hay from Bombay, which is much more bulky and less valuable than the compressed hay from England. No damage of any great extent can therefore ensue from the heaviest flood. There are two very large wooden stores, in which articles readily damageable by rain are housed; and there are two very large framework buildings erected, which only require the corrugated iron-plates.

Nearly opposite the commissariat a long wooden jetty is in course of erection. It is already completed for a considerable distance; but the water is so shallow, that it will have to be carried very much further out before boats can come alongside to load.

We have now completed our circular ride round the camp; and I must leave the camps and dépôts lying in the interior of the circle until another occasion, for I have not yet touched upon the immediate news of the day.

General Napier landed yesterday morning at half-past seven. A guard of honour of the 4th regiment was drawn up at the end of the pier, and the various generals here, with their staffs, and the heads of the different departments, received him. I had heard that he was going to land earlier, and went down to the waterside just at daylight.

Everything was quiet then, and not a breath of wind ruffled the water. Presently there was a sign of life in the men-of-war, the Octavia, Serapis, and Argus. Men began to climb the rigging, and to fasten man-lines above the yards. Then they came down again, and all was quiet on board the men-of-war; but the merchant-vessels were now making a move, and the native boats were putting off towards the ships they were told off to discharge. In the mean time the guard of honour and the officers took their places at the head of the bunder. Now a signal is run up to the mast-head of the Octavia, and, as if by magic, a crowd of white figures leap up the shrouds of the men-of-war, and run out upon the yards. Another minute of silence, and then a boat with an awning pulls out from the after-side of the Octavia, and a few seconds afterwards the thunder of her guns tells us that the Chief of the invading army has left the ship. Three minutes later the little guns of the mountain train proclaim that he has landed; the band strikes up "God save the Queen," the troops salute, and Sir Robert Napier has taken command of the forces here.

After all, this is more a ceremony than a reality, for the General has been ashore examining into all that was going on every day since he came into harbour. There is a great feeling of satisfaction at his arrival, as, in the first place, he is a most popular chief, and in the next, nothing definite could be decided upon as to the movements of troops or on the plan of the campaign until he arrived. The *on dit* now is that no more troops will be sent forward at present, but that the whole efforts of the transport corps and commissariat will be devoted to accumulating a six months' stock of provisions at Senafe. The 33d have already gone on; but it is now probable that no other regiment will move for another fortnight.

We have at last authentic news from the interior. A letter has arrived from the prisoners, dated Dec. 15th (I can hardly understand how, at the Shoho rate of travelling, it can have come so fast), in which they report that the King of Shoa, who was besieging Magdala, and upon whose assistance Colonel Merewether had built much, has retired from before the place, and that it is now open to Theodore. This is certainly bad news. Not that I have ever put the smallest trust in the assistance of any of these kinglings. On the contrary, I think that the policy which has been hitherto pursued with respect to the natives has been a mistake. We should have never asked for alliance or friendship. We are perfectly strong enough to go on by ourselves, and were we not it is certain that we could place no reliance upon any professions of friendship. Why, then, make the natives think we are weak by asking for allies? Say firmly to each king, "We are going on through your country to fetch the prisoners beyond. We are perfectly strong enough to do this, and anything beside which may be necessary. We go through and return without making any stay. In your country are many kings and many rivals. We need no assistance, and we know that if we enter into alliance with one chief we gain the enmity of another by so doing. We wish not, therefore, to enter into any alliance whatever. We are friends passing through your country. We require stores, cattle, &c., and we mean to have them; but we pay for everything we require, and that at prices which the imagination of the herd-and flock-owner of Abyssinia never before conceived even in his wildest dreams."

There are numerous rumours current in camp that the chiefs are forming an alliance against us, and that they intend to put their forces in motion to attack us. But of all this I cannot say that I believe one word. Nor do I consider it a matter of importance one way or another, for if they do come they will go away again at a vastly greater rate of speed than they advance, and will be very much more civil afterwards. After the landing of the Chief yesterday I went on board the Gomta, which has brought in nineteen elephants from Bombay, in charge of Captain Annesley, of the Land Transport Train. They all arrived in excellent condition, having been perfectly well during the whole voyage, except for two days, when there was a strong wind, which made them very unhappy. The debarkation was to begin directly the Commander-in-chief had landed. Accordingly, a party of sailors and marines came on board from the Octavia. The tackle had been already fixed, and the barge was alongside. It had been at first proposed that the animals should have been lowered over the ship's side into the water, and allowed to swim ashore; but the difficulty in relieving them of the slings would have been so great that it was determined, at any rate, to make the experiment with the barge. The animals were down in the hold, which was amply high enough even for the largest of them. They were ranged along on either side, with strong beams between each. They could lie down or stand up as they pleased. The operation of landing them was superintended by Captain Annesley, and by one of the officers of the Octavia. Large blocks were attached to the mainyard, which was strengthened by extra stays. One of the animals who was in the stall immediately under the hatchway was selected for the first experiment. The first difficulty consisted in getting the sling which was of the strongest canvas, with strong ropes along each side, under him. It was laid down upon the ground, and the mahout endeavoured to back the animal over it. Again and again he got him into the right position, but the instant the sailors pulled to the cords to lift up the sling the elephant made a rush forward. At last Sergeant Evans, who is one of the first-class inspectors in the transport train, succeeded in getting the sling under him in his stall, and then getting on his back, backed him under the blocks, the sailors keeping the sling in its place until they could get the hooks fast. Even then all was not finished, for the alarmed elephant continued trumpeting, and endeavouring to rush back to his stall. Sergeant Evans managed to get the breast- and hind-ropes fast, and then all that remained was for the men on deck to work the capstan. The fife struck up, and the elephant, protesting strongly but uselessly, was gradually lifted off his feet. Once in the air the great beast's strength was useless, and he swung an inert mass, except that as he went through the hatchway he got his hind-feet against it, and pushed with so much force, that it was feared for an instant that he would push himself head foremost out of the slings. In another minute, however, he rose above the hatchway, and was now beyond the possibility of doing himself or anyone else any harm. Up he rose, higher and higher, and then he was swung clear of the bulwarks, and lowered down into the barge. Here his mahout and attendant received him, stroked his trunk, and soothed him, and he allowed his slings to be taken off quietly, and stood quite tranquil until two more of his companions were raised from the hold and lowered to his side. Thus far nothing could be more satisfactory. Some of the others who landed later in the day gave more trouble, and had it not been for Sergeant Evans there would have been very great difficulty with them; but he is, without exception, the most resolute and fearless fellow I ever saw at work. Had it not been for him it is questionable whether the elephants would have been got on board at Bombay on the day fixed for their embarkation, and he was raised from the position of a third-class to that of a first-class inspector on the spot for his gallantry.

When these animals were on the barge it was determined to disembark them before lowering others down, in order to see whether they would walk on to the pier. A steam launch accordingly took the barge in tow, and steamed away to the landing-place. These little steam launches are the most handy and useful things here; no matter how large the barge or how long the string of laden boats, one of these little craft seizes upon it and rushes off with it without the slightest difficulty. On arriving at the wharf I saw at once that we should have a difficulty. The naval authorities who had charge of the landing had entirely disregarded the nature and instincts of the animals; and every child who has ever read anything at all about an elephant has heard that these clumsy-looking animals can get up and down the most difficult places, but that they have an invincible objection to trusting themselves upon any platform or bridge, and can only be induced to do so after many experiments as to its strength. The barge was nearly four feet above the level of the pier, and as the sides of the latter slanted somewhat, the side of the barge was distant about a foot from the jetty. But an elephant would have got down this as easily as a man would have done. Instead of allowing him to do this, some rails which had been landed for the line were put from the shore to the barge, the gangway used by the mules placed upon this, and the elephants were required to walk down. They naturally objected, especially as they were not allowed to pause and examine it, but were urged to walk straight on. This they refused pointblank to do, in spite of the efforts of the mahout, and the shoving and striking of the attendants behind them. They would not advance, but lay down to express their determination. At last one of them, on being forced close to the gangway, kneeled down, and with his head gave the whole structure a push which moved it several inches. He then stood up and walked away, having proved to his own satisfaction that we must be fools to expect an animal his size to walk along such a rickety structure as that. Still the heads of the debarkation were loth to give up their favourite idea of a platform. The gangway was taken away, and the marines and sailors brought rails and laid them tier on tier, gridiron-fashion, and placed the gangway on that; and thus having formed a sort of step or platform two feet high, they invited the elephants to step on to it. Again the elephants positively declined, and everything was again tried except patience, the one thing needed. Fortunately, just as the naval authorities were variously discussing the necessity of again slinging the animals and lowering them into the sea, to walk ashore, Captain Moore, interpreter to the Commander-in-chief, appeared upon the scene. At his suggestion the animals were allowed to approach quietly and to kneel down and inspect and try the structure upon which they were to trust themselves; and in another quarter of an hour they were all three safely landed.

An order of the day appeared yesterday thanking the pioneer force and Colonel Field at Senafe for their efforts. There are many remarks down here upon the fact that while the officers and men who marched up to Senafe, and have passed a comparatively quiet and pleasant time up there, have been thanked, there should be no word of praise for the men who have been working almost night and day down here. If any praise was to be given, it has certainly been earned by the men who have borne the heat and burden of the bad times at Zulla. This morning the mountain-guns, made at Woolwich, were out for practice. These guns have been fully described in the columns of the English press, I need not therefore enter into any details. The practice with shell was very fair, the little guns throwing the shell, which are nearly half their own length, with great precision, at 2000 yards. They appeared to me, however, to throw rather to the right. The troops were also out at exercise, and an order has been issued that all the regiments shall go for a march out every morning. This is as it should be: it will keep the men in health, and prepare them, to a certain extent, for the hard work they will probably have to go through when they once start.

Zulla, January 19th.

This has been a week altogether barren of events. No move of any kind has been made, or is at all likely to be made, for another fortnight at the very earliest. The transport train is exclusively employed in taking provisions to the front, and this is a very tedious process. The mules and ponies carry nominally a burden of two hundred pounds each, the camels four hundred pounds; but there are very few indeed of the former capable of bearing their proper burden, and I think I may say not one of the latter. Were an attempt to be made to load them to their full weight, the result would be that one-third of the animals at least would break down in the first two miles. A great number of animals are in hospital; but a vastly-greater proportion are still able to perform a certain amount of work, but nothing like their full quota. These are afflicted with coughs and lung-affections, which will, sooner or later, bring them into hospital, and thence to their graves, the victims of overwork, when in a weakened state, from irregular and scanty supplies of food and water. The transport train is at present so essentially the corps upon which the movements of the army depend, that it will not be out of place if I explain at some little length the constitution and duties of the corps and its officers. The transport train is commanded by Major Warden, and is divided into fourteen divisions, each of which, when complete, contains two thousand animals and twelve hundred men, including drivers, farriers and smiths, saddlers, &c. Each division is commanded by a captain, who has two subalterns. He has four inspectors or sergeant-majors, two second-class inspectors, sergeants; five third-class inspectors, corporals — all European soldiers. He also has two second inspectors and five third inspectors — natives; and one hundred native soldiers, who are supposed to act as assistants.

It will be seen that each division is as strong as three cavalry regiments; it is composed entirely of drivers collected hastily from all parts, Egyptians, Arabs, Italians, Greeks, Hindoos, &c.—all men without the smallest conception of military discipline; and to manage this vast body of men and animals there are a captain and two officers, and eleven white noncommissioned officers. Were each division stationary, or did it move in a body together, the task would be comparatively easy; but it is scattered over the pass, in convoys of from 200 down to little parties of twos and fours, with officers' baggage. The rules which have been drawn up for the regulation of the corps are admirable on paper, but utterly impracticable on service. Each native soldier is supposed to have control over twelve drivers and twenty-five mules, and is himself amenable to a head muccadum, or fourth inspector, he to a third, the third to the second, &c. "Each man in charge of a squad is to see that every animal brought in from duty is groomed, has the feet picked and cleaned, the provender put before him, the back well sponged with hot water." "The saddles will invariably, when taken off the animals, be placed upside down to dry, pads towards the sun, and afterwards neatly piled up with the equipments affixed to each, in rear of each squad, dressing from the right of the line." All these, and many similar rules, are admirable in theory; utterly impracticable in the field. A convoy arrives late at night. Its first task is to unload, and then to place food before the animals, and to water them if water is attainable; then drivers and animals lie down alike exhausted, and grooming, picking feet, and arranging equipments, dressing from the right, are alike unheeded. The officers of this corps have an almost impossible amount of work to get through. They are supposed to see their animals watered, to parade those which have to start, to see them fed, to see them groomed, to examine their backs, to see that the numerous convoys start at the right time, to look after the polyglot variety of drivers, most of them speaking Arabic, and other unknown tongues. Then they have to look after the native soldiers, to send in reports innumerable, and to keep office-books; they have to perform quartermaster duties and paymaster duties; they have the pay-sheets, family-payment rolls, returns of stores, equipments, defaulter-sheets, &c. to make out with their own hands, unless they take one of the few European inspectors from his work to act as clerk. "They are further responsible for the good order and condition of the cattle, and the due preservation and completeness of their equipments, and must see that each individual soldier, noncommissioned officer and inspector, does his work." In addition to all this, at present they have to be on the pier, seeing the animals landed, and to inspect the putting together and fittings of the saddles and equipments, and the issue of warm clothing to the drivers.

This is a slight sketch of the duties which these three officers have to perform for 2000 animals and 1200 men, with half-a-dozen European noncommissioned officers to assist them. The inspectors, too, have been in many cases selected by the officers commanding regiments, without the slightest reference to their acquirements. Very many of them can hardly speak a word of Hindoostanee, and are of course perfectly useless. All this greatly augments the labour and difficulty of the officer. To say that these last are at work from morning to night is nothing. It is one incessant round of toil, from five in the morning till seven at night, and then reports and accounts. If the officers could but do their work their own way, each for his own division, they would do it—roughly perhaps, but effectually; but it is this constant demand for reports, and the changes which are constantly being made in the arrangements, which make the work far too much to be got through. The great mistake which was committed was the sending any Hindoo inspectors and soldiers unless all, or at any rate the greater part, of the drivers had been also Hindoo. Hindoo drivers would have obeyed Hindoo inspectors and soldiers; the Arabs and Egyptians, who form the great proportion of the drivers, laugh in their faces. A Hindoo, too, is not an inventive man—give him his orders, be quite sure that he understands them, and he will carry them out as long as all goes straight; but he is a very helpless man if things go wrong. These mule-drivers are the most utterly reckless of men. If a mule breaks down, they leave him and his load upon the road. If one breaks down in a narrow spot they will be a good hour before they come to the resolution to pull him out of the way and continue their journey. If a cart-wheel gives out, there it may lie. If an animal has a sore back, or has the disease, or any other malady, it will never occur to them to say a word about it until he falls helpless. Altogether, the drivers of the train are a very reckless lot, who essentially want looking after. The pay offered to the inspectors of the different classes is very good, and there would have been no difficulty in obtaining volunteers from English regiments throughout India, it being of course made a *sine quâ non* that they should have had some colloquial knowledge of Hindoostanee. There should have been at least fifty to each division, and then no convoy of over twenty mules would ever have gone out without a European to look after them. If one of the animals had been ill or lame the inspector would report it; if a mule dropped he would see that the burden was divided among the others; if a wheel had broken he would make some shift or other to patch it up. He should have carried side-arms, and would have seen that the animals kept together without straggling, and would have prevented any looting on the part of the natives. In fact, he would have saved his pay twenty times over. It is this utter recklessness on the part of the drivers which has contributed largely to the great mortality among the animals. They will work the poor beasts with the most terrific sore backs, until in their agony they can go no further; then they will turn them loose and steal another from the lines, so that the veterinary surgeons only find out that animals are ill when they are utterly beyond work. Were sore backs, lameness, and disease only reported at the right time, a few days' rest and a little care would set most of the animals up; now, frequently the first intimation is received from someone who, riding along, has seen the poor beast lying down by the roadside dying.

There has been great discontent excited among these hard-worked officers of the transport train—some of whom have been at work in Egypt or India since August last; others of whom have borne the brunt of the worst time here—at the introduction of a number of other officers over their heads. The corps was constituted as a corps some months since, and the officers have been placed according to their regimental rank. According to all rule and precedent, every officer gazetted to the corps after that would hold rank—that is, local rank—according to the date of his gazetting into the corps. Instead of this, they have been placed according to their date of commission as captain, consequently the whole of the captains who have been at work here from the landing of the expedition—who have borne the toil and anxiety from the first—find two or three officers placed over their heads, and, in fact, if this procedure continue, will at the end of the campaign be six or seven lower on the list than they were before. This is the more inexcusable, as fourteen divisions were to be formed, and fourteen captains were gazetted, thus making the corps complete; and each man hoped, and had a right to expect, to have a division. Indeed, at first even the authorities recognised this; and these captains, who wished to come out to Abyssinia, but could obtain no other appointment, were gazetted as subalterns in the transport train; and as this was subsequent to the gazette forming the corps, it was naturally supposed by the other officers that they came in as junior of that rank. When, however, the first vacancy occurred in the captains, instead of the senior lieutenant obtaining promotion as he expected, one of these captain-subalterns was promoted to the vacancy; and, as he was an old captain, he actually not only jumped over the heads of all the subalterns, but over those of every captain who was here when he landed, and thus become second in command of the transport train. Since then other appointments have been made, and the original captains at present find themselves going gradually down instead of rising in their corps. This, after such work as they have gone through, is not a little hard, and is, I believe, quite without precedent in the service.

The arrangements for the position of the divisions have been so frequently altered during the past fortnight that I am quite unable to say where they are now posted. It was originally arranged by Captain Twentyman—at the time he was in command—that each division should have one station, and pass the stores from station to station. This was afterwards entirely altered, and it was ordered that each division should work from Koomaylo up to Senafe, and a captain was sent up to send the animals down for the purpose. Forty-eight hours afterwards another captain was despatched to entirely countermand these orders, and to make perfectly fresh arrangements, and these again have been altered during the last day or two. I need not say that these constant and needless changes add very greatly to the difficulties with which the officers of the train have to struggle. At present the stores from here to Koomaylo are carried by camels, and thence taken up by mules, oxen, and ponies from station to station.

Strangely enough, the through system, as it was called—that is, the sending animals right on for days with the same loads—was persevered in to the very end of the campaign, although it could be mathematically proved that the relay system was in every respect greatly superior. Captain

Ellis, of the transport train, sent in a table to the authorities, which proved conclusively that the same number of mules would carry one-sixth more goods in a given time by the "relay" system than by the "through." But the other advantages were even greater; an officer stationed at any given place had the men and animals of his division always under his eye. He would get to know both man and beast; he would soon find out which men did their work and which failed in it. The drivers and mules would each have its allotted place, and an infinity of confusion would be avoided; the arrangements for drawing forage for the animals, and food for the men, for cooking, &c. would have all been simple and practicable. Indeed, in every single respect, the relay system possesses immense advantages. It could not, of course, have been adopted beyond Antalo, but the saving of labour and life, the increase of efficiency, regularity, and discipline, from its introduction between Zulla and Antalo, would have been enormous.

I am unable to say how many animals are at present at work—probably nine or ten thousand, and this number, devoted entirely to the conveyance of commissariat stores as they are at present, would carry really large amounts forward, were it not that they carry their own forage, and were they of proper strength; but unfortunately a very large number of them have lung-disease, brought on by insufficient and irregular water and food. The number in hospital is terrible. There are at present about 700 mules and 700 camels in hospital, and the deaths are over 200 a-week. This is a terrible mortality; but were all the others in good working order, it would matter comparatively little; the worst is, that very many are poorly, and will fill the hospital ranks far quicker than death or discharge empty them. There are nominally ten veterinary surgeons to the force under Veterinary Surgeon Lamb, an officer of great experience; only five of the ten have arrived, and these are terribly overworked, as they have no staff, and have to inspect, prescribe, and administer medicines themselves. No time should be lost in filling up the ranks of the veterinary surgeons, and in giving them assistance, for when the numbers are complete they will have at least 100 such animals each to attend to, and these not trifling cases, but terrible sore backs, the last stages of lung-disease, and the local plague. The authorities appear to have thought the lives of the native drivers, officers, and non-commissioned officers, of no consequence whatever, for although there will be 280 Europeans and 18,000 native drivers when the corps is complete, there is not a single surgeon appointed for them! And this although the great part of the force will be stationed at small stations along the road, at which there will be no troops whatever, and of course no medical officer. The men are very liable to broken limbs and injuries from the kicks of the animals, and to illness from hardship and exposure; and yet to this numerous body of men, nearly equalling in number the whole of the rest of the expedition, there has not been a single medical man appointed!

The animals which appear to support the hard work and irregular food with the least deterioration are the bullocks. Of these a very small number indeed have been ill, and the deaths amount to only one or two weekly. They look in really good condition, and perform their work admirably. Indeed, the greater part of the mules and ponies look in fair condition, and they have certainly no lack of food, except at the up-stations. Very great credit is due to the commissariat department, who have done very well, and against whom one never hears a complaint. Since the first landing they have had an abundance of stores for the men; and no instance has, as far as I have heard, occurred of men being unable to obtain their proper rations. The Commander-in-chief is making every effort to strengthen the transport train, and has gazetted a number of unattached subalterns for it. He has also, I believe, applied to the native regiments here for volunteers for that corps; among the subalterns, I hear, there have been few, if any, answers in the affirmative. I understand that the European regiments have also been applied to for volunteers among the noncommissioned officers and men, to act as inspectors in the train. Among these, as among the officers, I hear the appeal has not been responded to. The work of the train is tremendously hard; and men fancy, and perhaps with reason, that they have less chance of going forward to the front in the train than they would have in their own regiments. There would have been no difficulty originally in obtaining any number of men from the regiments not coming to Abyssinia, as men would have volunteered for the very reason that makes the men here refuse to do so—namely, that they wished to see the war; in addition to which, as I have said, the pay in the train is really very good.

But, after all, what is most required by the transport train is a commanding officer of far higher rank than a major. The transport train is, as I have shown, a collection of fourteen divisions, each as numerous as three cavalry regiments, the whole equalling in men alone the rest of the expedition. To command this immense corps a brigadier-general of energy and standing should have been selected—a man who would see the work done, and at the same time insist on being allowed to carry out his plans in his own way, without interference from others. As it is, everyone has advice to offer to the transport train, and, while throwing the blame of everything that goes wrong upon their shoulders, men do little to assist them; think nothing of sending for transport animals, and then keep them waiting for hours; start at times which render it impossible that the animals can be watered; send in their requisitions at all sorts of odd times; and, in fact, show no regard whatever for anything but their personal convenience. Major Warden does his best, and works indefatigably; but it requires an officer of much higher rank and of great firmness and decision. The present would be a great chance for an officer to make himself a name. To have successfully managed so enormous a corps as the transport train under such extreme difficulties as have already, and will in future visit it, would be a feather in the cap of the most distinguished officer.

It is a moot question, whether it would not have been far better to have done here as in India—namely, to put the transport train under the commissariat; and the overwhelming majority of opinion is, that this would have been a very preferable course. In the first place, the commissariat have no responsibility whatever. They have simply to hand over at Zulla so many thousand bags of rice, sugar, biscuit, &c., and to say to them, "Deliver them in certain proportions at such and such stations along the road." This done, their responsibility ceases. If there is a deficiency anywhere, they have only to say, "We handed over the stores at Zulla in ample time, and if they have not arrived it is no fault of ours." I cannot but think that it would be far better for the commissariat to have a transport train of their own. In India they have proved over and over again that they are capable of carrying out their transport arrangements admirably. During the mutiny there was hardly a case occurred where the commissariat did not manage to have the food up ready for the men at the end of the day's march. For the conveyance of military stores and baggage, the transport train should be perfectly distinct from that of the commissariat. So many mules and drivers should be told off to each regiment, and that regiment should be responsible for them. One of the officers and a sergeant or two would be told off to look after them, and see that they were properly fed, watered, and looked after. The transport-train officer with the division would be in charge of spare mules, and exchange them when required for regimental mules which might have fallen sick by the way; in addition to which, a certain proportion of spare mules for casualties might be handed to each regiment. In case of a halt of a few days only, the mules would remain in charge of the troops; but if the halt were likely to be prolonged, the mules would be handed over to the transport officer, and by him used to assist the commissariat, or upon any duty for which they might be required.2

The elephants have been handed over to the commissariat train. They walk backwards and forwards between this place and Koomaylo, and take large quantities of stores forward. The natives are never tired of watching the huge beasts at their work, and wondering at their obedience to us. This astonishes them, indeed, more than anything they have seen of us, with the exception of our condensing water from the sea. One of them was speaking the other day to an officer, who is thoroughly acquainted with Arabic. "You say you are Christians," the Shoho said; "this cannot be, for you wear no blue cords round your necks. You are sons of Sheitan. You are more powerful than the afrits of old. They could move mountains, and fly across the air, but they could never drink from the sea, they could never change salt-water into fresh. You must be sons of Sheitan."

No troops have gone forward this week, with the exception of two companies of the 25th Native Infantry, who have gone out to Koomaylo to furnish guards and fatigue-parties there. No troops have landed, with the exception of considerable numbers of the Scinde Horse. I was anxious to see this regiment, which I have seen highly praised in books, but which Indian officers with whom I have conversed on the subject have generally spoken of in terms the reverse - of complimentary. I confess that their appearance is not imposing. The men are dressed in long green frock-coats, green trousers, black belts, and sabretasches, red sash round waist, and red turban. A picturesque uniform in itself; but the long coat has a clumsy effect on horseback. Their horses are, without exception, the very ugliest set of animals I ever set eyes on. A greater contrast between these men and horses and the smart 3d Cavalry at Senafe could hardly be conceived; and yet the men individually are a fine set of fellows, indeed are almost too heavy for cavalry. The great point which has always been urged in favour of the Scinde Horse is, that they carry their own baggage, and are independent of commissariat or transport train. This is, of course, a most valuable quality; and in India, where forage and provisions are purchased readily enough, it is probable that the regiment may be able to move about to a great extent on its own resources. Here it is altogether different, and the regiment have indented upon the transport train for just as many baggage-animals as other cavalry corps would require. The only use of the herds of ponies which they have brought with them is, to carry very large kits for the men's use—a matter of no advantage whatever to the public service, and, on the contrary, involving great expense, as these ponies were brought from India at the public expense, and have now to be fed and watered. I shall probably have to return to this subject during the campaign, as this system is one which has been strongly advocated and as strongly attacked among Indian officers. The railway continues to creep forward, and the first engine made a trial trip to-day upon it. Although there is little more to do than to lay the sleepers into the sand and to affix the rails, there is at present only a mile complete. One dry watercourse has been crossed, and here iron girders have been laid; but these nullahs should be no obstacle whatever to the progress of the work, as parties ought to be sent forward to get the little bridges, or any small cuttings there may be, finished in readiness, so that no pause may be occasioned in the laying the line. The country, with the exception of these little dry watercourses, which are from three to five feet deep, is perfectly flat; and the railway might, at any rate, be temporarily laid down with great ease and rapidity, especially with such a number of men as are employed upon it. As the work is being carried on at present without either method or plan or judgment, it is impossible even to predict when it will be finished to Koomaylo.

It is a great pity that the matter was not put into the hands of a regular railway contractor, who would have brought his plant, gangers, and plate-layers from England, viâ Egypt, in three weeks from the date of signing the contract, and who would, with native labour, have had the line open to Koomaylo, if not to Sooro, ere this. I am not blaming the engineer officers who are in charge of the railway. They exert themselves to the utmost, and have no assistance in the way of practical gangers and platelayers, and have neither tools nor conveniences of any kind. Indeed, the actual laying down of a line can hardly be considered engineers' work. An engineer makes the surveys and plans, and sees that the bridges, &c., are built of proper materials; but he is not a professed railway-maker, and is ill-calculated to direct a number of natives, who neither understand his language nor have a conception of what he is aiming at. It needed a body of thorough navvies, a couple of hundred strong, such as we had in the Crimea, to show the natives what to do, and to do the platelaying and skilled portion of the work themselves. When I say the railway has been, and will be, of no use to the advancing expedition, I of course except the line of rails down upon the pier and up to the stores, as this has been of the very greatest utility.3

The photographing party are up the pass, and have executed some excellent views of the gorge. The engineers have succeeded in sinking pumps at Guinea-fowl Plain, or, as it is now called, Undel Wells, and have got a plentiful supply of good water. This is most important and gratifying news. The journey from Sooro to Rayray Guddy, thirty miles, without water, was the trying part of the journey forward, and if the animals could speak not a few of them would lay their illnesses to that long and distressing journey. It is true that there was generally a little water to be had at the old well, but this was so deep and so difficult to get at, that, although a party of three or four animals could be watered there, it was quite impossible that a largo convoy could be watered. Now a large dépôt of provisions and forage will be established there, and the journey will henceforth be divided into five day's marches, of nearly equal length. Fresh animals arrive here every day, and the amount of stores of every description which is poured on shore is really surprising. Nothing could work better or more evenly than do all the departments here. There is no confusion of any sort, and the issue of rations and stores, and the general arrangements, work as smoothly as at Aldershot. The military bands play morning and evening, and all is as quiet and according to rule as if we had been six months and intended to stay six months more upon this plain, twenty-four hours' sojourn upon which was declared by our prophets of evil to be fatal to a European. The only thing in which we differ from a stationary camp is that there are no parades. Everyone is at work upon fatigue-duty. Every available man is ordered off to some work or other, and as we have with pioneers, coolies, hired natives, and soldiers, four or five thousand men here, we really ought to make considerable progress with our railway, which is now the only work of importance, with the exception of the wooden commissariat jetty, and the never-ending task of receiving and landing stores. Up to three days ago there was a piece of work in progress which was a great joke in camp. I mentioned in a former letter that the commissariat stores having been flooded, the engineers built a dam which was intended to keep out the sea, but which on the first heavy rain kept in the water and caused a fresh-water flood instead of a salt one. Colonel Wilkins then resolved upon a work on a large scale; on so large a scale, indeed, that there were reports through the camp that "he had determined on raising the whole African coast three feet," while others more moderate denied the exactness of this, and said that he was merely "seized with a desire to show the Bombay people how reclamations from the sea ought to be carried out." The last report was nearer to the truth than the first, for his intention was to raise the shore from one jetty to another, a distance of about 400 yards, the shore to be raised being thirty or forty yards in width, and needing three feet of additional height at the very least. The material to be used was sand. Accordingly, about a thousand men worked for a week with baskets at what their officers called mudlarking, and had not the sea fortunately interposed, they might have worked for another six months longer, with the certain result that the very first time a high tide, accompanied by wind, set in the work would altogether disappear; sand having—as most children who have built castles upon the Ramsgate sands are perfectly aware—an awkward knack of melting away when beaten upon by the sea. Fortunately, before more was done than making a sort of bank next to the sea, and when the labour of filling the whole shore behind this to the same level began to be apparent even to the most obstinate, the sea rose, came over the dam, covered the low ground behind three feet deep, entered the commissariat stores, and, as it could not escape, did considerably more damage than it would have done had the shore remained as it was before the labour of a thousand men for a week was expended upon it.

The rainy season, like most other things connected with Abyssinia, has turned out a myth. It was to have come in November, then it was postponed to December, then the 1st of January was named as the latest time, and yet, with the exception of one heavy shower, we have had no rain whatever. The dust is blowing again in perfect clouds. We taste it in all we eat and in all we drink. Grit is perpetually between our teeth. As for our hair, what with sea-bathing and what with dust it is approaching fast to the appearance of a hedgehog's back. Were it not for the evening bathe I do not know how we should get on. A great improvement has been effected in this respect during the last ten days. The end of the pier is now kept for officers only, the rest being devoted to the men. This is a great boon, and makes the end of the pier quite a pleasant place of assembly of an evening. Everyone is there, and everyone knows everyone else, so that it forms the grand rendezvous of the day. Our meeting-room is the sea, our toilet strict undress. I only wish that the water we use internally were as pleasant as the salt-water is for bathing, but the fact is, it is almost undrinkable. Why it is so no one seems to know; but there is no question as to the fact. It is extremely salt, and has a strong earthy taste in addition, and occasionally a disagreeable smell. Why it should be salt I know not, but can only suppose that the condensers are worked too hard, and that salt-water goes over with the steam. The earthy flavour and unpleasant smell which it sometimes has I attribute to the fact that the water which comes on shore from the ships must be bad. I have smelt exactly the same odour in water on board ship. The bad taste is so strong that it cannot be disguised or overpowered by the strongest admixture of spirits. By far the best water here is made by the condenser at the head of the pier, and this is served out to the European regiments, who are camped rather nearer to it than the native regiments are. Filters remove to a certain extent the earthy taste, but they do not alter the saline. A more serious matter even than the badness of the water is the fact that the supply has several times within the last ten days been insufficient, and hundreds of animals have had to go to their work in the morning, or to their beds at night, without a drop of water. It is this which lays the foundation of the lung-diseases, fills our hospitals with sick animals, to say nothing of the suffering caused to them. When the Scinde Horse, with their numerous baggage-animals, have moved forward, it is to be hoped that the naval authorities will be able to supply a sufficiency of drinkable water for the rest of the camp. The party of engineers have just begun a work which, when completed, will enable a much larger amount of stores to be landed daily than can at present be accomplished. They are driving piles so as to lengthen the pier some twenty or thirty yards, and to form a pier-head, on all sides of which lighters and boats can lie alongside to unload instead of only at one side, as at present. The commissariat wharf is also making considerable progress, and when this and the new pier-head are completed, the amount of stores which can be daily landed will be very large. As it is, it is wonderful what immense quantities of stores are landed and sent up the pier in the trucks by the commissariat, quartermaster, transport train, and engineer departments. Many hands make light work, and there is abundance of labour here, and a boat comes alongside, and its contents are emptied and placed upon a railway-truck in a very few minutes. Were a double line laid down the pier—which was specially built for it—and two or three connections or crossings laid down, so that full trucks could go out, and empty ones come in without waiting for each other, the capacity of the pier would be vastly greater than it is. Why this is not done no one seems to know. With the abundance of labour at hand it might be made in a day without interfering with the working of the present line. A great improvement has taken place in the conveyance of the post between this and Senafe. Ponies are in readiness at the various stations, and the mails are taken up in two days. Things are in fact getting into order in all the branches of the service, and with the exception of the water-supply and the ridiculously-slow progress of the railway, there is little to be wished for. The Punjaub Pioneers, whose arrival I mentioned in my last letter, are an uncommonly fine body of men. Their loose cotton dress and dark claret-brown turbans, and their picks and shovels slung across their shoulders, in addition to their arms and accoutrements, give them the appearance of a corps ready for any work; and this they have quite borne out. They have brought a number of ponies with them, and are fit for any service. The corps which have thus far arrived from Bengal and Madras have certainly done very great credit to these Presidencies, and make it a matter of regret that Bombay should have endeavoured to keep as far as possible the monopoly of an immense expedition like the present in her own hands. The Lahore division of the mule-train arrived here in the most perfect order. The saddles, accoutrements, &c., arrived with the mules, together with the proper complement of drivers, complete with warm clothing, &c. This division were therefore ready to take their load and to march up the very day after their landing, without the slightest confusion or delay. Of course the animals from Egypt and the Mediterranean could not arrive in this state of order, but there was no reason whatever why the Bombay division should not have arrived in a state of complete efficiency, instead of the animals coming by one ship, the drivers in another, the officers and inspectors in a third, and the accoutrements and clothing scattered over a whole fleet. Madras, too, has done well, although her contingent is a very small one. The Madras Sappers and Miners have greatly distinguished themselves, and the Madras dhoolie corps, which was raised and organised by Captain Smith, of the commissariat, has turned out of the very greatest utility. They have worked admirably, and have been quite willing to do any work to which they were set, however foreign it might be to the purpose for which they were engaged. Numbers of them have been transferred to the transport train; and, indeed, so useful has the corps proved, that orders have been sent to Madras for another of equal strength.

We had quite a pretty sight here the other night. The Pacha on board the Turkish frigate, which with two small consorts is lying in the harbour, invited Sir Robert Napier and the other generals, with their respective staffs, and the commanding officers of regiments and departments, to dinner. The frigate was illuminated with hundreds of lanterns hung along her shrouds and yards. The dinner was spread on the quarter-deck, which had awnings both roof and sides, so that it formed a perfect tent. The dinner was very good, and the fittings and ornaments of the table admirable. The sight, to men who had been for the last month eating off pewter and drinking out of tin cups, of a pile of porcelain plates, which were evidently some of Minton's or Copeland's best work, would be almost tantalising, and the dinner was enjoyed proportionately to its being so exceptional a circumstance. There was no making of speeches or drinking of healths, but the men-of-war and other boats as they left the frigate with their guests gave a hearty cheer to the Pacha for his hospitality. There is still a great want of boats in the harbour, and it is most difficult to get out to a ship to see a friend or to buy stores. Many of the ships are not unloading, and the men have nothing to do. It would be an excellent plan to authorise some of these vessels to send boats to shore to ply for hire, at a regular tariff. The men would like it, as they would gain good pay, and it would be a great boon to us on shore.

There is no news from the front, with the exception of that brought in just as the last mail was leaving, namely, that Theodore was moving towards Magdala, and that the Waagshum with his army was watching him. As Waagshum had neither the force nor the courage to hold the passes between Debra Tabor and Magdala—which, according to all accounts, a hundred men might easily hold against a thousand similarly armed—I do not think that the news that he was watching Theodore was of any more importance than if it had been "a troop of baboons are watching Theodore." I have not the least faith in these barbarian allies of ours. They will do nothing, and will demand great presents for it. Except that it amuses our "political agent," I do not see that the slightest possible utility can come from these native chiefs. The only king of any real importance is the King of Tigre, upon whose territory we are already encamped at Senafe. I hear that the purport of the message brought in by the ambassador or envoy who arrived before Christmas was to request that an envoy might be sent to him to enter into negotiations, and to arrange for a meeting between himself and the

Commander-in-chief. In consequence, Major Grant, of Nile celebrity, goes forward to-morrow, with Mr. Munzinger, our consul at Massowah, who acts as political adviser and interpreter. They will, I understand, go on from Senafe with a small guard of eight or ten cavalry. They will call upon the King of Tigre as official envoys, and will assure him of our friendship, and inform him that Sir Robert Napier is anxious to see him, and will meet him at Attegrat in a short time. I have now finished the news of the week, with the exception only of an adventure which befell Captain Pottinger, of the quartermaster's department. He was ordered to reconnoitre the passes leading from Senafe down to the head of Annesley Bay. He started with eight men, and had proceeded about forty miles when he was met by a party of armed Shohos, 100 strong. They ordered him to return to Senafe under pain of an instant attack. Of course Captain Pottinger, with his eight men, would have had no difficulty in defeating the 100 Shohos, but had blood been shed serious complications might have ensued, and he very wisely determined that it would be better to retire, as his mission was not one of extreme importance. This little affair is of itself of no consequence, but is worth notice as being the first time since our arrival here that the natives have in any way interfered with an armed force, however small. In my next letter I hope to be able to speak of at least a probability of a forward movement.

Zulla, January 22d.

Only three days have elapsed since I last wrote to you, but those three days have completely changed the prospects of things here. Then a move forward appeared to be an event which, we hoped, might happen somewhere in the dim future, but which, with the reports that provisions were scarcely accumulating at Senafe, but were being consumed as fast as they were taken up, seemed a very distant matter indeed. Now all this is changed, and "forward" is the cry. The 25th Native Infantry are already on the move, the 4th, "King's Own," are to go in a day or two, and the 3d Native Infantry are to follow as soon as possible. Sir Robert Napier goes up to-morrow or next day. Whether he will remain up there, and go forward at once, or whether he will return here again for a short time, is a moot point. I incline to the former opinion. From what I hear, and from what I see in the English papers, pressure is being strongly applied to Sir Robert Napier to move forward. Now, with the greatest deference for the home authorities and for the leader-writers upon the London press, I submit that they are forming opinions upon matters on which no one who has not visited this place is competent to judge. No one, I repeat, can form any opinion of the difficulties with which the Commander-in-chief has to contend here. The first want is the want of water, the second the want of forage, the third the want of transport. Twenty-eight thousand animals were to have been here by the end of December; not more than half that number have arrived, and of the 12,000 which have been landed 2000 are dead, and another 2000 unfit for work. The remainder are doing quite as much as could be expected of them, and are working well and smoothly; but 8000 are not sufficient to convey the provisions and stores of an army up seventy miles, and to carry their own forage as well. That is, they might convey quite sufficient for their supply from day to day, but they cannot accumulate sufficient provisions for the onward journey. The difficulties are simply overwhelming, and I do not know of a position of greater responsibility than that of Sir Robert Napier at the present moment. If he keeps the troops down here upon the plain, the increasing heat may at any moment produce an epidemic; and, in addition to this, the English public will ferment with indignation. On the other hand, if he pushes on with a few thousand men, he does so at enormous risk. He may take any number of laden animals with them; but if we get, as in all probability we shall get, into a country where for days no forage is obtainable, what is to become of the animals? It is not the enemy we fear—the enemy is contemptible; it is the distance, and the questions of provisions and transport. If a column goes on, it cuts itself loose from its base. With the exception of the laden animals, which start with it, it can receive no supplies whatever from the rear; it must be self-supporting. When Sherman left Atalanta he travelled through one of the most fertile countries in the world. We, on the contrary, go through one series of ravines and passes, and although there are many intervening places where we may count upon buying cattle, it is by no means certain that we can procure forage sufficient to last the animals across the next sterile pass. Altogether, it is a most difficult business, and one where the wisest would hesitate upon giving any opinion as to the best course to be pursued. I am sure General Napier will push forward if he sees any chance of a favourable issue; and if he does not, he will remain where he is in spite of any impatient criticism on the part of those who cannot guess at one tithe of his difficulties. Since writing the above I have received reliable information that the wing of the 33d will move forward to Antalo (a hundred miles in advance) in a few days. This is palpable evidence that at any rate we are going to feel our way forward. Personally I need not say how pleased I am, for living with the thermometer from 104° to 112°, in a tent, and surrounded and covered with a fine dust, existence can scarcely be called a pleasure here.

Sir Robert Napier is making great efforts to reduce the weight to be carried forward, and in this he is, without doubt, highly to be commended. The great curse of this army is its enormous number of followers. European regiments have quite a little host of sweepers, Lascars, water-bearers, &c. &c. Even the native regiments have a number of followers. Had English troops direct from England been employed, the weight to be carried would have been very much less than it is at present, and the men, being accustomed to shift and work for themselves, would have been more handy. It is said that the soldier's kit, now very heavy, is to be reduced; but at present the efforts are being directed almost exclusively against officers. An officer, whatever his rank, is to be allowed one mule only, and there is some rumour that even that allowance is to be reduced. I do not hesitate to say that that amount is insufficient. If an officer had his mule merely to carry his baggage it would be ample, but this is very far from being the case. On it he has to carry his groom's luggage and warm clothes, and those of his body-servant. He has to carry his cooking-utensils, &c., and the rugs, &c., for his horse; consequently he will be lucky if forty or fifty pounds remains for his own kit. This is not a campaign for a week or a month; it may, in all human probability will, last for a year, perhaps longer, and he has to carry clothes, bedding, &c., for a hot and a cold climate. It is simply impossible to do this in the limits of fifty pounds. Regimental officers are ordered to send back their servants to Bombay, only one to be kept for every three officers. Of course such officers will be able to get most of the work they require performed for them by their own men; but, at the same time, it is a hardship both to officers and servants. In all cases an officer has made an advance of from two to three months' pay to his servants; in all cases he has provided them with warm clothing; and it is very hard that he should lose all this, and be obliged to turn servants, whom he may have had for years, adrift at a moment's notice.

Senafe, January 31st.

After the heat and dust of Zulla this place is delightful. The heat of the day is tempered by a cool wind, and the really cold nights brace us up thoroughly. Above all, we have no dust. We are clean. One has to stop for a month upon the Plain of Zulla thoroughly to appreciate the pleasure of feeling clean. Here, too, there is water—not only to drink, but to wash in. After being dust-grimed and unable to wash, the sensation of being free from dust and enabled to wash at pleasure is delightful. Having with great difficulty succeeded in purchasing baggage-animals, I started early from Zulla, and arrived at Koomaylo in plenty of time to be able to examine the wonderful changes which have taken place there in the last three weeks. There were then some hundreds of animals there; now there are thousands. The lines of the mules and ponies extend in every direction; besides which are bullocks, camels, and elephants. Koomaylo is indeed the head-quarters of the transport-train animals. The camel divisions are here. They go down to the landing-place one day, are fed there, and come back loaded next day, getting their water only here. The elephants work in the same way, but they have to be watered at each end of their journey. The bullock division is here, and works upwards to Rayray Guddy, three days' march, taking up stores and bringing down Senafe grass when there is any to spare. Four mule and pony divisions are here; these, like the bullocks, work to Rayray Guddy and back. The sick animals of these six divisions are also here, and number nearly twelve hundred, including camels. The watering of all these animals morning and evening is a most interesting sight. There are long troughs, into which water is pumped continuously from the little American pumps. The different animals have each their allotted troughs. As they arrive they are formed in lines, and as one line has drunk the next advances. There is no bustle or confusion, for there is an ample supply of water for all. The water is very clear and good, but is quite warm, and most of the animals object to it the first time of tasting. Although the mules are in better condition than they were some time since, very many of them are still very weak, especially those that have been stationed at Rayray Guddy, where they get nothing to eat but the coarse Senafe hay, and have had very frequently to go without even this. The greatest difficulty of the transport train at present is most unquestionably in its drivers. The greater part were, as I have before said, collected haphazard from the scum of Smyrna, Beyrout, Alexandria, Cairo, and Suez. They are entirely without any idea of discipline, are perfectly reckless as to the Government stores, and are brutally cruel to their animals. By cruel, I do not mean actively cruel, but passively cruel. They do not thrash their mules much, they are too indifferent to the pace at which they travel to put themselves to the trouble of hurrying them. But they are horribly cruel in a passive way. They will continue to work their animals with the most terrible sore backs. They will never take the trouble to loosen the chain which forms part of the Bombay headgear, and which, unless it is carefully watched, will cut into the flesh under the chin, and in hundreds of cases has done so. They will jerk at the rein of their draught-mules until the clumsy bit raises terrible swellings in the mouth; they will say no word about the ailments of their beasts until they can absolutely go no single step further, and then, instead of taking them to the hospital lines, they turn them adrift, and report upon their arrival at night that the mules have died upon the way. There is, however, far less of this going on now than formerly, for a mounted inspector accompanies each train, and many of the large convoys have officers in charge of them. But not only for their cruelty and carelessness are these Egyptian, Levant, and Turk drivers objectionable; they are constantly mutinous. I saw the other day at Zulla a party of fifty who had arrived a few days before deliberately refuse to work. They did not like the place, and they would go back. Everything was tried with them; they were kept upon less than half rations and water for days, but they sturdily refused to do anything. The whole party might of course have been flogged, but that would not have made them work; and the first day that they went out with mules they would have thrown their burdens off and deserted with their animals. I was present when Colonel Holland, director-general of transport, endeavoured to persuade them to work. They steadily refused, and even when he promised that they should be sent back to Suez by the first ship, they refused to do any work whatever until the time for embarkation. As they stood in a circle round him, some gesticulating, but most standing in surly obstinacy, I thought I had never seen such a collection of thorough ruffians in my life—the picked scoundrels of the most lawless population on earth. I stopped one day at Koomaylo, and then came rapidly up the pass. The road is now really a very fair road for the whole distance, with the exception of four miles between Koomaylo and lower Sooro. This piece of road has not, by some strange oversight, been yet touched; but I hear that the 25th Native Infantry, one wing of which regiment is at Koomaylo, are to be set to work at it at once. It is along the flat of the valley, and only requires smoothing, and removing boulders, so that a few days will see this, the last piece of the road, completed. For the rest of the distance the road is everywhere as good as a bye-road in an out-of-the-way district at home. In many places it is very much better. Up the passes at Sooro and Rayray Guddy it is really an excellent road. The vast boulders, which I described upon the occasion of my first passing through it, are either shattered to pieces by blasting, or are surmounted by the road being raised by a gradual incline. Too much praise cannot be given to the Bombay Sappers and Miners, who have carried out these works. The same party, after finishing these passes, have now just completed a broad zigzag road from the bottom of the pass up to the Senafe plain. This was before the most trying part of the whole journey, now it is a road up which one might drive in a carriage and pair, and which reminds one of the last zigzags upon the summits of the Mount Cenis and St. Gothard passes. The whole of the works I have described are at once samples of skilful engineering and of unremitting exertion. No one who passed through six weeks ago would have believed that so much could possibly be effected in so short a time. Next only to the Bombay Sappers credit must be given to the Beloochee regiment, one wing of which under Major Beville at Sooro, and the other under Captain Hogg at Rayray Guddy, have made the road along those places where blasting was not required.

The Beloochees are a remarkably fine regiment, and work with a willingness and good-will which are beyond praise. Great regret is expressed on all sides that they have not been selected to accompany the 33d regiment upon its advance, especially as they are armed with Enfield rifles.

The Beloochees are deservedly one of the most popular regiments in the Indian service, and there is an *esprit de corps*—a feeling of personal attachment between men and officers, and a pride on the part of the latter to belong to so good a regiment—which the present extraordinary and unsatisfactory state of the Indian service renders altogether out of the question in the regular native regiments. There an officer forms no part of the regiment. He belongs to it for the time being, but if he goes home for leave, he will upon his return be posted in all probability to some other regiment. In this way all *esprit de corps*, all traces of mutual good feeling between men and officers, is entirely done away with. How such a system could ever have been devised, and how, once devised, it has ever been allowed to continue, is one of those extraordinary things which no civilian, and no military man under the rank of colonel, can understand.

At the station of Sooro and Rayray Guddy little change has been effected since I last described them, and about the same number of men are stationed there; but at Undel Wells, or Guinea-fowl Plain, as it was formerly called, the place was changed beyond all recognition. When last I was there it was a quiet valley, with a few Shohos watering their cattle at a scanty and dirty well. My own party was the only evidence of the British expedition. Now this was all changed. No city in the days of the gold-mining rush in Australia ever sprung into existence more suddenly. Here are long lines of transport-animals, here are commissariat-tents and stores, here a camp of the pioneers. The whole of the trees and brushwood have been cleared away. Here is the watering-place, with its troughs for animals and its tubs for men—the one supplied by one of Bastier's chain-pumps, a gigantic specimen of which used to pour out a cataract of water for the delectation of the visitors to the Paris Exhibition—the other by one of the little American pumps. Everything works as quietly and easily as if the age of the station was to be counted by months instead of by days.

I found that the telegraph is making rapid progress. The wire now works as far as Sooro, and is also erected downwards from Senafe to Rayray Guddy. It is a very fine copper wire, and in the midst of the lofty perpendicular rocks of the Sooro Pass it looks, as it goes in long stretches from angle to angle, with the sun shining bright upon it, like the glistening thread of some great spider.

It would have been long since laid to Senafe, but the greatest difficulty has occurred in obtaining poles, all those sent from Bombay having been thrown overboard to lighten the vessel in which they were shipped upon an occasion of her running aground. It has been found impossible to procure the poles for the remaining distance; and I hear that a wire coated with india-rubber is to be laid a few inches under the soil.

Senafe itself is but little altered. The 10th Native Infantry are still in their old camp. The 3d Native Cavalry have gone out about eight miles from here to a spot called Goose Plain, and the sappers and miners are encamped in the old lines of the 3d. The 33d lines are in a plain close to, but a little beyond, the old camp, and concealed from view until one has passed it.

On my arrival in camp I found that a deep gloom hung over everyone, and I heard the sad news that Colonel Dunn, the commanding officer of the 33d, had the day before accidentally shot himself when out shooting. The native servant who alone was with him reports that he himself was at the moment stooping to pour out some water, that he heard the report of a gun, and turning round saw his master stagger back, and then sink into a sitting position with the blood streaming from his breast. The man instantly ran back to camp, a distance of five miles, for assistance, and surgeons at once galloped off with bandages, &c., followed by dhoolie wallahs, with a dhoolie to carry him back to camp. When the surgeons arrived, they found Colonel Dunn lying on his back, dead. His flask was open by his side, his cap pulled over his face. He had bled to death in a few minutes after the accident. It is supposed that the gun was at full cock, and that the slight jar of putting the butt to the ground must have let the hammer down. There are very few men who could have been less spared than Colonel Dunn; none more deeply regretted. As an officer he was one of the most rising men in the service, and had he lived would probably have gained its highest honours and position. He was with the 11th Hussars in the Balaclava charge, and when the men were asked to select the man who in the whole regiment was most worthy of the Victoria Cross, they unanimously named Lieutenant Dunn. Never was the Victoria Cross placed on the breast of a more gallant soldier. When the 100th regiment was raised in Canada, he enrolled a very large number of men, and was gazetted its major. After attaining the rank of lieutenant-colonel he exchanged into the 33d, of which, at the time of this sad accident, he was full colonel, and was next on the list for his brigadier-generalship. He was only thirty-five years of age, the youngest colonel in the British service, and would, in all human probability, have been a brigadier-general before he was thirty-six. Known as a dashing officer, distinguished for his personal bravery, a colonel at an age when other men are captains, there was no rank or position in the army which he might not have confidently been predicted to attain, and his loss is a loss to the whole British army. But not less than as a soldier, do all who knew poor Dunn regret him as a man. He was the most popular of officers. Unassuming, frank, kind-hearted in the extreme, a delightful companion, and a warm friend—none met him who were not irresistibly attracted by him. He was a man essentially to be loved. In his regiment his loss is irreparable, and as they stood beside his lonely grave at the foot of the rock of Senafe, it is no disgrace to their manhood to say that there were few dry eyes amongst either officers or men. He was buried, in accordance with a wish he had once expressed, in his uniform, and Wolfe's lines on the burial of Sir John Moore will apply almost word for word to "the grave where *our* hero we buried."

Sir Robert Napier arrived here with his personal staff the day before yesterday, having been five days *en route*, spending one day carefully examining each station, inquiring, as is his custom, into every detail, and seeing how each department worked. Never was a commander more careful in this inquiry into every detail than is Sir Robert Napier. Nothing escapes him. He sees everything, hears what everyone has to say, and then decides firmly upon what is to be done. The army have rightly an unbounded confidence in him. He is essentially the man for an expedition of this sort. His reputation for dash and gallantry is well known, but at the same time he has a prudence and sagacity which will fit him for the extremely difficult position in which he is placed. If it is possible to make a dash into Central Abyssinia, undoubtedly he will do it; if, on the other hand, it cannot be done without extraordinary risk and difficulty—if it is next to impossible—no amount of outcry at home will drive him to attempt it.

It is believed here that, moved by the home authorities, a rapid dash is on the point of being made, and bets are freely exchanged that the expedition will be over by the 1st of April. For myself, I confess that even in the face of the approaching advance of the first division I have no anticipations whatever that such will be the case. Sir Robert, I believe, does mean to try. Urged on to instant action from home, he will despatch two or three regiments, with cavalry and artillery, and with the lightest possible baggage. But if the country at all resembles that we have already traversed, if it is one tithe as difficult and deficient in food and forage as Abyssinian travellers have told us, I am convinced that the column will have to come to a halt, and wait for supplies, and will have to proceed in a regular military way. I hope that I may be mistaken; I sincerely hope that the advancing column may meet with no insuperable obstacles; but, remembering that it is by no means certain that when we get to Magdala we shall find Theodore and the captives there, I am far more inclined to name nine months than three as the probable time which will elapse before we have attained the objects of our expedition,— that is, always supposing that Theodore does not deliver up the captives as we advance. It is quite certain that the advancing column must depend entirely upon themselves. They will be able to receive no supplies from the rear, for other regiments will take the place of those that go on from Senafe, and the transport train cannot do much more than keep Senafe supplied with provisions at present, even supplemented as their efforts are by those of thousands of the little native cattle. Indeed, had it not been for the quantity of stores brought up by the natives on their own cattle, there would not have been sufficient stores at Senafe to have supplied the troops who now move on. As some 1500 animals will be withdrawn from the strength of the transport train to march with the advance brigade, it is evident that the stores sent up for some time will not be much more than sufficient to supply Senafe, and that no animals will be available to send on fresh supply to the front. The brigade that advances, then, must depend entirely upon itself. It must not hope for any assistance whatever. To say the least, it is an expedition upon the like of which few bodies of men ever started. We have 330 miles to go, across a country known to be exceptionally mountainous and difficult. We have already learned that, with the exception of cattle, the country will provide us with no food whatever. The kings or chiefs through whose territory we march will be but neutral, and even if actively friendly, which they certainly are not, could afford us no practical assistance. To crown all, it may be that towards the end of the march we may have to fight our way through difficult passes, defended by men who, if ill-armed, are at least warlike and brave. History hardly records an instance of such an accumulation of difficulties. Pizarro's conquest of Mexico, perhaps, ranks foremost among enterprises of this sort, but Pizarro fought his way through the richest country in the world, and could never have had difficulties as to his supplies. There is no question about our conquering—the great question is as to our eating. If we were always certain of finding forage our difficulties would be light in comparison. Unfortunately our mules must eat as well as we, and we know that we shall have long passes where no forage whatever is procurable. If the mules were certain of their food it would be a mere arithmetical question—how many mules are required to convey food for 2500 men for forty days? As it stands now, we have no data to go upon, and whether our present advance succeeds or not is almost entirely dependent upon whether we can obtain forage for our animals. If we can do this, we shall get to Magdala; but if we find that we have to pass long distances without forage, it becomes an impossibility, and we must fall back upon the regular military method of forming dépôts and moving on stage by stage. In this latter case there is no predicting the probable limit of the expedition.

General Napier is taking the most stringent but necessary steps for reducing the baggage to a minimum. No officer, whatever his rank, is to be allowed more than one mule. Three officers are to sleep in each bell-tent, and one mule is allowed for two bell-tents. One mule is allowed to each three officers for cooking-utensils and mess-stores. Only one native servant is to be allowed for each three officers. No officers, except those entitled to horses in England, are to be mounted; they may, however, if they choose, take their own horse as a pack-animal instead of the mule to which they are entitled, in which case a pack-saddle will be issued to them. Similar reductions are being made among the regimental baggage and followers. The latter, whose name was legion, and who were at least as numerous as the fighting-men, are to be greatly curtailed. The Lascars, sweepers, water-bearers, &c. are either to be sent back, or to be turned into grass-cutters for the cavalry and baggage-animals. The European soldiers are to be limited to 35lb. weight of baggage, and part of this they will have to carry for themselves. All this is as it should be. In India it is policy as well as humanity to take every possible care of the British soldier. He is a very expensive machine, and although, as was found during the mutiny, he can work in the sun during an emergency without his health suffering, still at ordinary times it is far better to relieve him as far as possible from all duties whatever save drill and guard. Labour and food are so cheap in India that the expense of this host of camp-followers is comparatively slight. Here it is altogether different. It was known long before we started that the ground would be exceptionally difficult, that the difficulties of transport would be enormous, and that every mouth extra to be fed was of consequence; and yet in spite of this the European regiments arrived here with little short of 500 followers; and the native regiments have also hosts of hangers-on. As I have said, all this is now very properly to be done away with. The army will march as nearly as possible with European kit and following, and the transport train will be relieved of the incubus of thousands of useless mouths to be provided for. In speaking of the transport train, I should mention that Sir Robert Napier is in no way accountable for its absurd organisation and consequent break down. The Bombay authorities are alone responsible. When the expedition was first seriously talked of in August last, Sir Robert Napier drew up a scheme for a transport train, which I am assured by those who have seen it was excellent. This he sent in on the 23d of August. No notice was taken of it until the middle of September, when Sir Robert was told that a scheme would be prepared by the commissary-general. Another precious month elapsed, and then in the middle of October the present absurd scheme was hatched. It was sent to Sir Robert for his opinion, and he returned it with the memorandum that it was perfectly impracticable. The authorities persisted, however, in the teeth of his opinion, in having their plan carried out; and it was only upon Sir Robert's repeated and earnest remonstrances that they consented to increase the number of European inspectors and native overlookers to the present ridiculously-insufficient number. The result has abundantly proved the wisdom of the General, and the fatuity of the men who would interfere in every detail, and overrule the opinion of the man to whom everything was to be intrusted from the day of his leaving Bombay. Events have abundantly proved the error of intrusting the management of the expedition to civilians and men of bureaux.

And now, as to the advance brigade. Neither its composition nor its date of advance are yet known for certain. The Chief is not a man who says anything about his plans until the moment arrives when the necessary orders are to be given. It will probably comprise the whole or part of the 33d regiment, the 4th regiment—a portion of which is expected to arrive here to-day—the 10th Native Infantry, the Beloochees, the Punjaub Pioneers, the Bombay Sappers and Miners, the 3d Native Cavalry, and the Scinde Horse. Of these, two companies of the 33d regiment, and two of the 10th Native Infantry, are already at Attegrat, thirty-five miles in advance. Three more companies of each regiment started to-day. Brigadier-general Collings goes on with them, and will for the present command the advance. Part of the Pioneers are here, as are the Bombay Sappers. These go on in a day or two to make the road near and beyond Attegrat, the intermediate part having been already made by the 33d regiment. The Scinde Horse are some eight or nine miles away, and near them are the 3d Native Cavalry. I have omitted in my list of troops for the advance brigade to name the mountain trains, and three guns of the artillery, which will be carried by elephants. These animals are expected here in a day or two. I should be sorry to meet them on horseback in a narrow part of the pass, and I expect that they will cause terrible confusion among the transport-animals, for they have all a perfect horror of the elephant—that is, the first time that they see one. When they get to learn that he, like themselves, is a subjugated animal, they cease to feel any terror of him.

There is one pleasing change which has taken place since I last left Senafe, and which I have not yet spoken of. I mentioned that Sir Charles Staveley, when he was up here, ordered huts to be built for the muleteers by the 10th Native Infantry. These are now completed. They are long, leafy bowers, running along in regular lines between the rows of animals. They are very well and neatly built—so regular, indeed, that it is difficult at a short distance to believe that they are really built of boughs. They may not be as warm as houses, but they keep off the wind, and afford a great protection to the muleteers at night. The division here, that of Captain Griffiths, is the first which landed. It is now in very good order, and will accompany the advance brigade. The disease up here is, I am happy to say, on the decrease. The sick animals are out at Goose Plain with the artillery.

Yesterday, in the afternoon, there was a parade of the 33d, and 10th Native Infantry; small parties of the Royal Engineers, of 3d Native Cavalry, and of Scinde Horse were also present. Sir Robert Napier rode along the line, and the regiments then marched past. The little party of the 3d Cavalry came first, followed by the Scinde Horse, and offering as strong a contrast to each other as could be well imagined. The one was upon the European, the other upon the Asiatic model. The Scinde horsemen were much the heavier and more powerful men; and although they have not the military seat or the dashing air of the 3d, they had in their dark dresses, and quiet, determined look, the appearance of men who would be most formidable antagonists. Their horses, although ugly, are strong; and in a charge, it was the opinion of many of those who were looking on, that they would be much more than a match for their more showy rivals. The Scinde Horse are more discussed than any regiment out here; and, indeed, it is so famous a regiment, and is always stationed so much upon the frontiers, that its coming was looked forward to with considerable curiosity. Its appearance is certainly against it; that is, its horses are very ugly animals; but this is not the fault of the regiment, for its station is so far in Northern India that it cannot procure, except at very great cost, any but the native horses. I believe that this is almost the only objection which can be urged against the regiment; the men are remarkably fine; indeed, as I before stated, they are too heavy for cavalry. They are, as a whole, drawn from a much higher and wealthier class of natives than the men of any other regiment; they enlist in the Scinde Horse just as a young nobleman takes a commission in the Guards. There is a very great feeling of *esprit de corps*, and mutual good-feeling between officers and men; and all are proud of their regiment. The uniform, as I have said in a previous letter, is a long, dark-green coat, with red turban. It is the men's own choice, and is quite an Eastern uniform; their long curved sabres are also quite Asiatic. The men provide their own carriage; and from this point the transport train will not be called upon to assist them in any way beyond carrying their provisions. I alluded before to the wretched ponies they brought with them; but the case has been explained to me, and there is no blame to be attached to the corps on this score. The men were provided with camels to carry their baggage, and were told that these would do for Abyssinia. While upon their march down to the sea-coast a telegram arrived, stating that camels would not do; and the men were obliged to sell their camels at a sacrifice, and to buy any ponies they could get. I speak of the men doing so, because the horses, &c., are not the property of the Government, but of the men, or rather of some among the men.

The Scinde Horse are, and always were, an irregular cavalry, upon what is called the "sillidar" system. Government contracts with the men to find their own horses, accoutrements, arms, food, and carriage. This is the irregular cavalry system, upon which all native cavalry regiments are now placed. The sum paid is thirty rupees a month. Here, however, only twenty rupees are to be paid, as Government finds food and forage. The advantages of this system for frontier-work are enormous. The men are scattered over a wide extent of country in tens and twelves, and it would be manifestly impossible to have a series of commissariat stations to supply them. Whether the system is a good one for regiments stationed for months or years in a large garrison town is a very moot question, and one upon which there is an immense difference of opinion. These regiments would have no occasion for carriage. If they had to move to another town, it would be cheaper for them to send their baggage in carts than to keep up a sufficient baggage-train. When, therefore, the order to march on service comes, there are no means of transport. The 3d Native Cavalry are exactly a case in point. Four years ago they were changed from a regular to an irregular cavalry regiment; but, like all regiments, the 3d had its traditions, and stuck to them. They adhere to their old uniform and equipments, and are, at a short distance, undistinguishable from a European hussar regiment. They pay extreme attention to their drill, and are to all intents and purposes a regular cavalry. They are mounted on excellent horses, and are certainly wonderfully-cheap soldiers at three pounds a month, including everything. But they have been long stationed at Poonah, and consequently had no occasion to purchase baggage-animals, and came on here without them. When it was found that the regiment had arrived here without baggage-animals, there was, of course, considerable angry feeling in the official mind; and had it not been that the animals were dying in the plain, and that no other cavalry regiment was at hand to go up with the advance brigade, it is probable that they would have been kept in the rear of the army. However, they were badly wanted, and so carriage was given to them. I have already spoken in the highest terms of their bearing and efficiency. There is one point, however, in the sillidar system which strikes me as being particularly objectionable. It is not always with the men themselves that this contract is made; it is with the native officers. Some of the men do supply their own horses, &c.; but the native officers each contract to supply so many men and horses complete, buying the horses and accoutrements, and paying the men ten rupees a month. This, I cannot help thinking, is an unmixed evil. The man has two masters—the man who pays him, and the Government he serves. This evil was carried to a great extent in the days before the mutiny; and I have heard a case of a regiment at that time of which almost the whole of the horses and men were then owned by one native officer. Had that man been hostile to the Government, he might have taken off the whole regiment. Efforts have since been made to put a stop to this excessive contracting, and no officer is now allowed to own more than six of the horses. It appears to me that it should be altogether done away with, and that each man should find his own horse.

But I have wandered very far away from the parade-ground at Senafe. After marching past the regiments formed in close order, the General then addressed a few words to each. To Major Pritchard of the Engineers he said how glad he was to have his own corps with him again, and that he hoped some day to employ them to blow down the gates of Magdala. To the 33d he said a few words complimenting them upon their efficiency, and regretting that they would not be led by the gallant officer whose loss he and they deplored. The General then addressed the 10th Native Infantry, complimenting them upon their conduct and efficiency. Sir Robert spoke in Hindoostanee, a language of which my knowledge is unfortunately confined to about eight words; none of these occurred in the speech, and I am therefore unable to give the text. The regiments which go on are delighted at the prospect of a move, and the 10th Native Infantry cheered lustily as they marched off with their band at their head. Fresh troops arrive as fast as others move on. While I have been writing this a portion of the 4th King's Own have marched in, as also have the mule-battery with the light rifled guns from Woolwich. The most important, however, of to-day's arrivals has been that of a hundred bullock-carts. A string of camels has also come in, as I can tell by the lugubrious bellowings and roar which at present fills the air. The pass is therefore proved to be practicable, and the camels and bullock-carts will be a great assistance to us. The natives must be astonished at seeing this string of carts coming up a place which all their tradition must represent as almost impassable even for their own cattle, which, like goats, can go almost anywhere. Their ideas about us must altogether be rather curious; and as we know by experience how a story expands and alters as it goes, the reports which must reach the extreme confines of Abyssinia must be something astounding. Even here they are not contented with the facts. There is a report among them that the cattle we are buying up are intended to be food for a train of elephants we have coming to help us fight Theodore, and that we have also a lion-train, which will shortly be here. Our news from Magdala is as before. Theodore is slowly, very slowly advancing. He has got heavy cannon, and insists upon taking them with him. Waagshum, the king who has been besieging Magdala, has fairly run away, and the tribes around Magdala have all sent in their allegiance to Theodore. Theodore has been writing to Rassam as if he were his dearest friend, and Rassam has been answering him as if he were Theodore's grovelling slave. Theodore's letter runs in this style: "How are you? Are you well? I am quite well. Fear not. I am coming to your assistance. Keep up your head. I shall soon be with you. I have two big cannon. They are terrible, but very heavy to move." Rassam answers somewhat in this style: "Illustrious and most clement of potentates, I, your lowest of slaves, rejoice at the thought that your coming will throw a light upon our darkness. Our hearts swell with a great joy;" and more fulsome stuff of the same character. Dr. Blanc's letters to us are at once spirited and manly. "We are delighted," he says, "at the thought of your coming. How it will end no one can say. We are all prepared for the worst; but we have at least the satisfaction of knowing that our deaths will be avenged." Up to the last moment of doing this we have no day fixed for Sir Robert Napier's advance upon Attegrat. The 5th is named as the earliest date upon which a messenger can return from Grant's party, and say when Kassa, the King of Tigre, will be at Attegrat to meet the General. It is probable that the King will start almost immediately Grant arrives, and in that case Sir Robert will have to move forward at once in order to arrive first at the place of meeting. I go on to-morrow, unless any circumstance should occur to change my plan.

The scientific and the general members of the expedition are arriving very fast. Dr. Markham, the geographer of the expedition, has long been here. Mr. Holmes, of the British Museum, arrived yesterday, as archæologist; he is going off to-morrow to a church a few miles distant, to examine some manuscripts said to exist there. The Dutch officers arrive up to-day, and I hear two French officers arrive to-morrow. In reference to these foreign officers, I am assured to-day by a staff-officer, to whom I was regretting that more was not done for them, that they are not really commissioners. It may be so; but as, at any rate, they are officers who are paid by foreign governments, and are allowed to accompany the expedition, I confess that I am unable to see any essential difference. The staff-officer assured me, as a proof of the beneficent intentions of the authorities, that these foreign officers would not be charged for their rations. John Bull is indeed liberal. He is much more sharp as to the "specials;" for a general order was actually issued the other day, saying that "gentlemen unconnected with the army were to pay for a month's rations in advance." With the exception of the scientific men, who are all sent out by Government, and must, I suppose, be considered official persons, there are only four gentlemen here "unconnected with the army," namely, three other special correspondents and myself. I remarked to a commissariat-officer, with a smile, when called upon to pay my month in advance, that "I thought I might have been considered as good for the payment at the end of each month as officers were." "Ah," said the astute officer, "but suppose anything were to happen to you, whom should we look to for payment?" The reply was obvious: "But, on the other hand, suppose that unpleasant contingency should occur, of whom are my representatives to claim the amount for the days paid for but not eaten?" At whose suggestion this general order was issued I know not; but I do know that anything more paltry and more unworthy the general order of a large army was never issued. Who issued this order I know not, for I cannot but repeat that no one could be more kind and considerate than are Sir Robert Napier and every member of his staff to all of us.

I must now close my letter, for it is getting late, and my hand is so cold I can hardly hold a pen. I may just mention that colds are very prevalent here, and that at night there is an amount of coughing going on among the natives in the tents around, that is greater even than could be heard in an English church on a raw November morning during a dull sermon.

Senafe, February 3d.

When I closed my letter on the evening of the 31st ultimo, I had intended to start early the next morning. My plan was to have gone on to Attegrat, to have stopped a day or two there, and to have returned in plenty of time to have gone up again with Sir Robert Napier. After I had closed my letter, however, I heard that he would probably leave on the 5th; I should not, therefore, have had time to carry out my plan, and determined, in consequence, to wait here another day or two, and then to move on quietly in advance of the General, so as to be able to devote a short time to the examination of the country in the neighbourhood of each of the stations. I had another course open to me. The extreme advanced party are pushing on beyond Attegrat, on the road to Antalo. Should I go with them, or should I remain near head-quarters and report the regular progress of events? It was more amusing, of course, to be pushing on ahead; but it seemed to me that the interest of the public lay not in the road, but in the progress of the troops along that road. I have therefore made up my mind to jog quietly along with the main body of the army, the more especially as the meeting between Sir Robert Napier and the King of Tigre will be one of the most interesting events in the whole expedition.

Mr. Speedy has arrived in camp. He is to act as political adviser to General Napier, and his arrival is a general matter of satisfaction. Mr. Speedy was at one time an officer in the 81st Foot; he afterwards exchanged into the 10th Punjaubees, of which regiment he was some time adjutant. He afterwards left the service and wandered out to Abyssinia, where he entered the service of Theodore, and assisted him to organise and drill his army. Finding he was likely to share the fate of other British in this potentate's employ, and to be cast into prison, Mr. Speedy threw up his appointment, and has since been living in Australia. General Napier, having heard of him, wrote to beg him to come; and Mr. Speedy received the letter just in time to come off by the mail, with a kit, according to popular report, consisting only of two blankets. He is not, I am happy to say, an Abyssinian worshipper. Dr. Krapf, Colonel Merewether's adviser, is so. He seems to think that the black is a very much finer specimen of humanity than the white man; and that deeds which would be punished in the latter are highly excusable, if not laudable, when perpetrated by the former. Dr. Krapf is not singular in his ideas. Had his lines lain in England, I have no doubt that he would have been one of Governor Eyre's foremost persecutors. I am very glad that a healthier tone is likely to be introduced in our dealings with the natives. Mr. Speedy rode out yesterday, at the General's request, to some of the villages round, called upon the priests, and offered a present of money for the relief of the poor and distressed. The answer in each case was the same. The priests said that had it not been for our coming, a period of severe distress and suffering would probably have occurred. The crops had been devastated by the locusts, and the present drought would seriously affect the next harvest. Thanks, however, to the money which the English had distributed through the country in payment for cattle purchased by the commissariat, and for hay, wood, milk, &c., and for the hire of transport, the people were better off than usual; and therefore, with the exception of three or four dollars for the aged and infirm, they would decline with thanks General Napier's gift.

The Engineer Corps here have been very busy for the last few days practising signalling. The method used is Captain Bolton's system, which is in use in the Royal Navy. The method in which these signals are managed on land is, however, less known, and is specially interesting, as it is the first time they have been used in actual warfare. The present is, indeed, a sort of experiment; and if it prove successful and useful, it is probable that the system will be generally introduced into the army. The Engineers are giving lessons in the art of signalling to soldiers of the 33d regiment, and will teach men of each regiment out here, so that the system may be fairly tested. The signals by day are conveyed by flags; there are white, white-and-black, and black, according to the alphabet or method to be used. A single wave to the right means one; two waves, two; and so on up to five; the remaining four numbers are made either by waves to the left or by combination of wavings to either side. These numbers, like the flags on board ship, refer to a number in a book with which each signalman is furnished. Let us suppose, for example, that a general situated upon rising ground wishes to signal to any given division of his army. He makes the signal, let us say, "five." The signal is passed along by the line of signalmen to the fifth division, who all, by waving their flags, testify readiness. The signal is then passed, "1015." This means, "move to the support of the fourth division," which is instantly done without loss of time. Or the flags may be addressed to all the corps of the army; and the order, waved over thirty miles of country, might be, "Concentrate on the centre division." It is, indeed, astonishing how much time would be gained by using this method instead of sending a score of aides-de-camp scouring all over the country. At night the signals are conveyed by means of flashing lights. These are extremely ingenious in their construction. The signaller, who is always accompanied by a companion with a signal-book, has a brass tube some eight feet long, at the extremity of which is a lantern; in this lantern a spirit-lamp burns; underneath this spirit-lamp is a receptacle in which is placed a powder composed of magnesium, resin, and lycopodium, very much like the mixture with which stage-carpenters produce lightning by blowing it through a candle. This lamp acts on precisely the same principle. A bellows is attached to the brass tube. This bellows the signaller works, either in short or in long pressures; and the air, as it passes up, goes through the powder and forces a small quantity of it through a pair of nozzles placed close to the spirit-flame. The result is a brilliant flash, which is long or short according to the pressure upon the bellows. This light can be seen at a very great distance, and two or three parties of signallers placed upon hill-tops could convey an order a distance of fifty miles in a very few minutes. The difficulty, of course, lies in the liability to error. A single puff more or less might entirely change the order. 1021 might mean "Concentrate upon your left flank;" 1022 "Concentrate upon your right." It is all very well to say that each signal is repeated, and therefore that a mistake would be instantly corrected; but we all know what mistakes occur in telegraphic messages, even if we pay for their being repeated. The system appears as good and as little liable to error as anything of the kind could be; but when we consider that a miscounting of the flashes of light or of the waving of a flag might entirely alter the order given, it is evident that the risk is so great that a general would rather, if possible, despatch a mounted officer with written instructions. At the same time, the system for distant communication is undoubtedly adapted to expedite the movements of an army over a large tract of country. General Napier has taken a great interest in the experiments, and I have no doubt the system will be thoroughly tried during the present expedition. The apparatus for each signalling-party is singularly complete and handy; it is carried in two baskets or mule-panniers, and includes everything which could be required, comprising a light-tent, a canteen, flags, lanterns, a supply of alcohol and powder, a small case for writing in the rain, signal-books, &c. Each of these double panniers contains, in fact, everything required for the signalmen; and with twelve such apparatus, distributed among parties placed upon hill-tops, signals might be flashed at night from London to Edinburgh.

The elephants for the guns have not yet arrived, but are expected to-morrow, and in that case will go on with Sir Robert Napier; who, I believe, will positively leave in the afternoon. As several other bodies of troops move on the same day, it will make his entry into Attegrat quite an imposing affair. In fact, I should not be surprised if the sight of the elephants created quite a stampede among the natives. Speaking of elephants, a sad accident occurred a few days since at Sooro. These animals are to be met with in the mountains between that place and the sea, and three have been killed by officers of the Beloochees. Accordingly, Major Beville and Lieutenant Edwards went out to try their fortune, and were successful in finding a herd of them feeding in a valley. The animals scented them before they could get within fair shot, and began to run rapidly away; whereupon Edwards rushed out, crossed a small intervening nullah, and followed upon their heels. Elephants, however, are not animals that like being followed, and accordingly one of them turned and charged his pursuer. Edwards fired at him, but failing to check him, took to his heels. The animal overtook him in his descent of the nullah, seized him in his trunk, dashed him to the ground, and endeavoured to trample on him, but fortunately the slope of the ground rendered this a matter of difficulty. At this critical moment Major Beville arrived, and fired into the animal, who, most fortunately, upon finding himself wounded, quitted his victim and fled. Extraordinary to state, poor Edwards was not killed; but he has received some severe internal injuries, and is now lying at Sooro in a very precarious state.

The bullock-carts, which arrived the day before yesterday, aroused, as I anticipated, the admiration and wonder of the natives to the highest point. I believe that they never saw a wheeled vehicle before; and the apparition of the long line of carts, drawn by the splendid Brahmin cattle, coming up laden with stores, from a defile which all their traditions from time immemorial have represented to them as being impracticable even for their own sure-footed little cattle, completed their assurance that the English are truly sons of Sheitan. Our energy and resources must indeed appear something quite supernatural to this primitive people.

One of my principal grounds for objection to the Abyssinians is that they are such an intensely lazy race. Now, if people like to be lazy, and to eat the scanty bread of idleness instead of the large loaf gained by hard work, it is their own business, and a mere matter of taste, in favour of which there is much to be said. But the Abyssinian, although intensely lazy, is by no means satisfied to eat the bread of idleness. The noble savage is keenly awake to the value of labour, and insists that all the members of his family, with the exception only of himself and such of his sons as may be big enough to have their own way, work like the veriest slaves. You will see a great lout of a man walking lazily along towards the camp, armed with his spear and shield, while before him stagger his old mother, his wife, his sister, and his four or five children, carrying enormous bundles of hay. I am not exaggerating when I say that you will frequently see little girls not more than seven years old carrying bundles of hay of forty-five pounds weight into camp; and poor little mites of three or four years old carry a proportionate burden. The weight is never carried on the head, always upon the back, fastened by a thong of leather, which goes over the arms just below the shoulder and across the chest. The child or woman, as the case may be, walks bent forward, almost double. The men never carry loads; it is beneath the dignity of a noble savage. The whole of the work is done by the females and by the little boys of the family. My blood has fairly boiled many times, and I have longed heartily to lay my riding-whip across the shoulders of these lazy scoundrels, who are too lazy to work, but not too proud to drive their little children to work, and to live upon the result. The boys do, as I have said, a certain amount. When they are quite little they do nearly as much as their sisters, but as they grow up they do less and less, and it is rare to see a boy over twelve years old carrying a burden. The women here carry their babies on their backs, and not across the hip as the Hindoostanee women always do. The children are held in a sort of small shawl of leather, which is wrapped tightly round the mother, and only the top of the little thing's head is generally to be seen. In this way the mother has her arms free, and can carry about her bundle of wood or grass for sale; but in this case the burden is, of course, carried in her arms before her. I have often wondered that the children survive the double risk—of suffocation, from pressure against their mother's backs, and of sunstroke, from the sun coming down full upon the unprotected tops of their little bald heads. They do not seem to mind it, and I do not think that I have heard more than one or two infants utter a wail when being carried in that position. I can only suppose that the natural warmth of their mothers' naked backs is agreeable to them; but, with our present style of dress, it is not an experiment which I should recommend an English nurse to try with a fractious child, unless she wishes a coroner's inquest to be held upon it, with possibly other more unpleasant proceedings to follow.

The stores in the commissariat-yard here continue to increase, thanks to the amount brought up by the native cattle. At present there is, I understand, about a month's consumption for the troops here and in advance. The arrangements of the commissariat-yard are very good; as, indeed, most of the arrangements of that department have been throughout the expedition. At times this yard presents a most interesting spectacle. Here are large piles of rice- and flour-bags, and beside them the Parsees weighing out the rations to the numerous applicants. A little farther on is the butcher's shop, where the meat-rations are cut up and distributed. Here is a large enclosure fenced round with bushes, and containing cattle purchased for the troops from the natives. Here are some hundreds of mules unloading stores which they have brought from below. Farther on are more being loaded with grass, to go down for the sustenance of the animals in the pass. Here, again, are hundreds of women and children laden with grass, which an officer of the commissariat is weighing and paying for; giving, however, the money to the men; who, the instant the women have brought in the grass, send them off, and exert themselves so far as to receive the money. Near these is the wood-yard, where a similar scene is being enacted. Back again by the store-yard are a host of native cattle, which are waiting to receive stores to take forward to Attegrat. The contract price for this is a dollar and a half per head; and I am glad to say that we can obtain as many cattle as we like for the purpose. Here we have men; the only employment, indeed, which the Abyssinian men will undertake is driving cattle, or rather following them, for they never attempt in any way to guide or influence their movements, but dawdle after them with their eternal spears and shields, knowing well that the sagacious little cattle will always follow the beaten track. Close by is a space marked off for a market. Here we have groups of men squatted about everywhere among their cattle, sheep, and goats: there are a good many donkeys too, and a few mules. For these latter they have raised the price very greatly during the last month: then a good mule could be bought for fifteen dollars, now they charge thirty-five and forty. They are very independent too, and refuse to abate a single dollar in the price they ask: if they do not obtain the exact sum they demand, they will, after a certain time, mount and ride off to their villages, to return again next day with the price probably enhanced two or three dollars over that demanded on the first occasion.

I must now close this, as I am on the point of starting for Attegrat. I shall endeavour to send a few lines in from Goun-Gonna, the next station; for as the next mail starts in four days, and I shall be getting farther away every march, a letter from Attegrat could not get in here in time for the post.

Goun-Gonna, February 4th.

I feel quite glad to be again getting forward. Senafe has so long been my advanced post, that it seemed as if we were never going to get beyond that point. However, now I am once more *en route*, I hope that I shall have no further stop—beyond a few days at Attegrat, to see the meeting of the King of Tigre and the General—until I arrive at Antalo. Antalo will be about ten days' march from here, and, once there, half the distance to Magdala will have been accomplished. My ride yesterday afternoon was one of the most pleasant I have had here. The temperature was delightful—a bright sun and a strong cool wind; the road, too, for some distance, across an undulating plain, descending sharply into a magnificent valley, was a charming change after the monotony of the long valleys, up and down which I have been riding for the last six weeks, and the wide expanse of the sandy plain of Zulla. After leaving Senafe the plain falls for some distance, and after about five miles' ride we came down to the lowest point, where, in ordinary times, a small stream of water crosses the road, but which at present is perfectly dry, except where it has accumulated in large pools. By the side of one of these, about two miles to our left, we saw the camp of cavalry and sick animals. I may mention, by the way, that although the disease among the mules is much upon the decrease, and has altogether lost the virulence which at first characterised it, there are still, by the last weekly statement, two thousand six hundred animals, including camels, unfit for work, from one cause or other.

In this watered valley are immense herds of cattle. The plain is covered with a thick coarse grass, which has now been everywhere cut, either by the troops themselves for their horses, or by the natives for sale to us. Crossing the plain, we have a steep rise up the side of the hill, and then, surmounting the rise, we find ourselves at the head of a valley running nearly due south. This we descend; and from the number of villages perched on the eminences on either side, it is evident that water is generally found in this locality. It was probably, at some not very distant time, much more thickly populated than it is at present, for many of the villages are ruinous and deserted. This valley is very pretty, and, after the treeless plain of Senafe, is doubly agreeable, for the sides of the hills are everywhere clothed with the gigantic candelabra cactus. These are now just bursting into blossom. The blossoms grow from the extremity of each of the innumerable arms of the candelabra; and as their colour varies from white, through delicate shades of pink, to dark-red, the effect is very beautiful; indeed, with their regular growth, and perfect mass of blossom, they look as if they had just been transplanted from the grounds of the Messrs. Veitch to this country for some gigantic flower-show. There is a church in this valley, which is much venerated as being the scene of the martyrdom of some eight or ten Christians in the time of the persecution. My knowledge of Abyssinian history is, I confess, of too meagre a nature for me to give you an approximate date of this affair. Their bones are, however, still to be seen; and from this I should say that the event could not be very distant, as in a climate subject to great heat and heavy rains as this is, it is probable that bones would very speedily decay. The church is at some distance from the road, and is, like most of the churches here, upon a hill. I did not, therefore, turn aside to examine it, as

I shall have plenty of opportunities of examining churches hereafter, and, with the exception of the martyrs' bones, it presents no feature of peculiar interest. Descending the valley, we find it to be only a feeder of a wide valley running east and west. The valley was, like Goose Plain, covered with coarse grass, and contained immense herds of cattle. The side opposite to that by which we had entered it was very steep; the mountains are nearly bare, and near their summits present an appearance which, had I not seen it also upon the rock at Senafe, I should have said had been caused by a very slight fall of snow. I learn, however, that it is a very small lichen, which is abundant upon the rocks. I presume that this lichen is at present in flower or seed; for I did not observe the peculiar appearance at my first visit to Senafe, and it is so remarkable that I could not have failed to notice it had it existed at that time. We know now that we are near our destination, for we see the grass-cutters going along with great bundles of hay. We cross the valley and enter a smaller valley, which forks at a slight angle with the large one. As we fairly entered it, we saw near its extremity the camp of Goun-Gonna. A prettier situation could hardly have been selected. The hills to the right-hand are almost perpendicular, and upon a ledge about half-way up a village is nestled. The stream which flows down it has been used for the purpose of irrigation, and the bright green of the young crops was a delightful relief to our eyes. On the left-hand the hills are less precipitous, but are still very steep. The valley is less than a quarter of a mile in width, and ends abruptly with a semicircular sweep a short distance above the spot where the camp is pitched. What adds greatly to the beauty of the valley is, that it contains several of those immense trees with distorted trunks and bright-green foliage, whose real name is a moot point, but which are alike claimed to belong to the banyan, india-rubber, or tulip-tree species. At any rate, whatever be their species, they are one of the most picturesque species of tree I ever saw. They cover an immense extent of ground, and their trunks sometimes lie along the ground, sometimes rise in strange contorted forms. Their bark is extremely rough, and whitish-gray, and if seen without the foliage, would be certainly rather taken for strange blocks and pillars of stone than for the trunks of trees. In the camp we found a company of the 33d and the head-quarters of that regiment, who are upon their way to join the wing at Attegrat, and who had just come in, as had the mountain battery of steel guns under Colonel Milward, both having left Senafe two or three hours before ourselves. There was also a convoy of the Transport Train on their way to the front, and also a troop of the Scinde Horse. This station must be fifteen hundred feet below Senafe, and the difference of temperature is surprising. Last night I did not at all feel cold, whereas at Senafe it was next to impossible to keep warm, however numerous the wrappings in which one enveloped oneself. This morning I have been up a very pretty little broad valley, about a quarter of a mile in length. This branches off from the larger valley exactly opposite the camp, and it is down this that the little stream of water comes. The valley is clothed in shrubs and small trees, and the water falls into it over a perpendicular rock fifty feet high at its upper extremity. It put me very much in mind of a Westmoreland glen, with a little "force" at the extremity. Here, too, to increase the resemblance, I found some old friends whom I have not seen since I left England, namely dog-roses, common brambles, and honeysuckle. Down by the water's edge, upon the rocks, kept moist by the water-spray, grew maiden-hair and other ferns. The air was sweet with arbutus-flowers, and the plash of the water was most grateful to the ear after the dry plains of Zulla and Senafe. Here, too, we had the aloe in flower, with its long heads of reddish-orange blossom. Here we had a sort of scabius ten feet high, and a rush or water-grass twenty feet in height, with its plumy reed. Here over the shrubs crept the familiar clematis, with its great clusters of white downy reed. Here was a sort of tares, with their pink blossom, and growing straight and strong to a height of four or five feet. Upon the trees were perched wood-pigeons and doves, which called to one another with their soft coo. Altogether it was a lovely little spot, and it was with the greatest reluctance that I left it to come back to camp to write this letter previous to starting for Fokado, the next station.

You will see that, although the mail only goes once a week, I am, as long as I am moving forwards, obliged to write every three days, as for every day I move further the mail takes another day to come down. It is, in addition, no easy matter to find time to write when upon the march. One rises at daybreak, which is little before seven, and, using the very greatest diligence, it is nearly two hours before the tent can be struck, and the mules loaded and upon their way. I generally give them a start of an hour, and then ride on, overtake them, and see that all is going on well. If so, I ride forward, and use some friend's tent until my own arrives, which, if the distance is fourteen miles, will not be until nearly four in the afternoon; for my mules, with stoppages to readjust baggage, &c., do not make above two miles an hour. Then there is pitching the tent, drawing rations, and seeing the horses watered and fed; and by the time dinner is ready and our work done, it is past six o'clock. One generally puts one's rations with those of friends; and by the time the meal is over, and the succeeding pipe and glass of arrack-and-water discussed, one is far more fit for bed than for sitting down to chronicle the events of the day. My next letter will be from Attegrat, where I expect to stay for a few days.

Attegrat, February 7th.

I have been so long looking forward to arriving at Attegrat, that, being here, I feel that I have made a long stage into the interior of Abyssinia. I confess, however, that I am disappointed in Attegrat. It is foolish, I own. I ought by this time to have learnt the utter hollowness and emptiness of all statements connected with the country; and everything we have been told, everything we have been led to expect, has alike turned out utterly incorrect. Sometimes we have been told pleasant things, sometimes we have been threatened with dire calamities; but in both cases the vaticinations have turned out equally incorrect. Guinea-worms and tape-worms, fever and cholera, small-pox and dysentery, tetse-fly and sunstroke—all these have been distinguished by their absence: but as a counterbalance, so have Colonel Phayre's green fields and gushing springs at Zulla, his perennial water between Sooro and Rayray Guddy, and his emporium of commerce at Senafe, which turned out a village of six mud-huts. Still, in spite of previous disappointments, I confess I clung to the idea that I should find a town of considerable size at Attegrat. The place was marked in Roman capitals upon the maps. It had been spoken of as a town flowing with milk and honey; it was to be one of our main halting-places; and altogether one certainly did expect to find rather more than twenty hovels, a barn called a church, and another ruinous barn which was once a palace. But before I describe Attegrat, let me detail my journey here from Goun-Gonna. I sent my baggage off at seven o'clock in the morning, at the same time that the baggage of the headquarters of the 33d and Colonel Penn's battery of mountain guns started. I then explored the pretty valley I described in my last, and afterwards went into a friend's tent and finished my letter to you. At twelve o'clock I started for what I was told was an eleven miles' ride; but it turned out the longest sixteen I have ever ridden. Every officer and man to whom I have spoken—and among others I may quote Colonel Milward and Colonel Penn of the Artillery, and Major Cooper, and all the officers of the 33d—agreed with me that it was over sixteen miles. Colonel Phayre's and the quartermaster's departments' gross miscalculation of distances is becoming a very serious nuisance. It is absolutely cruel upon the men. If soldiers are told that they have a sixteen miles' march across a rough country, and beneath a hot sun, they will do the distance. It may be hard work; but they know when they start what is before them, and they make up their minds to it. But when they are told it is eleven miles, at the end of that distance they begin to look out anxiously for their camping-place. They become cross and impatient, and are infinitely more fatigued than they would have been had they been told the real distance that was before them.

I now resume my account of my day's march. For the first two miles the road mounted very steeply, until we were at least a thousand feet above

Goun-Gonna, and had gained the great plateau out of which the valley is cut. It must have been a very difficult ascent before the road was made by the Sappers and Miners and Punjaub Pioneers. I do not know which parts of the road between Senafe and Attegrat are to be assigned to each regiment; but I believe that the road between Senafe and Goun-Gonna was executed principally by the 33d, assisted by the 10th Native Infantry, and that beyond this point it has been entirely the work of the Sappers and Miners and the Pioneers. The road from Goun-Gonna to Attegrat has not been continuously formed, as it is from Zulla to Goun-Gonna. It is only made in very difficult places, where it would have been next to impossible for a mule to have passed without its burden getting over its ears or tail. In other places we have the mere track worn by the people of the country; but where we ascend or descend gulleys or ravines, or where the road winds along on the face of a hill, when a false step would have involved a roll of a thousand feet down, there a fair road has been cut, which, although frequently steep, is always safe and passable. The road, take it as a whole, from Goun-Gonna to this place, is about as good as a bridle-road among the Welsh or Scotch hills. There are some extremely-steep places, where one mule falling down would stop a whole force, and where the loads shift terribly; but there are no places which cannot with care be surmounted, even by a baggage-train of mules. But this has been the easy portion of the journey. From this place to Antalo the difficulties will be vastly greater; beyond Antalo still greater again. It is for this reason that I look forward to a time when my knapsack will contain my whole luggage, and when sleeping in the open air will be the rule for everyone. Upon getting fairly up to the top of the hill-side from Goun-Gonna, a flat of apparently almost illimitable extent stretched away before us. Two or three of the curious conical hills which abound in this country rose at a considerable distance, and in the horizon were the peaks of the most fantastically-jagged range of mountains I ever saw. Nothing in the Alps will give any idea of the varied outline of this range of peaks. They are serrated and jagged in every conceivable form. Single peaks and double peaks, peaks like a cavalry saddle, and great square-topped blocks with perpendicular sides. The plain itself was dotted with low bushes, and covered everywhere with a luxuriant growth of grass, or rather hay, which reached up to the horses' girths. The ground was strewn with loose stones, which, with the numerous small holes, made any progress beyond a walking-pace difficult and even dangerous. The stones, and indeed the whole formation of this upper plateau, are composed of a very white sandstone. In the pass up to Senafe the formation was entirely schist, broken and cracked-up in a wonderful manner, with numerous veins of quartz, and occasional walls of very hard volcanic stone traversing it. On the plain of Senafe, and throughout the whole country this side of it, we have a superincumbent bed of sandstone, which has evidently been exposed for a very long time to the action of water. The great rocks of Senafe are everywhere water-worn, and were islets, which rose above the level of a great sea, and resisted the action of the water, which has cleared away the sandstone around them to the general regular level of the plateau. Traversing the plain, we found that the seemingly almost boundless level was apparent rather than real, for the road constantly wound to avoid great valleys, which everywhere penetrated far into it. The sensation of coming suddenly upon a valley of 1000 or 1500 feet deep when apparently travelling upon a level plain was very singular. It quite upset all our preconceived notions of scenery. One found that the mountains to our left, which had appeared to rise a thousand feet or so above the plain, were really double that height from the bottom of the before-invisible valley which intervened between ourselves and them, and that the plain we were traversing was not a plain at all, but a succession of flat mountain-tops. Sometimes these valleys ran so far into the plateau that the road would have to diverge too much from the straight line to pass round their heads, and in these cases we descended some hundred feet and mounted up the other side. The view down some of these valleys was extremely fine, the mountains beyond frequently rising for miles in an unbroken perpendicular wall of two or three thousand feet. The finest view, however, was about two miles from our halting-place; and this, although I have seen much splendid scenery in my varied wanderings, was certainly the finest and most striking scene I ever beheld. Our path was winding along the face of a high mountain, along which our pioneers had cut a path some ten or twelve feet wide. We were perhaps a hundred feet above the general level of the plateau, but were passing round the head of a valley which lay some fifteen hundred feet below us. This valley was only a short branch of a broader valley which ran at right-angles to it, and beyond and in the middle of which a number of isolated hills rose up like islands; these were all flat-topped, and rose to the exact level of the general plateau. Some had sloping sides, others were perfectly perpendicular; and it required no stretch of the imagination to picture the time when a mighty river was sweeping down this great valley, and when these island-mountains breasted and divided its waters. To our right this valley was ten or twelve miles wide, and the numerous islands presented an extraordinary vista of precipice and slope. On the opposite side of the valley the plateau extended for a mile or two, and then rose into lofty rounded mountains; more to the left it stretched away for many miles, and the view was bounded by the extraordinary fantastic range of peaks of which I have already spoken. It was a most glorious view, and, broken by the lights and shadows thrown by a sinking sun, will always remain in my recollection as the most extraordinary and magnificent landscape I ever saw.

We arrived at Fokado at half-past four, getting in half an hour before our baggage, which had been eight hours and a half upon the road, and quite determined that in future, whatever labour it involved, we would not again let it out of our sight. The break-down of a baggage-animal, if one is at hand oneself to see that one's servants instantly and properly reload it, is an affair of ten minutes at most; but if the servants are left to their own devices, it will occupy over half-an-hour. First of all there are ten minutes wasted in deploring the calamity, another ten in undoing the cords, and at least twenty more in repacking and getting under way. Fokado, like all our camping-stations, lies in a slight basin; this basin is, like the rest of the plateau-land, covered with long grass. A dozen men with scythes could cut enough in a day to supply a cavalry regiment; but they would have to be very careful to choose such portions of the plain as are not covered with stones. As it is, the grass-cutters are supplied with very small sickles, which do very well to hack off a bunch of grass, but which are of little use towards getting in any large quantity. Fortunately the natives cut and bring it in in considerable amount, and I am able to purchase an abundance from them; for no forage is issued by the commissariat for our baggage-animals, and it would be out of the question to expect our syces to go out and cut grass after a long and fatiguing day's march. There is a well at Fokado from which plenty of cool and moderately-pure water is obtained. After having seen my tent erected and my rations drawn and on the fire, I walked on with two or three officers of the 33d to see the church. It stood, as most of the churches here do, upon slightly-rising ground, and was surrounded by a high wall, with the gateway entering beneath a sort of tower. Having paid my dollar — the modest tariff here demanded for admission — I entered the enclosure. It was in a state of the utmost disorder; loose boulders and stones were strewn everywhere, and I saw no signs whatever of graves. This was the case in the other three churches I have since visited, and is the more singular as the graveyards I saw and described coming up the pass, and which were those of the Mahometan tribes who inhabit that part of the country, were so carefully constructed and so religiously preserved. I have not seen a single grave since I entered the Christian part of Abyssinia. Near the church-door was a framework of three cross-poles, and from this were suspended, by straw ropes, two large stones of sonorous qualities. These were the church-bells. The church itself was a low edifice, built of rough stones, with large blocks forming the door-frame. Entering, I found myself in a low chamber, the roof being supported by four rough stone columns. The floor was littered down with rushes, and had exactly the appearance of a stable. On the wall was a rude half-length fresco of the Virgin, squinting terribly; and on the door leading to the next chamber was a skin or parchment with a somewhat similar painting. Having bowed deeply before each of these portraits at the request of the officiating priest, I was admitted into the next chamber, which was precisely similar to the first, but, having no windows, it only received such light as came in through the crevices of the doors. There was some demur as to my entering the next chamber, which indeed had been refused to all the officers who had been previously there; but I pointed to my white solar hat; and this and the fact of my not being in uniform convinced them, I believe, that I was a priest; for I should mention that the Abyssinian priests are distinguished by wearing white turbans, all the rest of the population going bare-headed. I was therefore admitted into the holy of holies. This was a more lofty chamber than the others, and was lighted by a window high up on the side wall. Across the room, at a distance of about a yard from the door, hung a screen about six feet high; this screen was made of roughly-embroidered canvas, and was apparently intended to prevent the eyes of the worshippers in the second chamber catching a glimpse of the *penetralia* when the door was opened. Looking round the end of this curtain, I saw an erection resembling a painter's easel. A parchment or skin was stretched across the upper portion, and on this probably was a painting of some sort; but as it was wrapped up in a cloth, I was unable to examine it, as I was not allowed to go beyond the line of the screen. Returning, I noticed in one corner of the first chamber some long sticks, with a double bend at the top; that is, resembling in form a cross, with the top piece broken off. These are used in the service. Near them, in a niche in the wall, were some pieces of iron fastened together so as to make a jingling noise when shaken. These, no doubt, supply the place of the bell at the raising of the host. I have omitted to say that in the churchyard were two rough fonts; they were round blocks of stone, about two feet and a half high and eighteen inches in diameter; the hollow at the top for water was about eight inches deep. I have seen no fonts in the other churches I have entered.

The following morning I started for Attegrat, a march of about eleven miles. For some distance the road kept along the top of the plateau, which was here undulating, and the road in many places was very rough. At last we came to the brink of a valley, into the bottom of which we had to descend. How anything like a laden animal ever got down before the road was made it is next to impossible to imagine. We came along a beaten track to the top of the valley, and we could see the path again going straight along below us from the bottom; but there was no trace of any track or path down the tremendously-steep descent; and I suppose the little bullocks, which are as sure-footed as goats, and the donkeys, were allowed to pick their way down as they liked best. Fortunately, we were not reduced to this alternative, which would certainly have ended in three out of our four baggage-animals breaking their necks, even if the fourth—a sturdy little Massowah mule, with the zebra-marks upon his back and legs—had managed to get in safety to the bottom. A road has been cut along the face of the hill by the Sappers and Pioneers; and this road, although exceedingly steep in some places, is yet perfectly practicable. It is, however, only six feet wide, and in two or three places even less, and consequently a train of mules are a long time getting down; for if the load of one shifts and gets over his ears, all the rest must wait until it is readjusted-no easy matter upon a steep incline. If one fall from weakness or disease, there would be no resource but to roll him at once over the edge of the path into the valley below. Fortunately, none of these contingencies happened to us. The loads all got on to the animals' necks, but our men and ourselves were able to keep them balanced there until we reached the foot of the hill, when all the loads had to be taken off and entirely repacked. Just at the foot of the incline was a village. During our journey across the plateau from Goun-Gonna to this point we had only passed Fokado and one other village. We saw many down in the deep valleys around whose heads we had skirted, but upon the flat level of the plateau we did not see a single habitation. There were numerous herds of cattle, but these probably come up to graze upon the thick grass during the day, and descend into the valleys for water at night. We also passed some curious piles of stones upon the plateau-land, which I omitted to mention in my description of that part of my journey. These piles were thirty or forty feet in diameter, and five or six feet high; they were of stones roughly thrown together, and had I met with them in England I should have supposed that they had been merely cleared off the fields; but here there were no signs of cultivation, and the stones were too thickly strewn everywhere to render it probable that any Abyssinian cultivator would have undertaken the labour of clearing piles of stones of this size off his land—a work which, without wheeled vehicles, would be very great. These heaps always occurred near the track, and were generally surrounded by bushes. I passed at least twenty of them. It is possible that these cairns may be burying-places; but the deserted position, the fact that they were far from villages, and the labour which they must have taken to make, all seem to negative this supposition. Besides which, there was hardly the regularity about their shape which one meets with in the burying-cairns of even the most savage nations. I confess that they are to me a perfect mystery. In the village at the foot of the descent was a church which was exactly similar to the one at Fokado. It had no fonts that I could observe, but boasted of a gong in addition to the sonorous stones for summoning the faithful to prayers. In the enclosure, lying among the stones, was a large volcanic bomb, the first of the sort I have seen in the country; it had apparently been brought there as something strange, and perhaps supernatural, and had therefore been put on holy ground; for the enclosure within the walls is holy in Abyssinian eyes, and we are always required to take off our hats on entering the outside gates.

From this village to Attegrat the road keeps in the bottom of a broad valley, the great part of which is ploughed up and ready for the seed, which is, I suppose, sown before the June rains. The soil is light and good, in many places a rich light loam, which would delight an English gardener's heart. The ploughs are drawn by oxen, and are exactly similar to those I have seen in parts of Italy, except that the share of this is broader and does certainly more work. Indeed, it is by no means badly adapted for shallow ploughing on a light ground. A ride of about five miles down the valley brought us to a slight rise in the ground, and on surmounting this, Attegrat lay before us. My first impression was that of disappointment, for, with the exception of its containing two or three larger buildings, it differed in nothing from the other villages we have seen. The valley, at the point where Attegrat lies, is about two miles wide, and the twenty or thirty flat-roofed huts, which, with the church and a ruined palace, constitute the city, stand on rising ground nearly in its centre. On the left of this valley, near the slope, is the British camp. Behind it the ground rises gradually, affording camping-ground, if necessary, for a considerable force. Indeed, with the exception of some ploughed fields round the town, the whole valley is well suited for a camp. The force at present here are the five companies of the 33d regiment, whose camp, with that of Penn's mountain battery of steel guns and the Royal Engineers, is the first we arrive at. Next to the 33d lines are the commissariat stores. A few hundred yards farther down in the valley is the camp of the six companies of the 10th Native Infantry. Their tents, like those of the European troops, are upon the slope. Beyond them this slope becomes much steeper, and accordingly the 3d Native Cavalry are camped in the bottom. Next to them come the Mule Train. The divisions here are the Lahore Mule Train and the A Division under Captain Griffiths. It was this division which first landed, and brought up the pioneer force. It has been ever since in the front, and is now in admirable condition. The Egyptian, Arab, Italian, and, in fact, all the drivers, except only the Hindoostanee drivers, have been during the last few days sent down to the coast to be returned to their own countries, and their places have been filled with the Hindoo dhoolie bearers, and others whose services will be no longer required, now that the regiments have all to march without followers. It need hardly be said that this will very greatly improve the efficiency of the division, for the Hindoo, if he has less strength than the Arab, Egyptian, or Persian, is yet amenable to discipline, and will, to the best of his power, carry out the orders he receives; whereas the other men were utterly reckless and disobedient, and could not be trusted out of reach of the eye of their officers. The camp of the Scinde

Horse is still farther down the valley, beyond the transport lines. Sir Robert Napier arrived yesterday afternoon. His camp had been pitched for him on some slightly-rising ground in front of the 33d lines, and distant three or four hundred yards. To-day, however, the tents are being struck, and will be pitched in a line with the 33d tents, and forming a connection between them and the artillery. His tent, therefore, is in the exact centre of the European line, with the artillery on his right, the 33d on his left flank.

I now proceed to describe Attegrat. The most conspicuous building, as seen from our camp, is a detached sort of fortress, which looks like nothing so much as the castle of Bluebeard in a pantomime. It stands on a rising knoll, and consists of a square building of two stories high. Upon the top, and greatly overhanging each side, are four extraordinary-looking erections, like great dog-kennels or pigeon-cots, but which must be six or seven feet square. Almost the whole of these constructions project over the walls. What may be the use of these curious appendages to the tower, it is impossible to say. Next to this square tower stands a building as incongruous with it in its construction as it is possible to conceive. It is round, and has a high thatched roof, like a beehive. In addition to these main structures are several low sheds. The whole are enclosed in a high wall with a tower in it, underneath which is the gateway. The buildings are, no doubt, of stone, but they are all plastered over with mud, and look as if made of that material. As I have said, it is exactly one's idea of Bluebeard's castle, and one expects to see sister Anne waving her handkerchief out of one of the pigeon-cots at its summit. Certainly, if the gate were to open, and a stout figure in an immense pasteboard head, with a blue beard trailing upon the ground, and surrounded by a host of retainers also with big heads—which their chief would, of course, belabour occasionally with his staff—were to issue out, it would be in such admirable keeping with the place, that one would feel no astonishment. And yet this fortress has its history, and has stood its siege. It seems that the king or chief of this part of the country used seldom to live in his palace in the town itself, and his brother had his abode there. The brother took too much upon himself, and the jealousy and ire of the chief were aroused, and he ordered his brother to move out of the palace. This he did, but constructed at half-a-mile from the town this formidable castle. A disagreement arose, and the king attacked the castle, which he took after twenty hours' siege. The castle is at present inhabited by the wife of a chief—I cannot say whether it is the same chief, for dates in Abyssinia are somewhat confused—who is a prisoner of Gobayze, King of Lasta. She has, I hear, taken a vow never to go out of doors while her husband is in captivity. Passing Bluebeard's castle, it is a good half-mile to the town. At the right-hand on a rising rock is the church, which at a distance exactly resembles a Swiss châlet. It is, of course, surrounded by its wall, and within the enclosure grow some of the gigantic candelabra cactus. The church itself is more lofty than any I have yet seen. It is square, and is covered with a high thatched roof, the eaves of which project all round a considerable distance, and are supported by poles. Upon paying the usual fee, I was admitted in the enclosure, and saw at once that this church was of far greater pretensions than any I had yet seen. The entrance was by a doorway of squared beams, with two arches, each cut out of one piece, and each ornamented with five rolls of wood underneath. Entering this, we were in a sort of lobby or hall. The walls of this were covered with frescoes representing the feats of the founder of the church, who was either the father or grandfather of the present chief. Here that redoubted warrior is represented spearing an elephant; again he is kneeling and taking aim at a lion, whose claws are of truly-formidable dimensions. Here there are two or three battle-scenes, in which he is defeating his enemies with immense slaughter. To judge by his portraits, the founder of the church was a fair, round-faced man, with short hair and a slight moustache. I passed from this vestibule into the church itself. Its construction differs entirely from the others I have seen, inasmuch as instead of the sacred chamber being placed beyond two others, it was in the centre of the building, and was surrounded by a passage, the walls of which were covered with frescoes representing events in Old and New Testament writing, and in the lives of the saints. Here we have St. George nobly spearing the dragon, while the King of Egypt's daughter and her maidens stand by with clasped hands and admiring eyes. Here we have St. Peter suffering martyrdom by being crucified head downwards; with a vast number of other martyrdoms. The biblical events all strictly follow the scriptural description; the only remarkable difference being that at the Last Supper thirteen apostles are represented as being present. In all these, as in the first frescoes, the faces of the actors are represented as white; while in the Temptation the tempter has his traditional sable hue. These frescoes are all in the early Byzantine style, and were they but really ancient, would be extremely curious and valuable; but as the church is not, at most, more than sixty or seventy years old, it is evident that they are the work of some Egyptian or Greek artist brought down for the purpose. I was not allowed to see what was in the central chamber. Leaving the church, I crossed the town, sixty or seventy yards, to where, at its other extremity, stands the ruined palace. It is surrounded by a wall, which encloses a considerable extent of ground. The principal portion of the palace far more resembles a church than do any of the actual churches of the country. It consists of a hall fifty feet long by twenty-five feet wide, with a small round room at the end opposite to the door. The entrance is underneath a porch; and along this, at about eight feet from the ground, there are built into it a line of bullocks' horns, with their points projecting outwards. The hall was thirty feet high to the springing of the roof, and must have been really a fine hall, country and place being taken into consideration. The greater part of one side-wall has, however, fallen; and the roof is entirely gone. Some of the great beams which crossed it lie on the ground, and it would be a matter of considerable interest to inquire whence, in a treeless country like this, these massive beams were obtained. The most interesting portion of the ruin is the room beyond the great hall, and which was probably the king's own room. It is entered by a double-arched door, of workmanship and design similar to that I have described at the church; the two buildings being coeval, and the woodwork unquestionably worked by some foreign artificer brought here for the purpose. The chamber itself is about fifteen feet across, with three deep recesses, each lighted by a small double-arched window of the same pattern as the door. The room was about twelve feet high, and was ceiled by a circular arched roof, which still remains. It is made of reeds or rushes sewn side by side, like the basketwork of the country, and dyed with a pattern in reel and blue. This was all worth describing in the palace; there were several other buildings attached to it, but none worthy of any special notice.

About a mile beyond Attegrat, upon the other side of the valley, there is another church, whose site might well have been selected by the monks of old for a monastery, so charming is the grove in which it is situated. This grove is of considerable extent, and consists of several sorts of really lofty trees: there is a thick undergrowth—with plenty of paths for walking, however—of all sorts of plants. There are some tall bananas with their broad, graceful leaves, the first I have seen since I left Bombay. There are roses and honeysuckles, wild figs and acacias; over all of which a thick cordage of various creepers twines in clusters. To add to the enjoyment, the whole air is heavy with the fragrance of the wild jasmine, which grows in great bushes, covered with clusters of its white star-like flowers. While sitting down with a party of three or four officers of the 33d enjoying the delightful shade and the charming fragrance, the priest with several natives came up to us, and taking seats, or rather squatting—I do not think an Abyssinian knows how to sit down—beside us, they entered into a species of conversation with us, inquiring particularly, as do all the natives, if we were Christians. Presently they made signs they would like to see some sketches I had been taking; but when they took them in their hands they were completely puzzled, turned them upside down and sideways, and even looked behind at the back of the paper: they could evidently make nothing of them. Presently the priest, with an air of great self-satisfaction, made signs that he could write, and demanded if I could do so. I had no writing at hand, but in my sketch-book I had a column of your paper which I had cut out for purposes of reference;

this I gravely handed over, and it was received with a perfect shout, first of astonishment, then of delight. They had never seen such even and perfect manuscript in their lives. The priest evidently thought I must be a priest of high grade, and he at once offered to show us the church, which he did without demanding the usual dollar from any one of the party. It was so similar to those I have previously described that I need not say anything about it, except that in the holy of holies, in place of a frame like a painter's easel, the shrine was composed of three poles, seven or eight feet long, inclining towards each other, and meeting at the top like a tripod: a piece of cloth was wrapped round the upper part of this frame. I cannot say whether it concealed anything, but it did not appear to me to do so. Below this a skin was stretched between the three legs, so as to make a sort òf shelf, and upon this were placed a number òf withered flowers. I should mention that, in the inner chamber of most of these churches, those who have entered with me have agreed that there was a faint but distinct odour of incense. It may be, however, that in all of them might have been some flowers, such as jasmine, the perfumes of which may have deceived us. It is rather singular that the grape has not been introduced into a country which would seem by its climate to be well suited for it. There is no wine to be obtained here; and the sacrament is administered by squeezing a raisin into a chalice of water. Raisins are, however, very scarce; and in some churches years have elapsed without the administration of the sacrament, owing entirely to the absence of even a single raisin.

In my description of Attegrat I have omitted to say, that although the town itself does not contain more than twenty or thirty houses, yet the population within a short distance is very large; for on the hill-side, behind the church I have just been describing, there are numerous villages, which are probably known in the local tongue as lower and upper Attegrat, new and old, eastern and western Attegrat. Attegrat, at any rate, is their centre; and judging by the number of natives one sees in and about the camp, and the number of houses in the various villages, there must be a population of six or eight thousand clustered in a circle of three or four miles from the town.

I have now described the general features of the place, and shall close and send off this letter, although it is only four days since I posted my last, and the next mail is not advertised to start for another eight days. I shall write again for that post; but my experience has taught me that the mail here is one of those charming uncertainties upon which it is impossible to calculate. Besides this, I may at any moment find myself compelled to push on; and, in that case, there would be no saying when my next letter would reach you. I hope, however, to be enabled to give you a full description of the visit of the King of Tigre, who is expected to-morrow or next day.

Attegrat, February 13th.

Our grand Christmas farcio-pantomime, entitled "Harlequin and the Magic Durbar; or the Ambassador, the Archbishop, and the Barbarian Cortege," has been played to an immensely amused and numerous audience. The title had been advertised as "The King, the Archbishop, &c.;" but, owing to the unavoidable absence of the principal actor, the Ambassador was at the last moment substituted for the King. The opening scene may be described as "The camp of the Knight Errant, Sir Robert Napier, with Bluebeard's Castle in the middle distance, and the town of Attegrat and the mountains in the background." Flourish of trumpets! A herald arrives, the part being enacted by Major Grant, who states that the King is unable to come in person to wait upon the valiant Knight, but that he had sent his dear brother, the Grand Vizier, together with his Archbishop, to assure the Knight of his friendship. Bustle and excitement in the camp. A pause. Sound of strange and barbaric music in the distance. This gradually approaches, and then, from the rear of Bluebeard's Castle—of which a full description was given in my last—enter the head of procession, consisting of—three men blowing upon cow-horns. These were inserted into the ends of long sticks, and in appearance were very like the long horns used by heralds of old. Their sound is lugubrious in the extreme. Next follows a man of tall stature, beating violently upon a tom-tom. Next follow the musqueteers of the body-guard; dress—dirty clothes miscellaneously draped; bare heads frizzled and oiled; arms—any stage-properties which might come conveniently to hand; old Portuguese match-locks, and new fowling-pieces from Liège; double-barrelled guns, and guns with one long and frequently crooked barrel, the large proportion quite incapable of being fired. Next follows the Ambassador of the King on a mule, with gorgeous caparisons of stamped green and red leather, bearing the tiger rampant, the arms of the great potentate his master. The Ambassador is clothed like his body-guard, in whity-brown cloth of coarse cotton, with red ends. With this, as a sign of his dignity, he envelopes not only his body, but his mouth and chin, as do the chiefs behind him. He wears round his neck a fur collar with long tails. The Ambassador of the great King is bareheaded. His hair is arranged, as is the manner of the chiefs of his people, in a series of little plaits, which run in parallel lines from his forehead over the head to the nape of the neck. This style appears to be copied from the Assyrian bas-relievos in the British Museum. Next to the Ambassador of the great King rides the Archbishop, upon a mule similarly caparisoned. The Archbishop is clothed in absolutely white robes, with turban to match. These dignitaries have both stirrups to their saddles, in which the great-toes only are placed, to, I should say, the imminent danger of those members if the mule should stumble. Behind these great personages ride the inferior chiefs. These, either from a feeling of modesty, or from a lack of animals, ride two upon each mule. Behind follow the spearmen of the guard on foot. These are about thirty in number, and are armed with lance, sickle, and shield. When this procession has fairly wound round the corner of Bluebeard's Castle, it halts to await the arrival of a herald from the good Knight. All this time the barbaric music continues to sound, and is answered by sister Anne and Fatimah in the castle, and by the women all over the country, by a prolonged cry on a single note, kept up with a quavering modulation for a considerable time. This is a welcome on the part of the people of the country to the ambassador of the great King. While the procession halts, the soldiers of the Knight Errant flock out to inspect them. Irregular chorus of soldiers: "My eye, Bill, if these are the sort of chaps we've come to fight, we sha'n't have much trouble with them." The remainder of the pantomime I will, for brevity's sake, describe as if it had been a real event in the expedition; but the reader must bear in mind that the whole piece, its accessories and appointments, were infinitely funny and amusing. After conferring with the Commander-in-chief, Major Grant and Mr. Speedy went out to meet the procession, and conducted them through the camp to the tent of General Merewether. During their progress the wild music continued to sound, and nearly effected a stampede of the whole of the animals in camp. In the mean time three companies of the 33d regiment, two of the 10th N.I., with the bands of both regiments, were drawn up in line in front of and facing Sir Robert Napier's tent, an interval of about fifty yards being left. On the flanks of the line two squadrons of the 3d N. Cavalry and of the Scinde Horse were drawn up. When all was ready, the cortége advanced, horns blowing and tom-toms beating. At their head strode Mr. Speedy, who is nearly six feet six inches tall, and who carried in his hand a sword nearly as tall as himself. As the procession approached, the military bands struck up and the troops saluted. The din at this moment was astounding. The bands played different tunes, and the cow-horns and tom-toms played no tune at all. Mr. Speedy with some trouble marshalled his ragged irregulars in line, and, this accomplished, led the two ambassadors to the chief's tent. The tent was one of the long narrow tents called native routies, and, being lined with scarlet, made a very good tent for the reception. Sir Robert Napier was seated with his helmet on at one end. The ambassadors were introduced by Mr. Speedy, who acted as interpreter, and after bowing very deeply, they shook hands with the chief. They then took seats upon the ground beside him; as many officers as could find room without crowding ranged themselves along the sides of the tent, and also took their places behind Sir Robert Napier, the back of the tent being open as well as the front. The conversation commenced by one of the ambassadors stating "that the King of Tigre, his brother, had sent him to assure the British Commander-in-chief of his friendship. The King would have come in person to welcome Sir Robert, but he had been just solemnly proclaimed king, and it was strict etiquette that he should not leave his capital for thirty days afterwards."

Sir Robert Napier replied that he was very glad to receive the assurance of the King's friendship; that we ourselves had come with the most friendly intentions to all in Abyssinia, with the exception only of those who held our countrymen captives; that in our progress we should violently interfere with no one; and that, our enterprise over, we should return at once to our own country. The Ambassador said "that the King and everyone in the country wished well to our cause; for that Theodore was a tyrant who had ravaged the whole country, and had murdered thousands of people, including his own near relations. Therefore, he hoped, that we should punish him for his wickedness." He then said "that the King was very anxious to see Sir Robert, and would be very glad if he would let him know how long he was likely to remain at Attegrat." The General answered "that he could not say when he should leave; that his preparations were not yet completed; but that when he was able to fix a day for his departure he would, if the King wished, send a message to let the King know; but that he feared he could not give sufficient notice for the King to arrive in time." The Ambassador then made a statement which showed that his last question was not *bonâ fide*, and that the King had really no intention of coming at all. He said "that the King had a large army—that as long as he was with them they behaved well, but that he could not leave them, for if he did so they would spread over the country and oppress the peasantry." The Chief replied that, "under these circumstances he could quite understand the King's reluctance to leave his army, but that he hoped on his return from Magdala he should have the pleasure of meeting his Majesty." There was then a pause in the conversation, and the Ambassador begged to know when he might be allowed to leave. Sir Robert answered that early in the morning he would show him our soldiers, and after that he could leave whenever he chose. A few trifling articles were then presented to the Ambassador and Archbishop as tokens of friendship, and after again bowing and shaking hands with Sir Robert Napier, they took their leave, and, surrounded by their guards, moved off amid the din of music which had greeted their arrival. The next morning at seven o'clock the whole of the troops turned out to a general parade. The Ambassadors were present. After riding along the whole line, the General and staff took up their position in front, and the 33d regiment were put through the bayonet exercise, which they performed exceedingly well, especially when it is considered that it is nearly four months since they last did it. They then went through the platoon drill; but the natives did not at all comprehend this. They heard the snapping of the locks as the Sniders were supposed to be fired in rapid volleys. When informed what was being done, they entirely disbelieved it, and plainly said so, stating that no guns could be fired so quickly as that. It is a very great pity that a small number of cartridges were not broken up and served out as blank cartridges; or better still, had a hundred ball cartridges been served out to ten men, to have been discharged as rapidly as possible against a rock on the hill-side. Weight is of course precious, but the lesson those hundred cartridges would have taught would have been cheaply purchased at any cost. It was emphatically a penny-wise-and-pound-foolish economy. Colonel Penn's batteries of steel guns were then examined, and these fired a few rounds with blank cartridges.

Our savage visitors, however, were more impressed with the artillery than they had been with the infantry. The guns, they said, were small, and did not make much noise; the infantry were pretty to look at, but of no use in a hilly country, and their long lines would be very easy to shoot at. These criticisms are very amusing on the part of the ragged savages, of whom I heard an Irish soldier of the 33d say, "And bedad it's ashamed I'd be to have to fire me rifle at such a miserable set of divils intirely. It 'ud be like killing a definceless brute baste." The general feeling in the camp, indeed, upon the subject was that of disappointment. It was exactly the reverse of "the stern joy that warriors feel in foe-men worthy of their steel." We did hope that if we were to fight it would be against something in some way or another formidable. We had heard a good deal about Theodore's army, who were said to be armed with guns and were drilled, and we did have a faint hope that our foe would not be utterly contemptible. But the first appearance of Abyssinian soldiery has quite dispelled any such idea. Mr. Speedy and our interpreters assure us that they are a fair sample of Abyssinian troops. Why, Falstaff's ragged regiment was a disciplined and regular body to this band of savages. As for their guns, I should say by their appearance that at least two-thirds would burst at the very first volley fired, and would be infinitely more dangerous to themselves than to anyone else.

If, however, our visitors thought very little of the infantry and artillery, they were greatly impressed by the cavalry. The Scinde Horse and 3d Native Cavalry made several charges, and these, they acknowledged, would upon level ground be irresistible. The horses themselves also struck them particularly. In Abyssinia there is nothing which could by the utmost stretch of courtesy be called a horse. They have nothing but little rawboned ponies, together with mules and donkeys. The cavalry animals, and those of the staff, therefore, strike them as being prodigies of strength and beauty. It is satisfactory to know that one arm of the service at least found favour in the sight of our military critics, who, however, qualified even that meed of approbation by adding that it was not likely that Theodore would fight us upon ground where the cavalry could charge at all. Our show, therefore, as a show, was completely thrown away, and they saw nothing of the one thing which would have impressed them—namely, an exhibition of the powers of the Snider rifle.

The next day the embassy took its departure with its barbaric music playing, and the strange quavering cries of the women answering it over the country. There is still a possibility that the King of Tigre may himself come to meet the Commander-in-chief either at Antalo or at some place on our march thither. I hardly think, however, that he will do so. These native kings are generally so faithless and treacherous among themselves that they do not like to trust their persons into anyone else's hands. Still, as the Ambassador was allowed to take his departure unharmed, it is quite upon the cards that the King will muster up courage and come in.

The following is a summary of the news from the front, as communicated to us by General Napier's orders:

"Letters were received on the 9th instant by General Merewether from Mr. Rassam and Dr. Blanc, dated Magdala, Jan. 17th, with enclosures from Mr. and Mrs. Flad, dated King's Camp, Jan 9th. All the prisoners are reported well up to date. A detachment of troops, which had left Magdala on Jan. 8th, had joined the King in his camp, and had received charge of a party of about 400 prisoners to escort from the camp to Magdala. The imprisoned Europeans were among the number. Their leg-fetters had been removed and handcuffs substituted, so that they might march. It is said Mr. Rosenthal would accompany them. The King was using every endeavour to get the road made, working with his own hands, and making the free Europeans help. He had made some slight progress, and had arrived at the bottom of the valley of the Djedda River. Mr. Rassam calculates he would reach Magdala about the end of February with his camp, though by abandoning the latter he could any day arrive there. The people of Dalanta continue submissive; but those of Davout had rebelled again. His soldiers had suffered from the scarcity of provisions and transport. It was reported at Magdala that Menilek, the King of Shoa, had again set out for Magdala, better prepared to act against Theodorus than on his former visit. A detailed communication from one of the captives, sent to his friends in England, and there published, has by some means reached the King's camp, and is in the hands of M. Bardel. Apprehensions are entertained that it may do injury there."

These letters add but little to what we knew before. Our last advice told us that Theodore was only distant a single day's march from Magdala,—which, by the way, is spelt Magdalla throughout the summary, but which is pronounced Māgdālā, the *a* being always long in Amharic,—and that he could at any moment ride in and fetch the captives confined in that fortress, or could send those with him to Magdala under a guard. He has chosen, it appears, the latter alternative. The captives have at least the melancholy satisfaction of being together. That the news of our coming has in no way influenced the tyrant's treatment of them is shown by the fact, that although their leg-chains have been removed to enable them to march, yet handcuffs have been substituted in their stead.

From rumours among the natives, we hear that his cruelties are more atrocious than ever. Women are being put to death by being thrown down wells, at the bottom of which spears are fixed point upwards. Men are executed by having their feet first chopped off, then their hands, then their legs at the knees, and then being left as food for wild-beasts. I do not vouch for the truth of these stories; but they have been brought by deserters from Theodore's camp, and are generally believed. I do sincerely trust that in no case shall we make a treaty with this demon which may save him from the punishment due to him.

The great question here is, first, whether Theodore will fight; and secondly, what we shall do if, when we arrive, he offers to deliver the prisoners to us as the price of our instant departure. As to the first point I can only repeat what I have before said, namely, that I am of opinion that he will fight, and I think fight at Magdala. The enormous trouble he is taking in conveying cannon with him to Magdala points conclusively to that result. If he only wished to carry his baggage and treasure into Magdala he might easily, with the force at his command, construct a mule-path in a few days at the latest; but he clings to his guns, and he can only require them so imperiously that he puts up with months of hardship for their sake that he may defend Magdala against us. These savages measure the offensive powers of a gun entirely by its size, and by the noise it makes. Thus Tigre's ambassador regarded our mountain train as mere pop-guns; and no doubt Theodore believes that with the great guns his European workmen have cast, and with the natural strength of the fortress, he can easily resist the attacks of the English. I believe that we shall find the King at Magdala, get there when we will; and that as he will offer no terms that we can accept, and as he will not assent to the demand for unconditional surrender which we are certain to make, we shall finally have to take the place by storm. The next question, as to what our course will be if he offers to deliver up the captives upon the condition of our instant retreat, is one which it is very difficult to predicate upon. No doubt Sir Robert Napier has instructions from home for his guidance under such a contingency; but I cannot bring myself to believe that these terms would be acceded to.

And now as to gossip about this place. The Abyssinians are celebrated by travellers in their country as being an intelligent people. Intelligent is by no means the word, nor is sharp nor cute; they are simply the most extortionate thieves that the sun's light ever shone on. Formerly the necessaries of life were extraordinarily cheap here. Mercher, the Tigre chief who acts as interpreter, tells me that, as an example, fowls could be purchased at forty for a dollar. I venture to say that, at the present moment, it is the dearest place in the habitable globe. I have seen three eggs offered for a dollar. This was, however, too much to be stood, and at present seven is the tariff; that is, as nearly as possible, eightpence apiece for very little eggs. An ordinary-sized fowl costs a dollar; and with great bargaining two very small and skinny ones can be obtained for that sum. Two pumpkins can be bought for a dollar: for a quart of milk a dollar is demanded, and I have seen it given. The commissariat give a dollar for about seventeen pounds of grain: if we buy it for our horses in the camp—which we are obliged to do, as there are no rations issued for our baggage-animals—we have to give a dollar for about twelve pounds. The price of a good mule before we came here was seven or eight dollars; this had risen to thirty-two or thirty-three, at which the 3d Cavalry bought a considerable number, and to thirty-seven, the average price at which Captain Griffiths, of the Transport Train, purchased a good many. General Merewether, however, by one of those masterly *coups* for which he is so distinguished, has suddenly raised the market price 25 per cent, by giving fifty dollars each for a lot of forty, among which were some very indifferent animals. After this, of course, fifty will be the current price, until General Merewether makes another purchase for the public service, after which there is no predicting the price at which they will probably arrive. It is all very well to say that they are cheaper here than they are in Egypt; that has, as far as I can see, nothing whatever to do with the question, any more than it would be to say they are cheaper than at the North Pole. The people were willing to sell them at thirty-seven dollars for picked animals; why, then, spoil the market by giving fifty? It is urged that we are in want of mules, and that, by offering even more than they ask, we shall induce them to send in larger quantities; but I cannot agree that it is so. We were before paying 700 per cent more than their ordinary price, and this would be sufficient temptation to owners of any mules within a hundred miles—and good mules are not common—to have brought them in. Every mule fit for the purpose would have come in, and by paying 900 per cent we can obtain no more. One source of irritation has been, I am happy to say, if not put down, at least rebuked. After the parade the other day the Commander-in-chief rode to the church, attended by most of the mounted officers. The usual demand of a dollar a-head was made, which Sir Robert very properly refused to pay, and through the interpreter said a few appropriate words to the priest as to money-changers in the temple. He refused, he said, upon that ground to allow the charge of a dollar a-head to be paid, but promised that upon his return from Magdala he would present an altar-cloth at the church.

I have not mentioned that oxen, for which even at the enormously-enhanced prices at Senafe we paid six and a-half dollars, are here charged sixteen and seventeen dollars; and this with the plains in many cases containing thousands upon thousands. Of course it is a great question as to how far we ought to put up with such extortion as this. It is certain that the French, under similar circumstances, would not do so; but then the success of the French against native populations has not upon the whole been brilliant; their case therefore is no argument in its favour. If we chose to take what we required, and to offer in payment the fair country price, or even its double, of course we could do so, and could thrash all Tigre if necessary; but, putting it in the mere pecuniary light, would it pay? Much as I hate extortion, dearly as I should like to punish the nation of thieves through whom we are passing, I yet do not think it would pay. It is hard to be cheated by a half-naked savage; but it is better to put up with it than to undergo the amount of labour, anxiety, and loss which savages could in our present circumstances entail upon us. They are at present driving a thriving trade by selling us part of the roofs of their houses. This sounds strange, but is absolutely the fact. Between this and Senafe—a distance of forty miles—not a single tree is to be met with which could be used for telegraph-poles: the engineers were completely at a nonplus. At last we struck upon the expedient of buying poles from the natives, and an offer was made to give them a dollar for every six poles. Since then Mr. Speedy, who has undertaken the negotiation, has a complete levée of natives with poles. These poles are perfectly straight, and must be fourteen feet long; they are slight, much slighter than ordinary English hop-poles, and they are very thin towards the upper extremity. The natives use them for the roofs of their houses; but where they get them from, or what tree furnishes them, is at present a mystery; certainly I have seen no tree since my arrival in this country which grows at all in the same way. Some of these poles look freshly cut, but others are old and have evidently been used in the roofs of houses. They would not be nearly strong enough for an ordinary telegraph-wire, but can easily enough carry the fine copper-wire used here.

Mr. Speedy has been requested by the Commander-in-chief to wear the native attire; and his appearance, although no doubt very imposing to the native mind, is yet extremely comic to a European eye. Imagine a gentleman six feet and a half high, with spectacles, wearing a red handkerchief over his head, and shading himself with a native straw umbrella. Round his neck he wears the fur collar with tails, to which I have already alluded as part of a chief's insignia; over his shoulders is the native white-cloth wrapping, with red ends; below this is a long coloured-silk garment; and below all this the British trousers and boots. Mr. Speedy is a capital fellow, and a general favourite with everyone; but his appearance at present is almost irresistibly inducive of laughter.

The climate of this place is as near perfection as possible. It is not so hot as Senafe during the day, although even here in a single bell-tent the thermometer registered 110° to-day at eleven o'clock. But there is almost always a fresh breeze; and excepting from nine to twelve, when the wind generally drops, it is never too hot for walking. At night it is not so cold as at Senafe; for although the glass goes down to 36° or 37°, there is no wind at night and very little dew, so that one does not feel the cold as one did at Senafe. It is really a delightful climate; and although 110° in a tent sounds hot, the sensation of heat is nothing approaching that of a sultry July day in England. There is no game here, with the exception of hares, which are very plentiful. Major Fanshawe, of the 33d, went out the other afternoon with his gun, and returned in a couple of hours with a bag of nineteen hares, an almost unprecedented amount of sport for two hours' shooting in an unpreserved country. The natives bring in leopard-skins for sale: where they shoot them I cannot say. They do not find any purchasers, for the amount of baggage allowed is so small, and will be smaller beyond Antalo, that no one will burden themselves with a pound of unnecessary weight.

The 33d went forward three days ago, and Sir Robert Napier himself starts for Antalo on the 17th instant. If the 4th regiment arrive in time they will accompany him. I close my letter rather hastily, as I have just heard there is a mail expected to go three days before the regular packet.

The Commander-in-chief has, since he started from the sea, shown every desire to forward our objects in every way. We were invited to be present at the reception of the Tigre ambassador, and Sir Robert very kindly sent in a *précis* of the information received from Magdala. I am very glad, for the sake of my readers as well as myself, that in future I shall have no fear of either being kept in the dark or of being debarred from accompanying any expedition which may be on foot. I am still more glad to be able to say that the position of the foreign commissioners has been also improved. They are now all forward here, and one of the Prussian officers has been placed upon the Chief's personal staff. This is much more as it should be. Now that we are fairly moving forward, bets are being freely exchanged as to the date of our arrival at Magdala. The first of May is the favourite time. I hardly think we shall be there as soon as that, but must delay the discussion of the pros and cons until my next.

Attegrat, February 17th.

Since I sent my letter off three days ago, nothing has occurred of any great importance; at the same time there is scarce a day passes here without some event of more or less interest taking place. A wing and the head-quarters of the 4th regiment have marched in, and have taken the place of the 33d regiment. The Beloochees are here, and a portion of these have already pushed on to improve the road. On the 15th we had quite a sensation in camp. Two elephants arrived, and 2000 or 3000 of the natives flocked around in a very few minutes. At first they kept at a prudent distance, but, emboldened by the sight of the Europeans standing round and giving the animals pieces of biscuit, they gradually closed in, and talked in tones of admiration and wonder, showing all their white teeth, as is their custom. Presently, however, one of the elephants, not approving of all this hubbub, wheeled suddenly round, his trunk high in the air, and trumpeting loudly. An instant scattering of the natives took place, the crowd flying in all directions as if an infernal-machine had exploded in their midst. They gradually reassembled, but never again ventured to get within familiar distance of the elephants. Yesterday the G-14 battery of Artillery arrived, and created an admiration among the natives that our mountain guns had quite failed to arouse. The guns are twelve-pounders, and have been brought as far as this upon their wheels, a fact which speaks equally for the practicability of the road and for the energy and perseverance of its officers and men. In many places the guns had to leave the road, and to be hauled up difficulties with tackle and handspikes. At the descent into this valley, which I described in a former letter, the road cut along the face of the hill was not of sufficient width for the wheels, and the guns had to be lowered down the steep descent into the valley bottom with tackle. Three hours were occupied in getting the six guns down. They will probably go no further than Antalo upon their carriages, but three will be thence taken on upon elephants; the other three will, at any rate for the present, remain here. This camp is in process of being turned into an entrenched position. The lines have been laid out by Major Pritchard of the Engineers, and the 4th are at present at work upon them. That regiment moves on to-morrow, but the next which takes its place in camp will continue the work. The entrenchments do not include the whole of the present camp, as the number of men permanently stationed here will, of course, be much smaller than at present. The lines will surround the commissariat stores and a portion of the water-pools; they also run round the summit of a steep shelf of rocks in the rear of the camp, and which, when thus strengthened, might be defended by 200 men against 500 similarly armed and disciplined, and therefore against any number of Abyssinians whatever. Even now that we have a strong force here, the people are exceedingly bumptious, and I have little doubt that there will be some row of greater or less importance when they see only a small body of troops stationed here.

Scarcely a day passes that they do not raise their war-cry about something or other. Some of the squabbles arise about our cutting grass; others about wood; others about their insisting upon wandering through the camp; and blows have been exchanged with fists and sticks upon all these and several other points. The noble Abyssinian is quite ready to cut and sell us any quantity of hay, and to charge us an exceedingly-remunerative price for the same. But although we have promised, and, indeed, have paid, a round sum for the privilege, they object strongly to our own men cutting hay, although it is of no use whatever to themselves. Consequently, a guard is always obliged to be sent on with the main body of grass-cutters. Any small parties who may go out in search of forage nearer to the camp than the regular grass plains are warned off, and driven back by the natives. There have been numerous rows on this score, and in some cases the natives have actually set fire to the grass rather than allow us to cut it. If they dared they would not allow a blade of grass to be cut except by themselves. The same questions arise as to wood. They will bring in large quantities of firewood themselves for sale, but they very strongly object to our men collecting it themselves, although there is not, of course, a shadow of pretence to say that our collecting dry wood can in any way damage them. There was a great hullabaloo yesterday on this subject. Two men had gone out for dry wood, and a priest and two or three natives came out and ordered them away. The priest told them that the grove where they were collecting the wood was sacred, and therefore they must not take it. The men of course did not understand a word he said, and expressed their determination to carry off their wood. He then called upon them as Christians to desist, and the men, being Hindoos, made some gestures of contempt or abhorrence at the name of Christians. An attack was then made upon them; but many of these Syces are remarkably strong, active fellows, and in a very short time the Abyssinians found that they had met with much more than their match.

They set up their rallying-cry, and a number more natives hurried up, and the Hindoos would have got the worst of it had not another grass-cutter come up with a gun. The Hindoos then retired, followed by a crowd of enraged Abyssinians. When they reached the camp the Abyssinians attempted to follow them in, and blows had to be freely exchanged before the point of their exclusion was maintained. The priest alone was admitted, and instead of conducting himself quietly he ran about shouting and gesticulating until one of the camp policemen seized him, and, after a struggle, made him a prisoner. When Sir Robert Napier, who was out riding, came into camp, he investigated the whole matter; and, finding that the Syces had been in the wrong by insulting the religion of the people, he ordered them to have a dozen lashes each. But here the Abyssinians really showed themselves to be Christians, for the priest and his witnesses, all of whom bore marks of having suffered in the skirmish, knelt down, and said they would not rise unless the culprits were forgiven, which accordingly they were. This certainly was a remarkable trait. Here were men who conceived that themselves and their religion had been insulted, and who had certainly been well thrashed, really and truly, while their wounds were still fresh, asking forgiveness for their foes. I fancy very few European Christians would have done it. It is pleasant to find a redeeming-point in the character of this nation of extortioners. It is also to be said for them that they are a very merry people, and are constantly on a broad grin. Quarrels among themselves are extremely rare; at least, I have not heard a single dispute since I arrived in this country.

The Abyssinians, too, are men with a strong sporting tendency. They bet freely on the speed of a horse or the accuracy of their aim. They bet, too, with conditions under which very few Englishmen would make a wager. They choose a judge, and the judge, whoever wins, takes the stakes, the loser of course paying. This system of betting, where one may lose and cannot win, is, as far as I am aware, without a precedent, and would do more, if introduced into England, to put down gambling than all the laws that Parliament could pass would do in a hundred years. Another thing to be said for them is that those who know them most like them best, and a stronger argument in their favour than this could hardly be used. Still, undoubtedly, they are fond of fighting, partly perhaps for its own sake, and partly because it would be manifestly impossible for them to put the whole of the hard work of the place on the shoulders of the women and children upon the plea of being warriors, and therefore privileged to do nothing, unless they really did do a little fighting occasionally.

This morning there was another row, which at one time really threatened to come to fighting. One of the natives came inside our lines when the men were at work upon the entrenchments. The policeman—a soldier armed with a stick—warned him back; but he refused to go. Having spoken several times, the sentry pushed him. Whereupon the native drew his sword and rushed upon the soldier, who met him, however, with a tremendous blow of his stick, which knocked him backwards into the ditch with a broken head. The man set up his war-cry, and the natives flocked up, shouting and brandishing their spears. They refused to retire when ordered by the officer to do so, and continued to threaten an attack until Colonel Cameron ordered fifty of his men to load and fix bayonets, and told the natives that unless they retired he should order his men to advance. This was sufficient; and the place was speedily cleared. These little fracas, although trifling in themselves, sufficiently show that the natives are an extremely independent race, and are quite ready for a fight upon the smallest provocation. At present we are so strong as to render any open attack upon their part a hopeless proceeding; but when this post is left with only four or five hundred men I should not be at all surprised if the natives came to blows with us upon some trifling matter or other. The three cannon which are to be left here will no doubt have a salutary effect. The natives are astonished at them, and say that they are much bigger than those of Theodore.

Three of the officers of the 4th regiment saw, the other day, at Fokado, an operation which was described by Bruce, but which has been denied by all subsequent travellers, and by the Abyssinians themselves. This was the operation of cutting a steak from the body of a living ox. They came upon the natives just as they were in the act of performing it. The unfortunate bullock was thrown down, and its four legs were tied together. The operator then cut an incision in the skin near the spine, just behind the hip-joint. He blew into this to separate the skin from the flesh, and then cut two other incisions at right angles to the first, and then lifted a flap of skin four or five inches square. From this he cut out a lump of flesh, cutting with the knife under the skin, so that the amount of flesh taken out was larger than the portion uncovered. The operator then filled up the hole with cow-dung, replaced the flap of skin, plastered it up with mud, untied the feet of the poor animal, which had kept up a low moaning while the operation was going on, gave it a kick to make it get up, and the whole thing was over. I should mention that the operator cut two or three gashes in the neighbourhood of the wound, apparently as a sign that the animal had been operated upon in that part. The officers observed that several of the other cattle of the same herd were marked in a precisely similar manner. They returned in half an hour, and found the animal walking about and feeding quietly. I have not mentioned that it bled very little at the time the operation was being performed. It certainly is very singular that, after so many years, Bruce's story, which has been always considered as a traveller's tale, should have been confirmed. All travellers have denied it. Mr. Speedy, who was a year among them, tells us that he never saw or heard of its being done, and that the Abyssinians, of whom he had inquired respecting the truth of Bruce's statement, had always most indignantly denied it, and indeed had asserted that it would be entirely contrary to their religion, for that they strictly keep the Mosaic law, to eat no meat unless the throat of the animal had been cut and the blood allowed to escape. Anatomists have denied the possibility of an animal when such an operation had been performed being able to walk afterwards. Here, however, was the indisputable fact. The operation was performed, and the ox did walk afterwards. It is true that it might not have been done by Abyssinians proper. The party may have been some wandering tribe belonging to the low country who might have come up for trading purposes. It is very unfortunate that neither Mr. Speedy nor any of the interpreters were at hand to find out the exact tribe to which these savages belonged.

I am unable to give you any reliable account of Major Grant's visit to the King of Tigre. He was, I know, hospitably received, and the horsemen of the King performed various feats, such as riding in and out between poles, and cutting at them; but I am unable to say more, as Sir Robert Napier, no doubt for some good reason of which I am ignorant, refused to allow us to see Major Grant's report, or to have a *précis* of it given to us. It is still reported that the King himself is coming to meet the General, and a place two days on our march towards Antalo is mentioned as the appointed place. We even hear that the King has set out from Adowa for that spot; but I confess that until I see his sable Majesty I shall not have much faith in his coming. Still, these very slippery men always do exactly the thing which one would expect that they would not do; and on this theory only is it quite possible that Kassa may appear *in propriâ personâ*. If he does come it will no doubt be a very much more stately affair than the pantomime I described in my last letter, and I hope that our elephants and cannon will open his Majesty's eyes to the fact that we are a people whom it would be vastly safer to leave alone.

I have been over to-day to the weekly fair at Attegrat. I was also there last Monday, but had no space to give to its description in my last letter. A more amusing sight I have seldom or never seen. Some two or three thousand people must have been present. The fair or market, as I suppose it should be called, is held upon a flat rocky slope on the other side of the village, and this is packed so close that one moves about among the squatting and standing groups with difficulty. At one end is the cattle-fair. The number each grazier brings into market is not large (seldom over two or three), and there they stand in little quiet groups surrounded by their master and several of his friends, and submitting to be felt, pinched, and examined as well as the best-behaved English cow would do. Here, too, are the donkeys, sturdy little beasts, not much bigger than a Newfoundland dog, but which will carry nearly as great a weight as a mule. I wonder our Transport Corps does not buy a lot of them for carrying commissariat stores. They will take two bags each, that is 150 pounds' weight, and require no saddles, for the bags are merely laid upon their broad little backs and strapped there with a few strips of hide; they require no grain, and very little hay, and cost only five or six dollars. Any number of them might be purchased. These, like the oxen, stand very quietly, and appear perfectly indifferent as to any possible change in their ownership. They not unfrequently have young ones by their side, little round rough beasts with disproportionately-long ears and shaggy coats. The goats appear to take matters with less indifference. Their masters endeavour to keep them in little circles, with their heads towards the centre; but they are continually trying to escape from this arrangement, and to make a bolt for it. They keep up a constant bleating as a protest against the whole proceeding. Near to them is the grain-market. Here are men and women with their grain-bags, made of skins of goats sewn up, and with only an opening at the neck. They sit about everywhere, while the buyers walk about among them and inspect the samples with a gravity and intentness which would do no discredit to Mark-lane. Their purchases probably will not exceed two or three pounds' weight, but they are as careful over the matter as a brewer would be who was going to make a bid for a ship's cargo. The grain is almost entirely barley, and splendid barley too. There are beside, however, a variety of other grain, of which I do not know the names. The natives distil a spirit from their barley, which is said to be something between gin and hollands in flavour. I have not yet tasted any. Very thick is the throng round a Parsee belonging to the commissariat, who is buying up all he can get for Government at a dollar for nineteen pounds. Near him is another little crowd: here another commissariat *employé* is similarly engaged in buying up ghee—that is, clarified or boiled butter— for the native troops. It does not look very nice, and what does not make the sight the pleasanter is, that the women, when they have emptied the jars into the commissariat casks, invariably wipe them out with their hands, and then plaster the remainder upon their heads. An Abyssinian does not consider himself properly dressed unless his hair is shining with oil, not put on or rubbed on, but plastered on, and running down his neck as the sun melts it. The idea is not, according to our notions, pleasant, but it is a matter of taste. When an Abyssinian really wants to make a great effect he uses butter, not ghee, and puts it on until his head is as white as that of a London footman. Then he is conscious that he has indeed done it, and walks with a dignity befitting his appearance. There were several swells of the period so got up at the market, and as they stood under the shelter of their straw umbrellas—for the sun would melt it and destroy the whole effect—I could not but wonder at and admire the different forms which human vanity takes.

Further on was the cloth mart. Here were women and men selling the black blankets which almost all women here wear, in addition to the ornamented skins, which form the only garments of the Senafe women. These blankets, which are very large, are worn wrapped round the body, and secured on one shoulder by a large iron pin. The blankets are coarse and thin, and have but little warmth. Officers have, however, bought large numbers for their servants, who feel the cold at night much. When we are stationary for a few days the followers construct some sort of tents with gunny-bags and clothes, but upon the march they have, of course, to sleep in the open air. Near to the vendors of blankets for the women are the sellers of the white-cotton cloth for the men. These are always men; I have seen no women engaged in selling cloth. I have no doubt they carry it to the market, but the men take the sale into their own hands. This is, perhaps, the busiest part of the fair. But beyond this we come to the largest and by far the most amusing portion of all. This is the miscellaneous market. Vegetables and herbs occupy by far the largest share of this. Here are women and girls with herbs of every sort and kind, of very few indeed of which I had any previous knowledge. Here, too, are women with tobacco, very coarse, and broken up roughly, instead of being cut. The tobacco, of course, is carried in the skins, which appear to be the receptacles for everything in this country. Here are men with salt, in shape and appearance exceedingly like a mower's whetstone. These serve as money, and are laid out upon the ground at so many for a dollar, but if the salesman sees a European approaching he will abstract a portion, and demand a dollar for less than half of the number which should be given for that amount. Here are men selling the blue string, which all Christians wear round their neck in token of their faith. Here are men selling the great iron pins, with a rough attempt at ornament upon their heads, which all women use to fasten their blankets upon their shoulders. Here are women with strings of beads, and pumpkins, and watercresses, and dried herbs, and chillies, and honey, and garlic, and potatoes, and young onions for sale. A miscellaneous catalogue, and sold quite as miscellaneously, for the goods are sold by barter more than for money, and each vendor will bring in half-a-dozen small baskets, which she places before her to contain the various articles which she may receive in exchange. Thus, for her beads she may get some grain, a few bulbs of garlic, and a bar or two of salt. Some of these, again, she will barter for a pumpkin, a chicken, and some dried herbs; and so the commerce is carried on. Imagine a large number of these dark-faced, scantily-dressed people, very grave over their purchases, but very merry, as is their wont, in their conversation with each other, the men generally walking about, the women squatting behind their wares, always in groups, and laughing, chattering, and looking after their children—strange little potbellied black figures, with half of their heads shaved, and their sole garment a very small piece of goatskin on their shoulder. Some of the girls are, as I have already said, really pretty, with beautiful brown eyes. They have no objection to be looked at and admired. They pretend, of course, to be very shy, and half hide their faces, and look the other way; but really are very amused and a good deal gratified when a European pauses to look at them. It is singular how similar is the constitution of the female mind in savage and in civilised countries. An English beauty certainly does not betray any consciousness of being looked at and admired, excepting, of course, if she be a milkmaid; but she is no doubt equally conscious, and perhaps just as pleased—except that the sensation is more a matter of course—as is the dark-eyed and dark-skinned Abyssinian girl sitting in her scanty leathern garment and shell-ornamented wrapper in the market at Attegrat.

I do not know when the rainy season begins; indeed, it is a moot point, authorities varying in their dates from April to July; but I know we had a thunderstorm here the other day which nearly washed us out of camp. It began at three o'clock in the afternoon, and found us quite unprepared, as we have had so many threatening-looking skies that we had ceased to believe in rain. However, this time there was no mistake about it. It came up in a dense black cloud from behind the mountain beyond Attegrat. The thunder roared, the lightning was for a while terrific, and for about an hour a tremendous storm of rain and hail poured down upon us. Being an old campaigner, one of my first cares upon pitching my tent had been to have a trench dug round it; but very many officers, relying upon the fine weather, had neglected taking this precaution. Knowing what the state of things would be, immediately the rain ceased I sallied out. The camp was completely under water. As I have mentioned in a former letter, it is pitched upon the gradual slope of a hill, and down this slope a perfect stream of water came nearly two inches deep. As the rain held up, a few figures might be observed peering out of their tents to examine the skies, and as soon as it was quite certain that the rain was over, the camp, which had five minutes before appeared perfectly deserted, was like an ant-hill suddenly disturbed. Great was the devastation the flood had wrought. Through many of the tents it had swept in a flood two inches deep, soaking everything placed upon the ground. Here we saw the servants bringing out a bed, which, having been placed upon the ground, was drenched with water; here was another party bringing out hay with which some particular man had carefully carpeted his tent; here was an officer emptying out his trunks to see if the things at the bottom had suffered. As I wandered about I met Major Minion, the principal commissariat-officer here. He was hastening to the Chief for authority to issue first-class flour instead of second to the troops, as a great deal of the first quality had got wetted, and must be issued at once to prevent its being spoiled. Of course the native followers and others who had no tents suffered most of all; and the camp in a short time presented the appearance of undergoing a general washing-day, so many were the garments hung out to dry. Of course, in accordance with the old proverb of shutting the door after the horse was stolen, there was at once a great demand for picks and shovels, and everyone who had not already done so set to work at digging a trench round their tents. The night after the storm was much less cold than the preceding one had been, and the whole country looks fresher and brighter for the washing. And now as to our most absorbing topic, the advance. It takes place positively to-morrow. Sir Robert Napier himself goes on, and is accompanied by the Artillery, 3d Native Cavalry, five companies of the 4th King's Own, and the remaining three companies of the 10th Native Infantry. The Beloochees were also to have gone forward, but there is not sufficient transport, and they will follow in a day or two. The little party of Engineers also go forward with the photographic and signalling apparatus. The two elephants will also form part of the train. The march hence to Antalo is eight days' journey, which are divided as follows: Mai Wahiz, 13 miles; Ad Abaga, 15; Dongolo, 12; Agula, 14; Dowlo, 19; Haig Kullat, 9; Afzool, 9; Antalo, 5: total, 96 miles. Colonel Phayre, who has again gone ahead, reports that the road presents no great difficulties; but it does not appear as if the first day's march were by any means an easy business, for the baggage-guard of the 33d regiment, which left here at nine o'clock in the morning, did not arrive at its destination until six o'clock on the following morning. The Commander-in-chief rode out next day, and found the road really impracticable at two or three places. He was exceedingly angry that the corps which has gone ahead nominally to make this road should have left it in such a state. A party of the Beloochees were at once set on, and it is to be hoped that by to-morrow they will have made it passable. The party of Bombay Sappers and Miners, who have done such good work in the pass, have gone on to-day, with instructions to keep a day's march ahead of the Chief. They will improve, as far as they can, any very difficult places; but as they will have to progress as fast as the troops, they will of course be able to do very little. The last two days' march even Colonel Phayre reports to be exceedingly difficult, as, instead of the flat sheets of sandstone over which much of the preceding day's journey passes, we here have to cross sheets of bare limestone, upon which horses can stand with difficulty. He states that it will be necessary to strew soil or sand upon the rocks to make them at all passable. It is evident, therefore, that we shall have some serious difficulties to encounter even between this and Antalo; still, we may expect to be at that town by the end of the month. From thence to Magdala it is 160 miles, or thereabouts; for it is impossible to reckon within twenty miles in a country where the mountains and gorges necessitate such constant windings. I mentioned in my last letter that bets were freely offered and taken that we arrive at Magdala by the 15th of April. The whole question is one of provision and transport; and the most casual examination of the question will show that it will be a very long time before the provision for the onward march can be collected at Antalo. I related in my letters a month since how hard a task it was to feed the troops at Senafe and along the pass, and to accumulate provisions in our advance to Attegrat. Senafe is only five days' march from Zulla; Antalo is sixteen; and, allowing for the mules to stop one day at Senafe, and one at Attegrat, to rest, which would be absolutely necessary, it is eighteen days from Zulla. We shall have twice as many troops to feed at Antalo as we had at Senafe; and as it is three times as long a journey, it will require six times as many transport-animals to feed the troops at Antalo now to what were required to feed the former force at Senafe. In addition to this, we shall have a body of troops at Attegrat, and another at Senafe, to feed. The Transport Train is more efficient now than it was a month since, but it is not greatly more numerous, as the number of fresh arrivals is almost balanced by the number of mules going daily into hospital, broken down with over-work, bad feeding, and sore backs brought on by the pack-saddles. The fact of the road being now practicable for carts to Senafe, is also an assistance to the Transport Train; but I confess that I cannot see how they will manage to provision all the line, much less to accumulate stores. It is, we have just seen, eighteen days from Zulla to Antalo. Supposing that the mules go regularly up and down, stopping two days at each end to rest, it will take them forty days to make the circuit. Putting the number of available transport-animals at 16,000, which is over the mark, there would be only four hundred a-day to start from the sea-coast. When it is remembered that these four hundred animals would have to carry their own food for those places at which grain cannot be obtained, that they have to carry the rations for their drivers for the forty days, that they have to provision the different minor posts, together with Senafe and Attegrat, it will be seen that the quantity of provisions which will reach Antalo daily will be by no means excessive. And yet, before we can move forward from Antalo, on a journey which, going and returning, and with a pause of a week at Magdala, can hardly be calculated as under two months, we must have accumulated there a sufficient amount of provisions for the whole time we may be absent; and this not only for the troops and animals who go, but for the force which will remain there during our absence. We must also have a supply accumulated at the posts along the road, as we shall take so large a portion of the transport-animals in our further advance, that we must be sure that a stock has accumulated sufficient to last some time. I hear that the number of mules which will go forward with us from Antalo will be about 6000, with two months' provisions for the column and a certain amount for themselves. Following out the calculation I have made, we prove mathematically that we never can accumulate this 6000 mule-loads at Antalo. Mathematical proofs, fortunately, occasionally are falsified by facts. It was mathematically proved that no steamer could ever cross the Atlantic. The feat was, however, somehow accomplished; and I have no doubt but that, in the teeth of mathematics, we shall somehow or other accumulate provisions at Antalo, and shall march on to Magdala; but it must be some time first. I think the 1st of May to be the very earliest date at which we can hope to leave Antalo. Of course much will depend upon the fruitfulness of the country in the immediate vicinity of that town. If we can only obtain sufficient grain to feed our animals, and to lay in a store of provender for them for the advance, it will greatly lessen our difficulties. As far as we have already come, such has not been the case. Even the extreme prices we have given have barely purchased sufficient grain for the daily supply, and animals upon the route have to be fed upon grain brought from Bombay. Still, we must hope for better things. The date of our advance depends almost entirely upon the state of the grain-market at Antalo. We start to-morrow morning at half-past six, and that means that we must be up and moving before five. I must therefore close this letter, but shall write again in time to save the post from Ad Abaga, where I believe we shall halt for a day.

Ad Abaga, Feb. 20th.

I cannot say that starting a convoy of baggage-mules off at half-past six in the morning is a pleasant operation. The order was "that all animals not off by half-past six must wait until after the departure of the column at seven;" that is, allowing for delays, that they would not be able to start until eight. I acceded to the suggestion of my travelling-companion that we should get our mules off early. At five we were up, completed our packing, had a cup of chocolate and a speedy wash, and then struck our tent, which was wet through with the heavy dew. Folding this up and getting it into a sack meant to contain it only when dry, was a long operation, trying to the temper and very destructive to the finger-nails. However, it and all our final preparations, including the loading the animals, were completed in time, and we were fairly *en route* at twenty minutes past six. We have long since come to the conclusion that the only way to get our baggage along is to be our own baggage-guard, and one or other of us, generally both, accompany it the whole distance. In this way we got into camp in the afternoon, from an hour and a half to two hours earlier than if we had trusted it only to the servants and drivers, and had we ridden on at our own pace we should only have had to wait doing nothing, and without a shelter, for three or four hours. On the present occasion my friend started with the baggage and I remained behind to see the column start. It was a pretty sight, and must have astonished the natives not a little. First came the 3d Native Cavalry, about three hundred strong, in their soldierly blue-and-silver uniforms. This regiment has had no easy time of it since their arrival at Attegrat, for we are exceedingly short of cavalry, and since the Scinde Horse went on, the 3d have had to furnish all the guards and escorts. For some days they had only eighteen men left in camp. I hear that two hundred horses have arrived at Zulla as remounts in the place of those they have lost by the disease. The strength of the regiment will then be raised to its original number of nearly five hundred sabres. I mentioned in a letter, some time since, that this regiment had been looked upon with some disfavour by the authorities for having started from Bombay without the baggage-animals with which, according to the terms of their agreement, they should have furnished themselves. This fault they have done their best to remedy by purchasing every mule they could get. They have now nearly made up their number, and upon the present march only had to draw thirty-five transport-animals, which they hope in a few days to be able to dispense with. Next to the 3d Native Cavalry came the Artillery, who had, at the last moment, received orders to take four guns instead of three. The guns were all drawn by eight horses. The greater part of the horses of this battery are very light grays, and two of the guns are horsed entirely by grays. They are in admirable condition, and look exceedingly well. Next followed the little party of Engineers. Behind them came the 4th King's Own, in their light-brown, or rather dust-coloured suits, with their band playing the "Red, White, and Blue." Colonel Cameron sets an excellent example to his men and officers by having his horse led, and by always marching at their head. The line was closed by the 10th Native Infantry, their band playing "Nelly Bligh." After the troops came the head of a long line of baggage-animals. Having seen the column pass, I rode on and rejoined my baggage.

The road, as usual, leads over the plateau, with occasional steep ascents and descents. Two of these ascents turned out quite impracticable for artillery, and the road as made reflects great discredit upon those who went on in command of the pioneer force to make the way. The roads are made with short, sharp zigzags, where it is impossible for the horses to draw. Had not the artillery been accompanied by a strong force of infantry it would have been impossible to have got the guns up. As it was, the guns were pulled up the straight places by the horses aided by the men, and then the horses were taken out, the guns unlimbered, and the gun was dragged up first, round the curve, by the infantry with ropes, and the limbers were taken up afterwards. The work of getting the guns up one of these ascents occupied over two hours. Sir R. Napier is naturally extremely angry, as, had he not been informed by the officer in advance that the road was perfectly practicable, he would of course have sent on a strong working-party some days previously. I reached Mai Wahiz at half-past twelve, the 3d Cavalry having got in half-an-hour before me. In the afternoon we had another severe thunderstorm, with heavy rain, which fortunately only lasted about half-an-hour. Our camp at Mai Wahiz, instead of being, as usual, on a plain, or rather a slight rise near the plain, was placed upon a hill. I hear that in future we are always to encamp on a hill, or at any rate, as far as possible, in a defensible position. This shows that our Chief places exceedingly little faith in any protestations the Tigre king may make, and that he thinks that, even if he does come in to the durbar at this place, yet that he is not to be trusted out of sight. Everything at Mai Wahiz is very scarce, and forage dearer than ever. I had to pay two dollars for about eighteen pounds of barley for my baggage-animals, that is, just sixpence a pound. Hay is equally dear. The commissariat served out no hay to the transport-animals, and all that they had after a hard day's work, with the prospect of another equally hard on the morrow, was three pounds of grain each.

From the foot of the hill we rode for some distance along a wide valley, with water in several places, and a good deal of cultivated ground. Then, after three or four miles of undulating plain we arrived at our camping-ground at a little after three o'clock. The natives here must be either a more warlike people than those whose villages we have passed since entering the country, or they must have much more warlike neighbours. For the villages are almost always surrounded by strong walls, and one or two were perched on eminences, and defended by walls and towers. One very curious castle we passed strongly resembling the old baronial castles one meets with in southern Scotland and the north of England. This was situated upon the edge of a precipice, and the rocks went sheer down from three sides of its walls for fifty or sixty feet. It must be impregnable in a country like this, where cannon are all but unknown. Another fort, which certainly looked of European construction, and if not must unquestionably have been built from a picture of a European fort, was perched upon the top of the mountain near where we descended into the valley. The precipice at its foot was at least a thousand feet down, but curiously enough the fort was in a sort of hollow, higher rocks at the distance of only a hundred yards on either side commanding it. If a European designed it, he certainly did not choose its position. It was a round fort, of perhaps fifty feet high, but it was difficult to judge its height from our position on the plain so much below it. Its diameter was about equal to its height. It had regular lines of loopholes, and appeared to have been built by some robber-chief to enable him to swoop down upon the caravans of traders journeying up and down the road we had just come. This camp is at about the same elevation as that at Mai Wahiz, and the climate is even more charming than that of Attegrat, for the heat is less during the day, and the cold last night was not at all equal to that which we experienced there. The *on dit* is that the King cannot arrive to-day, but will come to-morrow, and that we shall move out early and pitch our camp upon a plain six miles from here, and there receive him properly.

Dongolo, Feb. 26th.

The King of Tigre has turned out to be a living entity and not a mythical being, as we had begun to consider him. He was to have paid us a visit at Attegrat, but he sent us an ambassador in his place, and no one thought that we should ever hear any more of the King. However, he sent to say that he would meet us upon a plain near Ad Abaga, and we journeyed there, rather incredulous but still hopeful. The King was to have been at the appointed spot upon the day after we had reached Ad Abaga; but messengers sent out brought news that, although it was currently reported that he had started from Adowa, he had certainly not arrived anywhere in the neighbourhood. As it was most important that we should see the King, and remain upon friendly terms with him, and as it was certain that if he had started to meet us, and found that we had gone on without stopping to see him, he would feel grievously affronted, the Commander-in-chief determined to wait. Fortunately, any delay we might experience could be of no importance to us, as it will be impossible to move forward from Antalo until a large stock of provisions are accumulated there, and whether we waited a week at Ad Abaga or at Antalo was perfectly immaterial. Wait accordingly we did for three days, before any reliable news reached us. At last we heard for certain, as we believed, that the King was at Hanzein, twelve miles off. This was on Saturday, and the messenger said that of course the King would not move on Sunday, but that he would come in on Monday morning to Mai Dehar, the appointed meeting-place.

On Sunday Major Grant, Captain Moore, and Mr. Speedy set out to meet the King, and accompany him to the meeting-place. They rode out to Hanzein, and found a considerable body of armed men there, and some of the princes. They were told that the King was five miles further on, and five good miles they rode, and, again inquiring for his Majesty's whereabouts, found that the miles must have been Irish ones, for that the King was still five miles further on. They decided to return, and at Hanzein had another interview with the men in authority there. These worthies tried very hard to induce them to concede, on the part of Sir Robert Napier, that he would come as far as Hanzein to meet the King. Their object in this was, of course, to enhance the dignity of the King in the eyes of his own people, by making us come as far out of our way as possible to meet him; Major Grant, however, altogether refused to concede this point. He stated that we had already waited four days, and that unless the King moved forward at once, Sir Robert Napier would proceed upon his journey without seeing him. Major Grant then started with Major Pritchard of the Engineers, who had gone out to Hanzein with Lieutenant Morgan and his party of signallers, to return to camp. As it was dark when they started, they of course lost their way, and wandered about for some hours, leading their horses, which had two or three awkward falls. They arrived in camp at two o'clock in the morning. They did not pass any of the signallers' posts on their way, and consequently Lieutenant Morgan and his men remained up all night, to flash the news across the hills of the hour of the King's starting from Hanzein. Captain Moore and Mr. Speedy remained at Hanzein until the next day, and were hospitably, if not agreeably, entertained, with a repast, consisting of a large dish of half-baked bread, over which melted fat had been poured with a liberal hand. While they were occupied in endeavouring to find a morsel less saturated with fat than the rest, two or three of the chiefs showed them how the food should be eaten, by thrusting some exceedingly dirty hands into the mess, rolling up a large ball, and cramming it into their mouths. Captain Moore underwent a strong internal struggle, but conquered his desire to rush into the open air, and nobly shut his eyes and followed the example. Mr. Speedy—whose residence in Abyssinia has rendered him the reverse of dainty in matters of food—had already set-to with the grave complacency of a man who enjoys his repast.

On Monday a messenger came in who reported that the King had really arrived at Hanzein, and would come on to Mai Dehar early next morning. A native in our pay having verified this report, orders were issued for a move at daylight the next morning. The party was to consist of the four guns of Murray's battery, a squadron of 3d Native Cavalry, four companies of the 4th Regiment, one company of the 10th Native Infantry, the party of Engineers with their signalling and photographing apparatus, and two elephants. Although Mai Dehar was only five miles off, the troops were ordered to take their tents and baggage, as it was uncertain at what hour the proceedings might be over; and as the next march on to this place was only ten miles, they would be able to march straight through the next day, and would therefore lose no time by sleeping at Mai Dehar.

By seven o'clock we were all out of Ad Abaga, and by half-past nine the tents were pitched at Mai Dehar, which was not more than a four-mile march distant. Mai Dehar is a basin of about half a mile in diameter, with gradually-sloping sides, and possesses no picturesque effect whatever. A small stream runs through it, and the whole basin is covered with a long thick growth of hay. Orders were at once issued that no fires should be lighted or pipes allowed until the grass was all cut in the immediate vicinity of the tents, and for some little distance round the horses. This, of course, was a work which occupied some time; and at about eleven, before the fires were fairly alight, Mr. Speedy, who had gone straight on to meet the King, rode into camp with news that he had left him half an hour before, and that in a very few minutes he would arrive. In ten minutes a dark mass of figures showed upon the crest of the opposite rise of the valley, and presently a tent of bright scarlet colour rose in their midst, and showed that the King was present among them. Mr. Speedy again rode off to say that the Commander-in-chief would move forward to meet him in an hour. By that time the men had breakfasted, and at half-past twelve, when the bugle sounded the assembly, all were ready for any work they might be called on to do. They were formed in line a few hundred yards behind the tent, which had been pitched near the little stream for the durbar. Major Grant, Captain Moore, and Mr. Speedy now rode forward again towards the King's tent, accompanied by an escort of 3d Native Cavalry. Several officers who were not on duty, but who had come over on leave from the camp at Ad Abaga, also rode upon the flank of the cavalry, and among them I took my place.

The native army was ranged in line on both sides of the royal tent; they were not formed in any regular order, but stood thickly together, with the extremities of their line advanced in the form of the crescent of a young moon. There was no pressing or noise; all stood perfectly quiet as we advanced, and it was evident at once that we were in the presence of a greatly more formidable body of men than we had given Abyssinia credit for possessing. The only sound that broke the silence was the beating of a number of drums. These I afterwards had an opportunity of examining, and found them to be of the same shape, and as nearly as possible the same size, as our own kettledrums. Instead of being of metal, they were of thin wood, and were covered with skins with the hair on in the place of parchment. They were carried one on each side of a mule. There were six mules so laden, and the drums were beaten, some with small sticks, some with large and heavy ones. These last served as big drums, and kept time to the constant beating of the small ones. They played a sort of tune which, if rather monotonous, was by no means unmusical. The principal drummer had a red umbrella held over his head—a distinction enjoyed by no other person except his Majesty himself. When we had arrived within forty or fifty yards of the King's tent we halted. Major Grant and his party alighted from their horses and entered the royal tent, and the cavalry were drawn up in line parallel to the road the King would pass down on his way to the stream. Major Grant's mission was to inform the King that Sir Robert Napier was ready, and would advance to meet him as soon as he saw the King had left his tent. Some personages in authority now gave some orders, and a body of four or five hundred men took their places a short distance in front of the royal tent. Some of these men were on foot, some mounted; the great majority were armed with guns of some kind, and in addition carried shield and sword. The remainder had lances. There was a far greater variety of costume, and much more brilliancy of colour, among their body than we had any notion of seeing in Abyssinia. The majority, of course, had the whitey-brown cotton cloth of the country, with generally the red ends and fur tippets with long ends which are distinctive of a warrior of rank. Many, too, had a lion's mane over their shoulders, which is a sign that they have slain many enemies in battle. Very many too had on long shirts of state, reaching to the knees, and made of richly-brocaded silks, generally green, blue, or red, with yellow flowers. Some, the greatest dandies of all, wore mantles of velvet, violet being the prevailing colour. These reached a little below the waist, and were then cut into long tails of peculiar pattern, which, moreover, was always similar. These, who gave orders, and who were probably generals, were not bareheaded, as were all the rest of the Abyssinians, but had a coloured silk-handkerchief over and around the head, Bedouin fashion, and falling down upon the neck, with a sort of fillet or coronet of metal, which looked like tin, but may have been silver, round their foreheads. Of this body, which was evidently composed of chiefs and warriors of distinction, about equal numbers were mounted and on foot. Very many of the mules carried double, which is here considered by no means an *infra-dig.* method of travelling. In front of this body of men the band of drums took up their station, and in the rear five or six men blowing an instrument somewhat resembling a clarionet in appearance, except that it has only one note. Some of them were, however, pitched a tone above the others, so that the general result, although not so musical as that of the drums, was yet not discordant.

The King now came out of his tent, and mounted a mule. A dozen or so princes and personal attendants rode or walked near him, and two attendants walked one on each side, leaning against the mule, and supporting him, as it were, in his saddle. One held a large Magenta-silk umbrella over the King's head. Kassa is a man of seven or eight and twenty. He was plainly dressed in a swathing of native cloth, the only distinction between himself and an ordinary warrior being that, in place of a broad scarlet end, it had a sort of Cashmere pattern. The princes had similar borders to their robes. The King wore a fur tippet, and the cloth was wrapped round and round him, so that his arms were not visible, and he looked a mere bunch as he sat upon his mule. The cloth was brought up round his chin and mouth. He was bareheaded; his hair was plaited in lines from the forehead to the back of the head, in the peculiar manner I have before described, and which exactly resembles that upon some of the Assyrian wall-paintings in the British Museum. These plaits are each tied at the end, and form a little bunch of tails at the back of the neck. Kassa has a mild and rather irresolute face, and was evidently nervous at the unaccustomed ceremony he was about to go through. I believe that his face does not belie his character, and that he is quite guided by three or four of his principal advisers. Puppet kings are not confined to Abyssinia. Major Grant rode by the side of the King, and conversed with him through the medium of Mercher, the interpreter. The mule ridden by the King, and those of the principal personages, all had the gay green-and-red embossed leather trappings I described as adorning the mule ridden by the ambassador who came in to Attegrat. There were several priests in the train, distinguished as usual by their turbans and the whiteness of their robes. In my description of the King's dress I have said nothing of his leggings or shoes, for the reason that he, as well as everyone of his nation, had bare legs and feet. Immediately the King had started, I closed-in with the unattached officers behind him, and the 3d Native Cavalry came on behind us. In the rear of them, and keeping a perfect line, came the main body of native troops—horsemen in front, footmen behind them. The whole effect was extremely picturesque, and, as seen from the opposite side of the valley, must have been most striking. As soon as we were in motion, we saw Sir Robert Napier approaching from the opposite camp. He rode in a howdah upon an elephant with scarlet trappings; behind followed the other elephant, and his staff rode around him. The troops remained in a line at some little distance in rear of the durbar tent, the 10th Native Infantry being drawn up as a guard of honour in front of the tent. When we were about three-quarters of the distance down the slope upon our side of the hill, the body-guard in front of the King halted, and fell back upon each side, leaving a road, through which the King and his personal following rode. The 3d Native Cavalry followed, but the natives formed line again in the rear and halted. Sir Robert Napier arrived first at the stream, but the elephant refused to cross, and the General then alighted and mounted his horse, and again advanced to meet the King, who had by this time crossed the stream. Sir Robert and the King shook hands, and then rode together to the durbar tent. There everyone dismounted, and as many as the tent would accommodate entered. I was fortunate enough to be one of these. The King and the Commander-in-chief took seats in two chairs. Five of the principal princes sat upon the ground. The King's shield-and-spear-bearer stood behind him, and several other native attendants stood near. About a dozen European officers ranged themselves round the sides of the tent. At the moment of entering the tent, the guard of honour and the artillery fired a salute, which caused a great commotion among the horses, and I have no doubt rather startled and alarmed the King of Tigre's army, which had all remained upon the other side of the stream. Throughout the day the greatest discipline prevailed upon this point, not a single man crossing the stream, with the exception only of the King's personal attendants.

The conversation between Sir Robert Napier and the King was interpreted by Mercher and by his brother, who formed part of the King's retinue. Both these brothers are Tigre chiefs, who were curiously enough sent to Bombay to be educated, and to learn the English language. The conversation was of the most formal kind. Sir Robert expressed his hope that the King was not fatigued with his journey. The King replied that he was never tired when he came to see his friends. Here the conversation languished a little, and then Sir Robert expressed the pleasure that we English, who sent missionaries to all parts of the world, experienced at finding a Christian nation here in the midst of Africa. To this the King replied, that he did not wish to see strangers in his country, but that if strangers came he preferred that they should be Christians. This was a decided damper; but Sir Robert, after a pause, rallied nobly, and said that we had a most friendly feeling for all the Abyssinians, with the exception only of the bad men who held our countrymen captive. The King replied that Theodore was our common enemy, and that he hoped we should punish him as he deserved. The General then inquired the names of the princes present, and found that one was an elder brother, and two were uncles of the King. These were all intelligent-looking men, with fine faces for Abyssinians. The King's elder brother is a much more resolute and determined-looking man than the King. These men, as well as the King, we could now see, upon their sitting down and getting their arms a little free from the wrappings of cloth, had very large golden armlets, or rather wrist-ornaments, of exactly the same shape as a lady's gauntlet. Sir Robert now said that he wished to present the King with some presents, to demonstrate our friendship. These were a double-barrelled rifle by Purday, some handsome Bohemian glass vases, and the horse upon which he himself rode when he met the King. By the way, I question much if the King will ever trust himself upon the horse, which is a high-spirited and rather restive animal, and which upon our leaving the tent completely overpowered the native to whom it had been delivered, and had finally to be taken up to the royal tent by its own syce. The meeting now was over, that is, it was over as a public meeting, and all retired from the tent except two or three confidential officers on either side. What had preceded was merely a formal opening, and the interview was now really interesting. I am, of course, unable to give the details, but the general substance was that the King now entirely threw aside his reserve, and said that he hoped for our support in the disputes which will arise upon Theodore's defeat. Sir Robert Napier "assured the King of our friendship, but stated that his Queen had sent him here solely with the design of rescuing our countrymen, but that she had given him strict orders on no account to take any part in the unfortunate dissensions which were taking place in the country. We have, as we marched onward to this place, seen everywhere the signs of these unfortunate wars, in the fields lying uncultivated, and in the deserted villages, and he hoped to hear that with the destruction of the power of Theodore, this most unfortunate state of things would cease. At the same time he assured the King that he might rely that if we could give him no support we should also abstain from giving any assistance whatever to his rivals." Kassa afterwards, in answer to a request of the Chief, promised that he would send messengers to the principal towns upon our route, ordering the inhabitants to do all in their power to furnish us with provisions and supplies. After the interview was over, the King and princes were supplied with wine and spirits, not, however, without some difficulty, for there are very few bottles of wine remaining in the camp of the advancing column. There was then a pause of an hour or two, after which our troops were paraded, and went through a few manœuvres before the King. These were not of much interest, as no powder was expended, and the ground, being full of deep holes, hidden by long grass, was most unfavourable for the movements of either artillery or cavalry. The action of the Armstrongs was also explained to the King. After this the troops returned to camp, and Sir Robert Napier and his staff crossed the stream with the King to pay a return visit to the royal tent. The natives, who had been clustered by the stream, all rose at his approach, and the drums struck up their strange music. We were now enabled, riding as we were among a dense throng of natives, to judge more accurately of their number and appearance than we had hitherto been able to do. The general opinion was, that there must have been about three thousand, three-quarters of whom were armed with guns. They were a fine, active-looking set of men, and in a rough country would make formidable antagonists even for trained soldiers. These men are known to be brave, and are fairly armed, but Theodore's army has always defeated them. Theodore's army must, therefore, have been by no means despicable antagonists; and although that army has now dwindled to four or five thousand men, it is probable that that four or five thousand are the most desperate characters and the most warlike warriors of his original force. Strong as Magdala naturally is, and garrisoned by a few thousand such men as these, it may possibly be a hard nut even for a British army to crack.

Arrived at the King's tent, which is of considerable size, Sir Robert Napier entered with the King, princes, and as many of his staff as the tent would accommodate, and took seats upon the carpeted ground. Here refreshments, small flat bread, and native liquors of fermented honey and herbs, and native spirits, were served round. Sir Robert Napier was declared by the King to be a good warrior, and the King presented him with his own lion-mane tippet, his own sword, shield, and spear, the mule he had himself ridden at the interview, with its saddle and trappings, and a silver gauntlet. After about half an hour the Commander-in-chief took his leave.

As I rode up towards the tent I was smoking a cigar, and this attracted the greatest attention and astonishment from the natives who were crowding round. It was evident they had never seen a cigar before. I gave away several to the chiefs, who, however, were quite in the dark as to what to do with them when they had got them. I offered them my cigar to light those I had given them from; but they had no idea what to do with it, and were on the point of putting it into one of their mouths, when I rescued it, and struck a light with a vesuvian. This astonished them even more than the cigar. However, they lit their cigars, and smoked them with manifest content, occasionally lending them to their friends for a whiff. Numbers of applications then poured in upon me, which, however, I was obliged to refuse, for cigars are very precious articles here. I left when Sir Robert Napier did, as it was nearly six o'clock, and I wished to get back to Ad Abaga, where I had left my tent and baggage, before it became too dark to follow the track.

The opinion of the King and his principal warriors respecting our troops is similar to that expressed by the natives at the review at Attegrat, namely, that our troops would be invincible upon a plain, but that they would have no fear of us upon a mountain side. Our cannon are not so large as they had expected to see; but they said that they had heard great things of our rockets, which rush through the air with a tremendous noise, and destroy those who are not killed by their explosion by a noxious vapour which is fatal to man and beast. They are thoroughly convinced that we have great power of enchantment; and this will probably do more to retain their neutrality than any fear of our arms would do. They say that by enchantment we have tamed the elephants; by enchantment we have kept the rain from falling near the sea-coast, and interrupting our work in the pass; by enchantment we have made the locusts disappear the moment we came up on to the high country; and therefore that were we offended, we should by enchantment also prevent rain from falling over the whole country, and thus create a dreadful famine in the land.

As the natives are impressed by enchantment, and are not at all impressed by our soldiers, I should propose that in any future war of the same kind there should be an officer appointed under the title of magician to the forces, and that he should have subordinate officers as assistant magicians and deputy-assistant magicians. The duty of these officers should be to exhibit signs and wonders. Mr. Anderson might perhaps be induced to undertake the control of the machine tricks and general magic; Mr. Home would do the spiritual business, and could astonish the native mind with the sight of elephants floating in the air, or could terrify a negro potentate by tweaking his nose at a durbar by invisible fingers. One of the deputy-assistant magicians should be a pyrotechnist, whose duty would be to light up the camp with unearthly fire, and to place strange portents in the midnight sky. Certainly, had this department been organised before the expedition began, and had a few of its officers been present, we might have dispensed with several regiments, and the cost of the expedition would have been greatly lessened, however munificent the remuneration of the chiefs of the department might have been. Should Government adopt this suggestion, and I have no doubt they will do so, I shall expect a valuable appointment in the corps.

On the day after the last mail left we were favoured with a *précis* of the letters from Magdala which had arrived three days previously. They contained nothing of any great importance. Gobayze and Menelek were both near King Theodore; so near, indeed, that the camp-fires of the former could be seen from Theodore's camp. They were both evidently afraid to attack him; but Gobayze had sent him an insulting message, and Theodore had at once put the unfortunate herald to death. Theodore was making very slow progress; and it was thought that he would not arrive until the end of March at Magdala. He was ten hours' ride from that fortress, which would mean about twenty-five miles. Even if he travels at half the reported rate of speed, he will be there before us. The opinion is general now that we shall have a fight at the end of our journey.

Doullo, February 29.

We arrived here yesterday afternoon, after three days' marching. On the 26th the troops went from Mai Dehar to Dongollo, fifteen miles; on the 27th to Agula, nine miles; and on the 28th to Doullo, fifteen miles. The road has lain across a much more undulating country than that over which we have previously passed. On the first day's march we had one very long and steep descent. This tried the mules; and many were the upsets of packs, many the tired animals who lay down, and refused to move until unsaddled, upon the narrow ledge. Fortunately, however, although long and steep, it was straight, and so the artillery got down with comparative ease and without any accident. The camp was in a valley, where the water was very good, and where there was one pool of deep water nearly 200 yards long, which afforded excellent bathing. There were a good many fish in it, and several were caught of over a pound in weight. This is curious, as it shows that the Abyssinians are by no means skilful fishermen; for Mr. Speedy tells me that during his residence in the country he never saw nor heard of a fish more than three inches long being caught.

The next day's march was a short and rather easy one. The last was not only long, but it had some very long and difficult ascents and descents; indeed, it was one succession of hills for the whole distance. The country has throughout been thinly populated. We have come across several ruined villages, which have probably been destroyed in the constant wars which are raging in this country. The churches, however, have generally been respected; and whenever a really fine clump of trees is to be seen, there is always a church to be found in their shade. Where the villages have been destroyed, the churches are of course deserted, and are more or less falling into ruins. This camp is pitched in a wide valley, and we are procuring more supplies than usual from the natives. Yesterday we bought 1500lb. of grain, and to-day we are obtaining an even larger supply. Grass, however, is comparatively scarce, and the water is by no means good. Cattle, as usual, are in abundance. We are going on again to-morrow, and shall reach the camp beyond Antalo in two days. I hear very good accounts of the state of the supplies there, and am told that we have bought, in addition to grain, &c., considerable quantities of flour and bread.

This is by far the most satisfactory intelligence we have yet received since we landed in Abyssinia, and if these supplies continue to come in, it will very greatly shorten the duration of our campaign. The great question is to accumulate supplies sufficient for us to march to Magdala. As long as we have to consume the supplies the mules bring up, the process of accumulation must be a very long one. Flour and meat are the only two articles of diet which are of material weight. The preserved vegetables, tea, sugar, and salt, amount together to under six ounces per diem per man; and one mule would therefore carry the rations of 500 men of these articles. When we reach Antalo and join the advanced force our number will not exceed 1200 Europeans, and 50 mules will carry three weeks' rations for them, exclusive of meat, which we can always purchase, flour, and rum. At present the ration of rum is one drachm a day, but it is possible that at any moment this may be stopped; and it is at all events probable that no rum will be carried beyond Antalo. If, therefore, we can purchase flour and meat along the march, and the Europeans of the advance force number 3000, we shall only require six mules a day to carry their rations, or 186 mules for a month's supply. Of course this calculation will not hold good for our journey, as it is most improbable that we shall succeed in getting flour or bread along the road; but if we can only buy sufficient quantities for our consumption while we are stopping at Antalo, it will be an immense relief to the transport-train. The native bread is not at all bad. It is baked in cakes about an inch thick and eight inches in diameter. It is dark in colour, and sometimes sour; but I have tasted some as good bread as one could wish to eat. The price I have paid here is a dollar for five of these loaves, weighing about a pound and a half each. Wood is very scarce, a dollar being charged for four bundles of sticks weighing under ten pounds a bundle.

The pause of to-day is made partly to enable the artillery to repair a wheel of one of their store-wagons, which broke in coming down the last descent, partly to rest the animals, which now, after four days' work, greatly needed a day's rest. We require more cavalry with us. The 3d Native Cavalry have had tremendously hard work; what with marching and picket-duty, the men never get more than two nights in the week in bed, and sometimes not more than one. It is surprising how the animals, with so great an amount of work and with insufficient food, keep in such good condition as they are at present. All the animals will, however, be improved by a short stay at Antalo.

The weather has very much changed since we left Ad Abaga. We have a strong and really cold north-wind blowing all day, and between five and eight o'clock of an evening it is most cutting. At night it drops; and the temperature is then not so cold as it was either at Senafe or Attegrat. The natives generally are affected with coughs and colds; and the amount of coughing which goes on at night in the vicinity of our tent is both astonishing and disagreeable.

Sir Charles Staveley came up from Zulla, and joined us on the day of our leaving Ad Abaga. He has taken command of the advanced brigade. I hear that, owing to the quantities of stores taken up by the trains which accompanied General Collings's column and our own, the supplies at Senafe and other places along the line were very low; so much so, that the troops who were ordered up have been kept back at Zulla until further stores could be accumulated. I trust that by this time a large stock has been collected at Senafe, as Captain Griffiths, who commanded the portion of the transport-train which went forward with General Collings's column, has just passed downward with his mules to fetch up another supply.

Antalo, March 4th.

When I wrote, four days since, from Doullo, I mentioned that we had news of flour and other stores being purchased in considerable quantities at Antalo, and that if supplies continued to come in, the prospects of the expedition would be altogether changed. But I certainly did not anticipate that we should be able to advance from here under three weeks or a month. Two days before we arrived here, indeed, there were rumours of a much earlier move than had been anticipated; and an order was issued that in all probability we should be compelled to go forward without either rum, tea, or sugar. Of course everyone is prepared to make great sacrifices, and to submit to every hardship which may be absolutely necessary. Every reduction of kit, the dismissal of the native followers, and the diminution of carriage, has been received not only without a murmur, but with actual satisfaction by everyone. The reductions were felt to be necessary; for in no other way would it be possible to penetrate this inhospitable country. It was considered probable that beyond Lât we should have to go without tents, and with only a blanket and one change of clothes; and I have not heard an expression of repugnance or complaint at the prospect: but this order to proceed without rum, tea, or sugar, was received with the gravest dissatisfaction by men and officers of all ranks. It was not as a matter of comfort that it was objected to, but as a matter of health. Rum is an article difficult of carriage, and can be dispensed with; sugar also might be done without; but tea is upon a campaign like this an absolute necessity, if the men are to have no rum. It is not that the tea is nice, for it certainly is not; it is positively nasty. It bears no resemblance whatever to the herb we drink in England as tea; at the same time it is an absolute essential. The mornings and nights are very cold; the troops are on the move at half-past five in the morning, when everything is saturated with dew; they are hard at work all day; their picket-duty is very severe; and to give them with their breakfast in the morning and their supper at the end of their day's work nothing but cold water to drink, was simply to send the whole army into hospital. Were the water good, the results might not have been so disastrous, but it is almost always drawn from stagnant pools, and is the reverse of wholesome. Officers generally drink the water only after filtering, but the men never think of taking the trouble. Boiling the water is no doubt even superior in its effect to filtering it; but the men would certainly not boil the water if they had nothing to put in it. They would drink nothing but impure water, which in a country where the changes in temperature are so great and so sudden as they are here, would most certainly bring on dysentery in a very short time. The privation of their rum would in itself be much felt among the men. They have all been some years in India, where rum forms part of a soldier's regular ration. They are accustomed to its use, and no doubt would feel somewhat its sudden privation. Had they been troops fresh from England, it would have mattered comparatively little. Our adjutant-general, Colonel Thesiger, is a total abstainer; I believe that is the polite expression for a teetotaller. Of course his theory is, that men are much better without spirits; and the present will be a great opportunity for testing the effects of a Maine Law. I believe, however, that officers and men would give up their rum and their sugar without a murmur where tea is but allowed them; but I am sure that bad water alone will lay up half the troops. Nor will there be any saving in carriage by leaving tea behind. We shall have to take a greater weight of medicines than we should of the tea. The reason given for thus leaving behind what everyone feels to be, bad as it is, the most precious portion of our stores, was, that we can procure any amount of native carriage, but that the natives will only carry flour and grain, and refuse to undertake the carriage of rum, sugar, and tea, partly because of the greater responsibility, and partly because of the shape of the barrels and casks, which are inconvenient to pack upon the little oxen and donkeys. Everyone asks, Have we, then, no carriage of our own? Have we no available transport-mules besides those carrying the tents? One mule will carry from 150 to 200 pounds weight, which would give 500 men their day's ration of tea. The advance brigade will not contain much over 3000 men, and consequently fifty mules will carry two months' rations of tea for them; and it is an extraordinary thing if, out of the 15,000 baggage-animals in the transport-train, fifty cannot be spared to carry an article which everyone feels to be all-important both for the health and comfort of the troops. I am sure that Sir Robert Napier himself consented with the greatest reluctance to the proposition, and that he shares in the general satisfaction which is experienced at the report that the commissariat find that some of the natives are consenting to take on tea, if it is packed in skins or in stout bags, and that therefore a proportion of tea will at any rate be taken on.

I began this letter by saying that the news of the purchase of flour and grain would, if true, completely change the whole prospect of the expedition. I am happy to say that the news we heard is now more than verified, and that the commissariat are purchasing at the rate of 12,000 lbs. or 14,000 lbs. of flour a day. In addition to this, they are buying sufficient bread for the daily consumption of the troops. Very large convoys of native baggage-animals have also come in during the last few days, and we find ourselves with two months' provision of all kinds, and four months' provision of flour already in hand for the whole of the advanced division. This is a more forward state of things than I expected to have seen in another two months, and entirely alters the prospect of the campaign. Had we found the same dearth of food here which we experienced all along the line, we must have waited so long that it would have been an impossibility to have returned before the rain. Now there is a chance of our so doing.

Sanguine spirits even mention the 1st of April as the probable day for reaching Magdala. If we are there at the end of the first week in April, we shall, should Theodore await us and no hitch occur, start upon our return march by the 15th, pass through this place by the 7th of May, and be at Zulla in another month, that is, before the rains begin. I have, however, seen so many unforeseen obstacles, so many unavoidable delays occur since we first landed, that I cannot put any faith in this sudden express speed. When we arrived here two days since, the intention was that we should march on the 6th. I hear that our advance is now postponed, at any rate, until the 9th; and I should not be surprised if we were here for a week after that date. The fact is, no one knows anything whatever about the roads in front of us. All travellers, with one exception, who have journeyed here have turned to the right at Antalo, and have gone down the valley to Socota. The one exception is Dr. Krapf, and his report of the road is far too vague to be of any practical utility. It only requires a look to the southward of this camp to give us a notion of the country we are going to travel through. A chain of rugged mountains with peak rising beyond peak extends in an unbroken line. Over or through them we have somehow to get, and at present we know next to nothing about them.

A pioneer force of two companies of the 33d, some of the Beloochees, some Punjaub pioneers, sappers, and miners, and the Scinde horse have gone on ahead to make roads, and the reports we have at present received from them are the reverse of favourable.

Lât is our next halting-place; and until we hear that the road to that place is practicable for mules, it is no use advancing from here, where we are living upon the country and consuming no stores.

I now return to the narrative of our march here. From Doullo to Icullot was only an eight-miles' march across a by-no-means difficult country. The next march on to this place was twelve miles, and the country was very undulating; but such an excellent road had been made by the advanced brigade that the mules had no difficulty whatever in crossing it. This road was better than anything we have traversed since we left Senafe. The Commander-in-chief, however, did not go by the same route, but turned off to visit Chalicote, a considerable town lying a little distance out of the line of march.

Chalicote is more prettily situated than any town we have hitherto seen. It lies in a well-wooded valley. The church is in precisely the same style as that at Attegrat, with frescoes drawn apparently by the same hand. I so fully described the church at Attegrat, that any details respecting this would be superfluous.

The Chief was accompanied by some of his staff, and by Mr. Holmes, of the British Museum, who had hoped to acquire some old manuscripts there, especially as he had heard of one said to be of great value, and bound in silver gilt. It turned out, however, to be quite modern; and up to the present time Mr. Holmes, although he has been indefatigable in his search, has not succeeded in finding any manuscript of great antiquity; he has, however, heard of some at a place a little distant from our line of march, which he hopes to acquire upon our return, and which, if they correspond to the description given of them, will be of very great value. It was hardly to be expected that, skirting as the line of march does upon the very edge of the table-land of Abyssinia—a portion of the country remote from the principal towns, and exposed to the constant devastation of border warfare—any remains of very great antiquity would be met with. Had our course led through Axoum, which was the capital of that strange Greek possession of which Adulis or Zulla was the seaport, we might have expected some interesting discoveries to have taken place. There is yet a possibility that we may see Axoum; for although, if there is any chance of getting out of the country before the rainy season, we shall of course make every effort to get back in time, there is a rumour that, if we are obliged to pass the wet season here, a portion of the force will go back by Axoum and Adowa.

This camp is called Antalo, but it is a mere name of courtesy, like that of a good many English railway-stations. It is nearly six miles from the town of Antalo, going by the most direct and most difficult road; eight miles fully by the more accessible path. The position of Antalo was certainly selected more with a view to its defensibility than for its convenience. It lies upon a small undulating plain six or seven hundred feet above the general level of the valley, and at the foot of a very lofty and precipitous hill which rises nearly sheer up fifteen hundred feet above it. This hill is accessible only at one or two places, and walls are built across them; so that it forms a safe retreat for the inhabitants of Antalo in the event of their being attacked by a superior force. This hill fortress is called Amba Antalo. A position such as this is no unnecessary protection in this part of the country, for Antalo lies at the very edge of the territory of the warlike Gallas. These tribes, whenever their harvest is a bad one, gather together and make a foray upon the villages of the plain, and sweep off crops and cattle. Everywhere on the plain are ruined villages, which attest the frequency and ferocity of these forays; and Antalo itself has evidently, and at no very distant time, contained four times as large a population as it does at present. I rode over there the day before yesterday to the weekly fair.

I described fully the market at Attegrat in a former letter; and as this was precisely the same scene upon a rather larger scale, I have little to add to what I then said. Very large quantities of flour were brought in, and the commissariat secured a considerable supply. Numbers of mules, donkeys, and cattle were also there. The small-goods market too was crowded, and herbs and grain of all sorts—onions, chillies, cloth, and most of the other articles I mentioned as having seen at Attegrat—were here, with the exception only of pumpkins, of which I did not see a single specimen. I, however, bought three pounds of coffee, which I look upon as a great prize, as it will be a change from the excessively bitter herb termed by courtesy tea. The commissariat have purchased a considerable quantity of coffee, and I am told we shall find it much more plentiful as we go forward. This will be a very great boon for the men.

I think that the people here are more merry and full of fun than those at Attegrat; they enter, or rather attempt to enter, into conversation much more freely, and really seem anxious to do anything for one. I had at least a dozen of them yesterday all talking together, and endeavouring to make out what I wanted to find out about some small packets of lead-ore which were used as a medium of exchange. It was a rich flaky ore, containing quite eighty per cent of lead, and marking paper freely. I was very desirous of finding out which part of the country it came from; but neither my pantomime nor the united endeavours of the lookers-on to understand me availed to elicit the required information.

During my progress through the country I have not seen any sign of mineral ground, with the exception of some very rich samples of ironstone. During the last three or four days' march the formation has changed several times from sandstone to a hard blue limestone, and *vice versâ*. On the faces of these bare hills it would be easy even at a distance to detect the change of colour or the rising ridges which generally indicate the existence of a vein of mineral; but, as I have said, although I have carefully examined the country as I passed through it, I have seen no mineral indication whatever.

To return to the fair. The scene, as at Attegrat, was very amusing; and the attitude of the groups—the women sitting about everywhere with their baskets, the men leaning upon their spears, the cattle standing about in groups—the whole scene reminded me strongly of an Irish fair, barring only the absence of the friendly pig, with his agonised shriek of expostulation and disgust.

Antalo consists of four or five villages, each standing upon the summits of small rises. They were formerly connected together, and even now are surrounded by ruined huts. The last blow Antalo suffered was three years ago, when it was attacked by the Gallas, incited and led by a rebel against Kassa, named Waldo Yasus. Both Antalo and the villages on the plains suffered greatly at that time; and a terrible attack of cholera, which swept over the country shortly afterwards, completed their ruin. The houses have all high conical roofs, thatched with rushes. Each house has a courtyard surrounded by a high wall. The women here are less picturesque in dress and less pleasing in feature than those of Attegrat. Their morality is lax in the extreme. "A virtuous woman is a crown to her husband:" I fear there are very few crowned heads in Abyssinia. I had left my horse at the foot of the ascent from the plain up to Attegrat, and had walked the last two miles. It was a very hot day, and one of our first inquiries upon reaching the fair was for "tedge." We were conducted to what answered to a public-house. Here we entered, and passing through a sort of outer passage, found ourselves in almost outer darkness. It was some time before we could see sufficiently to avail ourselves of the invitation to be seated, but presently descried two seats or couches, built up of stone and covered with skins. The room was semicircular in form, and very lofty, going up to the thatched roof, which was lined with bamboo; on either side were small chambers, which appeared devoted to miscellaneous purposes; for after we had been some minutes in the place, and were able to see a little, we made out that a donkey was standing placidly at the door of one of these chambers, and that a goat and a fireplace were the principal articles of furniture in the other. The walls of the room were smoothly plastered, and as an abode it no doubt possessed the advantage of coolness, even in the hottest weather. Tedge, as I have before said, is a liquor made from fermented honey and water, with herbs, and tastes like a mixture of small beer and lemonade made from mouldy lemons, and was brought in in a flask very like a Lucca oil-flask, but rather flatter, and with a larger neck. From the neck of this flask we drank by turns; and as it did not hold more than half a pint, and as we were four in number and the day was hot, we demanded more. It seems that no more was strained; so a large jar was brought, the wife of the proprietor put a fold of her very dirty garment over its mouth, and strained the liquor through it into the flask, and we drank it. In calmer moments and in other climes, it is probable that we should not have done so—probable even that a feeling of sickness would have overpowered us. I am happy to say, however, that the army in Abyssinia has altogether overcome any feeling of squeamishness.

I have seen some rum drank in which several cockroaches had committed suicide; and I have assisted to eat honey which was black with ants whose appetites had caused their untimely death. As for cooking, I confess that I avoid the cooking-fires. I have seen sights which have tried my philosophy to the utmost, and am now quite content to eat the very excellent dinners our servants prepare from rations, and not to think of the processes the meat has undergone. My tent-companion and myself pride ourselves much upon our cooks. They are two Goa Portuguese, and are, we flatter ourselves, beyond all comparison the best cooks in camp. Their soups are excellent, their cutlets the best I ever tasted, their preserved potatoes, baked in cakes, delicious. They sent up birds in as good a style as I can get them in a London club. Their pumpkin-pie—when we could get pumpkins—was the talk of camp; the fame of their baked sheep's head, with brain cutlets, came to the ears of Sir Robert Napier himself. Imagine, then, our feelings, when the stern decree was emanated—all native servants whatever are to be sent away; each officer is to carry 75 lb. of luggage, including bed, cooking-utensils, and plates and dishes; and three officers are to be allotted to each bell-tent. Heads of departments only are to be allowed a bell-tent between two. At first we had believed that this order did not apply to us; that having our own baggage-animals, and providing our forage, &c. at our own cost, and the tent being our own property, we thought that it was a matter which concerned no one but ourselves as to what or who we took on with us. But we were deceived. Quartermaster-generals, eager to effect the greatest possible cutting down, had their eyes upon the special correspondents and the scientific gentlemen who accompany the camp; and we were officially informed that we must be amenable to the same rules as others. We pointed out that we found our own carriage, and therefore that the weight we carried mattered to no one; but were sternly informed that if we purchased grain for our animals, there was so much the less available for the public service. To a certain extent this was true; and so we said that we were ready to go on with the weight that other officers were allowed, but that the tent in the first place was our own, and that it would be quite impossible for three men to write in a tent together. We were ready, therefore, to carry less than the permitted 75 lbs. of baggage, in order to have half a tent each; so that our total kit, including tent, would not exceed the prescribed 140 lbs. Our friends in the quartermaster department were quite unable to grant us this request, and it was only upon a personal application to Sir Robert Napier that we gained our point, as, upon our stating the case, he at once consented to our retaining our own tent to ourselves. The next question was that of servants. "All servants to be sent back, a grass-cutter only being allowed for each horse." At first we thought we should be obliged to send our servants back. Fortunately, however, a grass-cutter is allowed for each horse; and as we have each two horses, we have retained our cooks under the title of grass-cutters for our second horses. We are not singular in our management, and there are very few staff-officers who have not managed in some such manner to retain their servants. The fact is, that a rule of this sort bears very much more hardly upon a staff-officer, or a civilian living as we are, than it does upon a regimental officer. A soldier-servant is allotted to each officer upon application, and regimental officers who pick handy men from their own companies, and who live three in a tent, have their three soldier-servants between them as usual. It is far otherwise with a staff-officer: he may obtain a soldier-servant from a regiment; but that soldier does not know him, and will not work for him as he will for his own officer. In the next place, the soldier has certain regimental work to do, which will take him away from his master's tent for a considerable portion of the day; and lastly, a staff-officer is liable to be sent away on duty from the camp where the regiment to which his servant belongs is stationed. In our own case a soldier-servant would be useless; we might wish at any moment to push on to the pioneer force, or to accompany the Commander-in-chief upon a short expedition, and we should then be left without any servant whatever. At any rate, the order is generally evaded. Were it not that two months must elapse before a copy of this letter can come out to us, I should not speak so freely upon this point, as we should be having a special committee of officers of the quarter-master-general's department assembling to consider the question of "evasion of the general order relating to servants by officers and civilians attached to the army."

Antalo, March 7th.

I am happy to say that Major Minion, of the commissariat, arrived here early this morning with a large convoy, carrying among other stores a large quantity of rum; and it is now finally decided that a certain quantity of both rum and tea shall be served out daily to the troops on the advance. This happy state of things has been principally brought about by the energetic remonstrances of all the medical officers, and by their representation of the disastrous effect which the sudden privation of tea and rum would have upon the health of the troops, especially under the circumstances of the water being so bad. Sir Robert Napier himself was, I know, most averse to so extreme a measure; and nothing but the most urgent feeling of the necessity of pushing on in the lightest and most speedy manner could have induced him to consent to it; and I am sure that he is as pleased as anyone that he is able to continue the issue of what are really essentials to the soldiers.

It is still intended that we shall march on the 9th instant; indeed, orders were issued for a forward movement for both yesterday and to-day. The orders were, however, countermanded, for the road is not practicable for more than one day's march. As to the state of the road beyond, we receive contradictory reports. Colonel Phayre, with his usual happy, sanguine way of seeing things, states, I hear, that it is not a very bad road; while the engineer officer, on the other hand, reports that it will require a great deal of work to make it practicable for baggage-animals, especially for the elephants with the guns. The reason why the order was given for the troops to march forward at once was, that Colonel Phayre sent in to say that Waldo Yasus, the destroyer of Antalo, had sent in to say that he should oppose our passage. It caused quite an excitement for a time. But I learn to-day that Brigadier-general Field, who commands the pioneer forces, has sent in a letter to say that the whole thing is a mistake, and that Waldo Yasus is perfectly friendly, and that some of the Scindees have already gone on.

M. Munzinger, whose name I have frequently had occasion to mention as French consul at Massowah, and as accompanying the force as political adviser and interpreter, has gone on ahead on a mission to Gobayze. M. Munzinger has been some years in the country; he has married an Abyssinian woman, and owns villages and land near here. He is therefore well known to the natives, speaks their language, and is in every respect very well fitted for an expedition of this sort. On the other hand, there is some dissatisfaction among members of the staff, who say that an officer ought to have been selected for a mission of such importance, and should of course have been accompanied by an interpreter. It is urged, too, that the French look with great jealousy at our proceedings, and that their interests are totally opposed to our own; and that therefore a gentleman, however eligible in other respects, who is a French official should not have been intrusted with so important a mission. From all I have heard of M. Munzinger, I think there need be no objection upon the latter score; but I confess that I agree with those who think that a British officer—Major Grant, for instance—ought to have gone as our ambassador, or at least should have accompanied M. Munzinger. M. Munzinger was, I believe, sent forward by Colonel Merewether without Sir Robert Napier's knowledge. As M. Munzinger went forward, he had an interview with Waldo Yasus, who expressed some little fear that we, as the friends of Kassa, might intend to attack his amba, or fort, which stands on a lofty rock immediately beside the defile through which we pass. M. Munzinger, however, tranquillised him upon that score, and assured him that we should in no way interfere with any dissensions in the country. Waldo expressed himself as perfectly satisfied. M. Munzinger has now nearly reached Lake Ashangi, and his report of the road is decidedly favourable.

The gentleman to whom this expedition is most greatly indebted, and who has done infinitely more with the natives than the whole of our so-called politicals and interpreters put together, is Mr. Speedy. I have already mentioned that Mr. Speedy was sent for from New Zealand to accompany the expedition, Sir Stafford Northcote having strongly recommended him to Sir Robert Napier. The summons arrived somewhat unexpectedly to Mr. Speedy, for he had already written to Colonel Merewether volunteering his services, which had been declined by that officer. Mr. Speedy, however, came off in three days after he received General Napier's communication. His services here have been simply invaluable. Almost every useful negotiation with the natives has been conducted by him. He speaks the language exceedingly well, and is unwearied in his work. He hears complaints, receives chiefs, and is in fact at present our great medium of communication with the natives. He may be said to have completely extinguished the little light of our former politicals. Unquestionably he would have been the man to have sent to Gobayze; but even had not Colonel Merewether sent off his emissary, M. Munzinger, without consulting Sir Robert Napier, the Commander-in-chief would not have parted with Mr. Speedy, who is now his right-hand in all his communications with the natives. Among the other stores which have arrived to-day is some tobacco. The quantity is quite insufficient for the wants of the troops during their advance; but even a small supply per man will be a very great boon, for at present there is hardly any tobacco left among them. Even the officers' supplies are beginning to run short, and they as well as the men will soon be reduced to smoke the country tobacco, which is a disgusting mixture of tobacco and cow-dung formed into flat cakes.

The generals of the advanced force are Brigadier-general Field (who has only just been promoted), who commands the pioneer force; Brigadier-general Schneider, who has the first brigade; and Brigadier-general Wilby the second. Brigadier-general Collings, who has hitherto commanded the advanced brigade, is to be left behind here. This has naturally given rise to very strong comment. General Collings is far senior in the service to any of the men who have been thus chosen for the post of honour, and he has seen probably as much active service as the other three officers together. He is in every respect an excellent soldier and a most popular man; and there is a general feeling that his being thus passed over is a most undeserved slight, to put it in the mildest form. There is another reason why he should have certainly formed part of the advance. The first division is composed almost entirely of Europeans; and yet two out of the three officers chosen are Indian officers who have never commanded an English soldier during the whole of their service. General Collings has not, as far as I have heard, in any way neglected his duty; and his case is a matter of regret and sympathy with every officer with whom I have spoken—I mean, of course, outside the charmed pale of the official circle.

The general health of the troops continues excellent. There have been a few cases of dysentery, but the hospitals are all but empty.

Antalo is low, that is, in comparison with some of the places we have marched through: it is little over 6000 feet above the sea, that is, 3000 feet lower than Ad Abaga. The nights are consequently much milder than those we have lately experienced. The sun is hot between eight and ten in the morning; but at the latter hour a breeze springs up, which continues to blow with violence all day, and renders the heat of the sun, which would otherwise be great, bearable and even pleasant. The spirit of the troops is no less good than their health. Men who were marching up with the first wings of the 4th and 33d would suffer anything from sore feet rather than say a word on the subject, lest they should be left behind. One case of this illustrates the feeling even more strongly. The day upon which we marched out from Attegrat, three of the men of the 4th in some way obtained some liquor, and were convicted of drunkenness upon the line of march. This is a serious military offence, punishable by fifty lashes; but Colonel Cameron told them that, as they were all good-conduct men, he would only punish them by sending them back to the wing behind. The men all came forward and requested as a favour to be flogged instead of being left behind. Nothing could speak in stronger terms for the spirit of the troops than this. I am glad to say that, in consideration of their previous good conduct, Colonel Cameron felt himself enabled to pardon them. This fact, in itself, is a better answer to those who argue for the abolition of corporal punishment in the army than a hundred pamphlets would be. The only cogent reason of any force which the objectors to corporal punishment can allege is, that it degrades a soldier in his own eyes, and that he is good for nothing afterwards. Now, this is not the case. I have at various times spoken to hundreds of soldiers on the subject, and their answer is almost invariably the same: "It is not the punishment in which is the disgrace; it is the crime. If a man is flogged for stealing, he gets it thrown in his teeth afterwards that he has been flogged for being a thief; but if he gets a drop too much, and perhaps is impudent to a sergeant or officer, he may be flogged, but he will never have it brought up against him as a disgrace afterwards." The present instance proves this. These three soldiers, all good-conduct men, who had seen seven years of service, all considered that there would be much greater disgrace in being sent to the rear than in being flogged.

There is not very much shooting in this neighbourhood; a few guinea-fowls and grouse, and an occasional hare, have been bagged, but even these are scarce. As for the wild-beasts, of which we were to see so much, they simply are not. The rhinoceroses, who were to dispute the passage of the defiles; the alligators and hippopotami, who were to lurk around the watering-places, and to render the fetching a jug of water a service of as great danger as was the drawing a goblet from the enchanted fountain in our dear old fairy tales,—all these monsters are unknown here. We hear of lions, indeed, but somehow they are never found in the parts of the country we traverse. The hyena and jackal are the only animals met with which could, even by courtesy, be called wild-beasts. These, indeed, swarm; and their numerous holes are a serious hindrance and danger to riders; beyond this they are harmless, and one would as soon think of shooting a fox as a jackal. Sportsmen are seriously disappointed; almost everyone has brought out either rifle or gun, and many have carried both. Now, when our luggage is limited to seventy-five pounds, the weight of even one rifle, with its bullet-mould and a good stock of lead and powder, is a very material consideration; and, after the sacrifice of many little comforts to retain the rifle, it is very hard to find that it is quite useless. There is still a faint hope that we may find large game near the Ashangi Lake; but, considering that it is over 5000 feet above the sea, I can hardly think it is likely that we shall find any large game there, except perhaps elephants. The owners of fowling-pieces are better off. There have been few camping-grounds where a good shot might not get a guinea-fowl or two in an hour's ramble; and a guinea-fowl well cooked is one of the best game birds I know. Powder and shot are very valuable; indeed, they cannot be bought at any price, unless one is fortunate enough to find some one who, in the readjustment of his baggage, finds that he cannot possibly carry on all his stock of ammunition.

The plains here are singularly devoid of flowers: I never travelled in any country, indeed, where there was such a complete absence of wild-flowers; excepting, of course, the little watered dells, which I have described in previous letters. There is one solitary sort of flower, however, which I have met with in the plains in the neighbourhood, and which differs from any I ever saw before: it is a pea. The flower is of the size and colour of the "everlasting-pea;" but, instead of growing as a climber, the flower grows upon its own stalk from the ground. These flowers grow in clusters; but there are no leaves or stems, with the exception of the flower-stalk itself, three or four inches in height. The flower has a scent exactly resembling that of a violet, but less powerful: the seed is contained in a long, narrow pod, like that of a wallflower.

Scorpions are rather abundant here; and so, I am sorry to say, are white ants. It is not that one has any peculiar objection to white ants. They are certainly repulsive-looking insects, with their flabby white bodies and their big yellow heads, but that is of little consequence; and if they would but content themselves with walking about the tents and climbing over everything, as do other ants, together with spiders of every size, and a few beetles, one would not wish to interfere with their pleasures. Unfortunately they will not amuse themselves in this harmless way: they shun the light, and work in darkness, and their work consists in eating holes in the bottom of one's portmanteau, or in the waterproof-sheet under one's bed, or one's saddles, or books, or anything else which may come handy to them.

Now, as we are going to leave most of our portmanteaus and luggage here until we return, this propensity of theirs becomes a grave inconvenience. I fancy that we shall find our luggage, when we return, in a very dilapidated condition. There is only one satisfaction,—our clothes are rapidly getting into a state beyond which even white ants can effect little further damage.

The remaining wing of the 4th Regiment arrived two days ago, and the second wing of the 33d marched in this morning. We have therefore all the troops now collected in readiness for the forward move, with the exception only of a portion of the Beloochees, the 3d Dragoon Guards, and the elephants with the six-inch mortars; together with the elephants to carry Murray's guns. All these will, it is said, be here in two or three days. There is another thing of some slight importance lacking: this is money.

The commissariat have purchased such enormous quantities of flour and other stores, that the money brought up is exhausted. Fortunately another treasure-convoy is expected in a day or two.

This morning, at a quarter to six, General Staveley had all the troops out for a field-day. A deserted village upon a rising ground was attacked and carried in excellent style; but the manœuvres would have no interest to a general reader beyond those of any garrison field-day.

Antalo, March 11th.

When Colonel Phayre went ahead on the day of our arrival at Antalo, and reported that the road was rather bad, but not impracticable, every one looked at the range of peaks ahead of us and had serious misgivings. An order was issued for our march upon the 7th, and a party of pioneers were sent on to clear away any slight obstacles which might occur. The report of their commanding officer as to the state of the road was most unfavourable, and a wing of the 33d were sent out to assist. In consequence of the reports which came in, the march was postponed to the 9th, and Captain Macgregor, of the quartermaster's department, was sent out to report. On the evening of the 8th a joint report from this officer and Captain Goodfellow, of the Engineers, was received. It stated, "that they knew nearly every pass in India, but that in their experience they had met nothing whatever to compare to this defile, and that the Sooro pass was child's-play in comparison. With the 800 men at work, it would, they calculated, take another ten days' labour to make it practicable for mules." All this time Colonel Phayre was still in front, but his reports gave us no idea of the true state of things. In the mean time we were receiving reports from Mr. Munzinger, who, as I stated in my last, had gone ahead to see Gobayze, and he said that the road, although difficult in places, was by no means bad. Of course, on the receipt of the reports of Captains Macgregor and Goodfellow, the march was again postponed. Everyone was indignant. Sir Robert Napier, I have reason to know, was more indignant than anyone, for his heart is set upon getting onward as fast as possible. On the 9th arrived an officer from the front, with the astounding intelligence that he had just ridden down the other road, which was known to exist; that it was six miles shorter; it passed over the mountain range at a point 1500 feet lower than the other, and presented throughout its whole distance no serious difficulties whatever. This it appeared, was the very route that Munzinger had travelled, and the discrepancies between his accounts and the real state of things were at once explained. At first the news was received with absolute incredulity. It seemed impossible that the quartermaster-general could have kept the troops at work for a week upon an impracticable road, when a good one lay ready at hand. The road, too, which Colonel Phayre had not explored is called the Royal road, which in itself was sufficient to show that it was the best and most frequented of the two. But the fact was, our political officer had heard that a rebel chief had a fortress upon this road; the same chief whom I mentioned in my last as having been reported by Colonel Phayre as opposing our way. The man really is perfectly friendly, and was at first rather more afraid of us than our quartermaster-general was of him. However, the mere fact of his being there was assumed to be a good reason for our not taking the road. And so a precious week has been wasted, and all the labour thrown away. The new road is, of course, not yet passable for the elephants with the heavy guns, but Sir Robert will push on with the 4th Regiment and the steel guns, and the 33d and the pioneer force will set to work and get it in order for the rest of the force as soon as possible. It is not often that we find a pioneer force engaged in making a road after the head-quarters and part of the army have gone by. Our first march is only eight miles. The distance thence up the pass is nineteen. I believe that the troops will do it in two days, but that Sir

Robert Napier, with an escort, will go straight through to Attala, in order to judge for himself of the real state of things.

Our items of news from the rear are but of slight general interest. Captain St. John reports, I am told, that the natives have ceased to damage the telegraph-wires; but as a *per-contra*, he says that the wires are frequently broken by the baboons, who climb up the poles, and hang on the wires by their tails. I am assured that this is an absolute fact. One of the mule-drivers near Attegrat shot a native the other day. The man, who was armed with a gun, attempted to rob the mule; but the driver resisted, wrenched the gun from his hand, and shot him. The robber is not dead, but lies in a precarious state. The lesson was greatly required; but instead of being rewarded for his conduct, the mule-driver got a dozen lashes! I hope that the next driver whose mule is attacked will allow it to be looted, and that the functionary who has just so ably instructed mule-drivers not to defend the public property will be ordered to pay the cost of the stores stolen. Tents have been erected here for the reception of such luggage as cannot be carried on under the present regulations. I sent my portmanteau in this morning, and had the pleasure when moving it of finding that the white ants had eaten a large hole in the bottom. I do not expect to find any remains of it, or of its contents, upon my return. Captain Moore, the Commander-in-chief's interpreter, has gone on ahead to pacify the local chiefs, and to assure them that we have no intention of molesting them. No better man could have been selected for the office. Captain Moore speaks almost every known language, and has had as much experience of native potentates as any man living. Major Grant has gone on to Attala, to buy provisions, &c. An officer of his African experience and standing would have been far better employed as an ambassador to King Gobayze; while bargaining with natives would have been much more in accordance with Mr. Munzinger's experience and powers. Some tobacco has come up, and has been distributed among the troops, to their great satisfaction. During the last few days the troops have been exercised in turning out rapidly on the alarm being sounded. The sentries have, too, been placed and instructed as if in front of an enemy, who might at any moment make a night attack.

The natives here unanimously express their hopes and wishes that we should take possession of the country and become their masters. Our style of paying for everything we require has taken them entirely by surprise. It is altogether contrary to their experience. There is no doubt that they are extremely poor, and terribly ground down, and many of their very numerous vices are, to a certain extent, excusable upon this score. They are so poor that they will sell anything for dollars—their corn, their flour, their donkeys, their cattle, their wives, or their daughters. They are a terribly priest-ridden people. I should say that no people in the world pay such extortionate dues. The priests claim two-fifths of the gross produce; of the remainder one-third is claimed by the King; then comes the local chief: so that finally the unfortunate cultivator gets less than one-fifth of the crop he has raised. It is no wonder that the people are poor, and that in times of drought, or when the locusts sweep over the land, or the rebels, more destructive still, carry off crops and herds and flocks, famine stalks through the land. There is no doubt that our mastership would be an unmixed blessing to them, but it would certainly be the very reverse of advantageous to ourselves. From our landing at Zulla to the present time we have passed through a country more barren than any I ever traversed. Except for grazing purposes it is absolutely valueless. Here and there, in the valleys, are little patches of cultivation by the side of the streams; but in the whole two hundred miles we have passed through, looking east and west as far as the eye can reach, I do not think that we have seen, in all, five hundred acres of cultivated land. Taking the two hundred miles north and south by, say, ten miles east and west—in all, two thousand square miles—I would not take the fee-simple as a gift. I am not, of course, suggesting that the ground we have traversed is to be taken as a fair sample of Abyssinia. Unquestionably it is not so. It would be as fair to land in the north of England, and to skirt the sea-coast, keeping on the Cumberland, Westmoreland, Lancashire, Welsh, and Cornwall hills, and then to pronounce England a sterile country. Still, by what we have seen, by the ranges of mountain-summits discernible everywhere in the far west, it is evident that a very large portion of Abyssinia is mere grazing-land; and it is probable that the valleys and low-lying plains, which are extremely fertile, would be unhealthy for European constitutions. Whatever ideas may have been entertained at one time as to our taking possession of a country so rich, so fertile, and so salubrious as this was represented to be, the experience of this expedition must have entirely dispelled this notion. The general aspect of the country is so bare, the fertile portions so distant from the coast, the roads so impracticable, that any idea of English colonisers settling here, as suggested by Mr. Dufton and others, is simply preposterous; and in addition to all this, a very large force would be required to keep a warlike and turbulent people in order. We see by the English papers that "A British Taxpayer" has been writing indignantly, demanding why two or three thousand men were not sufficient for this paltry business. If the British Taxpayer had been out here, he would not have asked such a question. British soldiers are by no means men to overrate difficulties, or to hold their enemies at higher than their real value. But the universal opinion here is, that we have not one man too many in the country. The tribes of Shohos on the sea-coast; the King of Tigre, who can summon 20,000 or 30,000 men to his banner; the fierce Gallas, through whom we have still to pass,—all these have been, and probably will be, friendly. But why? Simply because we are strong enough to keep them in order. No one doubts for a moment that if they thought that they were strong enough, they would fall upon us instantly for the sake of plunder. If the three thousand men who, according to this critic, would have been amply sufficient, could have been endowed with the agreeable faculty of going for three months without food, and if their horses had been similarly gifted, they would without doubt have been amply sufficient. Three thousand British soldiers, as long as they keep together in a compact body, could march from the Mediterranean to the Cape of Good Hope. But, unfortunately, men and animals who can go for three months without food are scarce in these degenerate days. Our experience here is that, with the exception of meat, no food whatever is procurable between Zulla and our present most advanced post, with the solitary exception of Antalo. Grain for the animals is almost as scarce. We have bought small quantities, indeed, at most of the stations, but we never get it for the first few days after our arrival. It is only after we have been at a place for a short time, and when the people find out how large a sum we pay for it, that they bring in even small quantities. Then the problem would present itself: these three thousand men must be fed. To be fed, they must carry supplies with them. These supplies must be conveyed upon baggage-animals. These baggage-animals must be fed. But there is no food to be obtained as they march on direct. Therefore, it is evident that dépôts must be formed, and these must be guarded; communication must be kept up, roads must be made to some extent, for there are many places perfectly impracticable for loaded animals. And so the three thousand men would be frittered all over the country, and would be harassed to death by overwork and watching, and it is certain they could never penetrate to Magdala. Has a "Taxpayer" ever read the history of the French campaign in Spain? Has he any idea of the number of hundred thousand men who marched into that country, and of the numbers who returned to France? A very small proportion of the deficit fell under British steel and lead. They were accounted for by the peasantry. They died, shot down upon baggage-guard, cut off when in search of provisions, surprised when in small parties, harassed to death by overwork. Such would have been the fate of three thousand men landing in Abyssinia. The people here are as brave as the Spaniards, the country is beyond all comparison more difficult, and the resources which, it offers to an invader are as nothing to those of Spain. Our force, as it is now constituted, is sufficient to overawe the country, and it is fortunate that it is so. For I say fearlessly, and there is not an officer here who would not support me in that opinion, that if the people were hostile, we could not even with our present force have ever hoped to reach Magdala. It would have been a sheer impossibility. A mere passive resistance, the driving away of flocks and herds, and the burning of the grass, would have brought us to a standstill at Senafe; while the bare idea of defending our communication, and guarding the enormous trains required for our march of three hundred miles through a barren, hostile, and most difficult country, is so supremely ridiculous as to be laughable. The experiment of the three thousand men, had it been tried, would have ended in a disaster such as, with the exception of Cabul, the British arms have never experienced, and it must afterwards have been retrieved with a force of three times the strength even of our present one, and at an expenditure which might have taught even the "British Taxpayer" that penny wisdom is an equivalent for pound foolishness.

A general order has just appeared regulating the whole distribution of the troops; and as this is a final arrangement, it will no doubt be interesting to all who have friends in the army here.

First Division.—Major-general Staveley, K.C.B., in command; Colonel Wood, deputy-adjutant-general; Major Baigrie, deputy-quartermaster-general. Pioneer Force: Brigadier-general Field. Troops: forty sabres 3d Native Cavalry; forty Scinde Horse; 3d and 4th company Bombay Sappers and Miners; two companies 33d Regiment; two companies Beloochees; one company Punjaub Pioneers.

First Brigade, Brigadier-general Schneider.—Troops: Head-quarters wing 3d Dragoon Guards, 3d Native Cavalry, Scinde Horse, G battery, 14, Royal Artillery, A battery 21st company Royal Artillery, 4th King's Own, Head-quarters and eight companies 33d, 10th company Royal Engineers, Head-quarters and two companies Beloochees, Head-quarters wing 10th Native Infantry.

Second Brigade, Brigadier-general Wilby.—Wing of 12th Bengal Cavalry, B battery 21st Royal Artillery, two 8-inch mortars, with detachment 5th battery 25th Royal Artillery, Rocket Naval Brigade, K company Madras Sappers, seven companies Punjaub Pioneers, wing of Beloochees.

It will thus be seen that the 1st Division consists of four entire infantry regiments—the 4th, 33d, Beloochees, and Punjaub Pioneers—and a wing of the 10th Native Infantry, of the 3d Native Cavalry, the Scinde Horse, a wing of the Dragoon Guards, and a wing of the 12th Bengal Cavalry, three batteries of Royal Artillery and two 8-inch mortars, and three companies of Sappers and Miners and one company of Royal Engineers; an admirably-selected force, and which, as long as it kept together, would be invincible.

Another general order has also been promulgated, which I have very great pleasure in giving, because it does full justice to a most meritorious and hardworking body of officers. I have the more pleasure in giving publication to the order, as it thoroughly indorses the opinion I have all along stated that the transport officers were in no way to blame for the confusion which took place at Zulla:

"General Order.—Head-quarters, Camp Antalo, March 4th.—The Commander-in-chief has lately received from the Director Transport Train, Abyssinia field force, a full and particular report of the service rendered to the corps by the officers under his command. His Excellency has perused this report with much satisfaction, and it is most gratifying to him to find that, in spite of the numerous and extraordinary difficulties with which the officers of the transport-train have had to contend, and notwithstanding the hard and unceasing work they have had to perform, they have, almost without exception, displayed an amount of steady determination to do their best which is beyond all praise. The Commander-in-chief begs to assure Major Warden and the officers under his command that the work performed by them has not been overlooked, and shall not be forgotten. His Excellency trusts that one and all will remember that upon their individual exertions depends, in a great measure, the success of the expedition. The transport-train, for reasons far beyond the control of the officers belonging to it, has just commenced to assume that military organisation so requisite to its well-being, and for want of which at first it suffered so severely.... The Commander-in-chief is well aware how much the services of the officers of the transport-train have been depreciated, and how unfairly blame has been attached to them for shortcomings beyond their control. His Excellency, however, assures them that he has never for a moment lost confidence in them, nor has he ever doubted that their exertions would eventually bring order and regularity out of confusion and indiscipline.... All cannot of course work under the eye of the Commander-in-chief, and comparatively few can accompany the advanced force; but his Excellency will make no distinction when the campaign is over between those who were in front and those who were necessarily in the rear. All by good work can contribute materially to the success of the campaign, and it will be by that standard, and by that alone, that his Excellency will be guided when making hereafter his report upon the services performed by the officers under his command.—By order of his Excellency the Commander-in-chief. Fred. Thesiger, lieutenant-colonel, deputy-adjutant-general."

Never was liberal praise more deserved, and it will be most gratifying to the men who have slaved and toiled almost night and day in the face of every possible discouragement.

Meshech, March 14th.

We have advanced two days' marches into the Abyssinian hills, and at every step forward we see more clearly the difficulties with which we have to struggle. The first day's journey was to Musgee; an easy march of eight miles across an undulating plain. At Musgee we found the two companies of the 33d, two of the 10th Native Infantry, and the Sappers and Miners, who constitute the pioneer force. They had just come in, recalled from the hard and unprofitable labour in the defile, and now prepared to set to work anew upon the new route. They report the pass as a tremendous defile, and say that the detachment of Scinde Horse have lost no less than seven horses either from falls or from over-fatigue. We were amused at the natives who came round, and absolutely made fun of the soldiers for their unsuccessful attempts at making roads in impassable places, when there was a good road ready at hand. The head-quarters and the other three companies of the 33d, and the company of the Punjaub Pioneers, were near the other end of the defile, and they had orders to push straight on to Attala, and begin to improve the road from the other end. At Musgee we had clear running water, which was really enjoyable after the stagnant stuff we had been drinking at Antalo. On the morning of the 13th Sir Robert Napier started with his staff and an escort at seven o'clock. The rest of the force left at ten precisely. The march was eight miles—a short distance apparently; but when I state that a great number of the animals did not arrive until eight in the evening, it will be at once seen that it was very much harder work than it appears at first sight. The first three or four miles of this road, or rather track, led along the hill-side, and then as the valley narrowed in, and its sides became very precipitous, it kept along the bottom. There we crossed and recrossed a little stream at least a dozen times; and much of the delay and confusion was caused by mules insisting upon stopping to drink, and thereby of course bringing the whole line to a stop. This part of the march was by far the prettiest and most English we have seen out here. We were travelling in a grove of trees, with a thick underwood, except just where a path was cut wide enough for a single mule to pass. A really good-sized streamlet of clear water wound here and there, with quiet pools, and bright tumbling little cascades. Under our feet was a cool greensward, over our heads a shady screen of foliage. Imagine the charm of such a scene to us, who, except in an occasional secluded dell, have scarcely seen a tree, or felt shade, or heard the plash of falling water for months. How we should have liked to have halted, and to have enjoyed the turf and the shade for an hour or two! All our attention was required, however, for the work in hand, for in many places we had very rough bits, and the wood-nymphs and dryads must have been sorely startled at the shouting and tumult which arose in their quiet shades. On each side of us the mountains rose to a great height, crowned with perpendicular precipices, on one of which, seemingly accessible only to a bird, was the stronghold of some border chief. Presently the mountain sides receded a little, and we emerged into a small plain. In the centre of this ran the stream, and by its side were some very large trees, which I can best describe by saying they resemble oaks with willow-leaves. Here we encamped.

The troops had taken four hours to do the eight miles; but the commissariat animals, as I have stated, were more than double that time upon the road. Both at Musgee and here there is a great lack of grain for the animals. One pound of grain was all they got yesterday, and to-day at twelve there is to be a similar large issue. If this sort of thing continues, the animals must inevitably break down. The drivers, after their day's work was over, did go up into the hills and cut some grass; but the coarse grass contains very little nourishment, and the horses refuse to eat it. The mules eat it, indeed, but it can do them very little good. I have all along in my calculations of the probable duration of the campaign argued that we must expect to come to places where forage was not procurable, and that if we came to a place where for four days' marches we could get no grain and but little grass, that we must come to a standstill and form dépôts. Of course the difficulty will be proportionately greater when we have the whole advance force, with its thousands of cavalry-horses and baggage-animals with us. We were to have started this morning at seven o'clock; but a messenger arrived at two this morning with a letter from the Commander-in-chief to General Staveley, saying that the road was so bad that we must halt for a day to enable the pioneer force to smooth some of the most impracticable places. We have also news of the head-quarters and three companies of the 33d who had pushed on by the "Phayre" road to Attala. They had a distance of fourteen miles to go, four of which they had comparatively cleared. They started early, and they got in the following day at twelve o'clock, having been twenty-eight hours on the road. The pioneer force is hard at work upon the road ahead, and to-morrow morning we start for Attala. It is stated to be an eight-mile march; but I hear that the opinion of those who have gone on is, that it is a good thirteen. At Attala I anticipate that we shall wait some days-that is, if forage is obtainable. Everything must now depend upon this vital point. We must push-on to some place where abundant forage can be obtained, and we must then wait for the remainder of the force to come up. This must entail a halt of some days, whenever it is; for the 3d Dragoon Guards and the 12th Bengal Cavalry were both some marches' distance from Antalo when we left, and they will, of course, have to make a halt of a day or two at that place upon their advance, to rest their animals. I hear that in the neighbourhood of Lât there is plenty of forage; in that case Lât will probably be our halting-place, if we find we cannot obtain sufficient grass and grain at Attala. Sportsmen have been looking forward to our arrival at Lake Ashangi, as game is likely to be abundant in that neighbourhood, especially wild-fowl. We have received a letter from Mr. Massinger, which shows that any attempt at wild-fowl shooting either at early dawn or at dusk is likely to be attended with some little danger. It is, he says, very difficult, and even dangerous, to approach the shores of the lake. They are very flat, and the whole surface of the ground has been broken up into chasms and crevasses, which are filled with soft mud, and are not easily distinguishable from the surrounding soil. A long stick plunged into the soft mud found no bottom, and a person falling into one of these would, unless immediate assistance was at hand, be inevitably lost. The natives say that these crevasses were all formed by an earthquake which took place about three years ago. Previous to that time the lake had an outlet through which the overflow water made its way into the Tacazze. This outlet is now stopped, and the water has risen and filled all these chasms made by the earthquake.

Mahkan, March 16th.

My last letter was dated from the pretty camping-ground bearing the scriptural denomination of Meshech. Thence to Atzala was a march of thirteen miles. The road led up the valley, as upon the previous day, for about six miles, and then we had a long, but fortunately tolerably gradual, climb up the saddle of the ridge. On the right of the summit of the pass is the Amba of Waldo: it is considerably the highest peak in the neighbourhood, — isolated, four-sided, and apparently perpendicular. As far as we could see, there were no walls or artificial defences. The huts which contain the garrison are built on ledges upon the face of the rock. Ledge is hardly the proper expression; for a ledge is a projection, whereas the huts are built in deep scores which run round the face. The rock overhead completely overhangs them; so that they are to a certain extent sheltered from the wind, which would, at an elevation of 12,000 feet above the sea, be otherwise almost unbearable in such an exposed condition. Waldo himself was at the top of the pass when we went along. He is a man of about thirty-five, with a very intelligent and pleasing face. A number of his warriors attended him, and he was very much interested in our various uniforms and appointments. He chatted for some time with General Staveley, who fired-off his revolver for his edification. The articles, however, that pleased him most were telescopes and field-glasses, and he expressed a strong desire for one. He was evidently acquainted with their use, for he shut one eye and examined the country through my telescope with a nautical air which would have done no discredit to the most aspiring midshipman. The Commander-in-chief presented him with an excellent glass on the following day; and he will now from his eyrie be able to see any advancing foe in ample time to make his preparations for defence.

The descent from the top of the pass was much steeper and more severe than the ascent had been, and the train of mules was a very long time making its way to the bottom. Every animal that fell, every load which shifted, brought the whole line to a standstill. However, patience and care will effect wonders; and we got to the foot of the steep portion without a casualty among the animals.

At Attala, or Atzala, as I find it is more correctly spelt, we found the Commander-in-chief encamped with the head-quarter wing of the 33d and a small escort of Scinde Horse and the 3d Native Cavalry. The Commander-in-chief intends, I believe, in future to accompany the Pioneer Force, and to judge for himself as to the capabilities of the roads, and to direct the work to be done to make them passable by the main body. Colonel Phayre will, however, still continue a couple of days' march ahead, with a small escort. Sir Robert Napier gets through an immense quantity of work in the course of a day; and the following order, which has been lately issued, shows that he is unable to trust the political business, such as it is, out of his own hands, but is compelled to be his own political officer, as well as his own explorer: "The Commander-in-chief directs that in future all reports forwarded for his information by officers in the intelligence department may be sent to the political secretary, through the general or other officer commanding the division or post in which they may be serving. In special cases, where a more immediate communication to his Excellency may seem expedient, reports may be sent direct; copies of them, however, being at once furnished to the officer's immediate military superior. All instructions for the guidance of officers in the intelligence department will be sent to them by Captain Tweedie, political secretary, who must be considered as the sole officer authorised to convey to them his Excellency's commands."

Atzala is situated in an extensive basin, apparently surrounded upon all sides by lofty hills. The abundance which we found at Antalo still continues, and the commissariat are able to purchase grain for the animals. I found upon my arrival in camp that Sir Robert Napier intended to push on at once with the Pioneer Force, leaving Sir Charles Staveley to follow, with an interval of a day or two, to allow the road to be improved. Sir Robert has also sent back for the light guns of Twiss's Mountain Train, and for the Naval Rocket Brigade, both of which formed part of the 2d Brigade, according to the published list. There are two explanations of this order; the one being that he finds the roads so bad that he thinks it will perhaps be impossible to bring the heavy guns of Murray's battery on without great loss of time; the other theory is, that he is now convinced that we shall have to fight at Magdala, and wishes to arrive there with as strong a force of artillery as possible. The advices from Magdala tell us that Theodore had received exact intelligence of our whereabouts and rate of moving; and that whereas, believing us to be nearer, he had decided upon waiting at Dalanta; and he has now pushed on with the greatest energy, and arrived with his guns and convoy quite close to Magdala. This is, I think, the best news we could receive. Theodore has evidently made up his mind to await us at any rate in his fortress. He may fight, he may pretend friendship, and offer us the prisoners; but, at any rate, he will be there: whereas, if he had not been able to reach Magdala, he might have retired at our approach; and if he had ever taken to the hills, our expedition would have been almost interminable: once in Magdala, and surrounded, we are sure of him. Magdala may be, and I believe is, very strong, and may hold out for weeks; but we know that sooner or later we must have it. I believe that the guns we have will be useless, except for their moral effect upon the enemy. A shell thrown on to the summit of a rock fortress when the garrison were sheltered behind great boulders, or in caves or crevices, might alarm them, but would probably do very little harm. Our stock of missiles is very limited, and we shall probably have to take the place at last by assault. If Magdala at all approaches Waldo's fortress in strength, an assault in the face of some thousands of determined men, commanded by a desperate chief like Theodore, will be no child's-play even for British troops. A few stones rolled down would sweep the path of a whole line of stormers. A breastwork of great boulders rolled into position from above would baffle the bravest. People talk lightly of Magdala and its savage garrison; but if they prove true to their king, it will prove as hard a nut as British prowess ever had to crack. Officers speaking to me upon the subject have argued Magdala is probably not so strong as many of the hill-forts in India which we have in our time taken. This is no doubt true; as is the fact that the defenders of these hill-forts were as brave, and were in addition much better armed than are the garrison of Magdala. But, on the other hand, the defenders of Indian hill-forts knew what British troops were; they knew that our power was almost infinite; that we were the masters of all India; and that sooner or later we could accumulate force enough to capture even the most seemingly impregnable fortress. It was, they knew, a mere question of time with us. However physically brave, the knowledge that final over-throw is certain, will to a great extent paralyse the efforts of any body of men. The reverse of all this is the case with Theodore's soldiers. They have never fought but to conquer; they have a fanatical persuasion of the might of their leader, and believe in his star; they have been always told that Magdala is impregnable. For their enemies they have neither fear nor reverence. The few white men they have seen have been men of peace—missionaries and such-like—living but by their sufferance, and now for years held in the degrading position of captives. Theodore has impressed them with the belief that we are a mere nation of traders, and that although we manufacture good guns, and can use them at a distance, yet that we are wanting in courage, and no match for his men in a hand-to-hand fight. Doubtless, too, he will impress upon them the fact that we cannot have brought a large stock of ammunition for our guns across this long and difficult route; and that therefore his men have only to keep quiet and let us expend our missiles, and that then our power of doing harm will be at an end. He has, too, promised that they shall divide among themselves all our treasure and spoil; and as by this time they have probably heard that we are absolutely strewing the country with dollars, their idea of our probable spoil must be something magnificent.

However, the problem of war or peace will soon be solved. At the rate at which we are now proceeding, another three weeks will see us in front of Magdala. Indeed, if we continue to press forward at the present rate, we should be at our journey's end in a fortnight, or, rather, we should be there if the whole of the mules did not die. To-day's march has been fifteen of the longest and heaviest miles ever traversed, with scarcely a mile of level ground the whole distance. The difficulty began at the very start, for we had at once to climb a high and steep hill, and to descend at once on the other side. So long a time did this occupy, so many were the stoppages and breakdowns, that although the first of the train started before seven, it was ten before the last of the convoy of six hundred had even commenced the ascent. The Commander-in-chief was not to start till one o'clock, and a small party of mules would leave at that time with his tent, &c. I therefore had, very fortunately as it turned out, resolved not to start my animals until the same time. After passing over the first hill, we came to another, which was the highest we had yet come to, being two hundred feet higher than the summit of the pass upon the preceding day. The ascent, although very long, was not very steep; indeed, all the hills we have crossed are much more precipitous on the southern than on the northern side. Here our difficulties commenced; for at the top of the hill were numbers of the animals who had started five hours before us. The descent was blocked up, and for ten minutes at a time everyone was brought to a stand-still. Great was the noise, tremendous the shouting in various languages. Once upon the descent of the hill, everyone kept in single file; but the confusion was greatest at the top, as everyone strove to get his own animal first upon the track. Here were Beloochees, Scinde Horse, Engineers, 33d men, and 3d Native Cavalry, all trying to insinuate the animals of which they were in charge into the straight line. Not unfrequently some unfair effort to interlope ended in well-merited punishment, by one of the mules getting jammed between others, and his load pulled back over his tail. At last we got our animals fairly on to the descent, which was very steep and winding, and then there was nothing for it but patience. With our own animals we had no trouble, for we had long ago found out that although a string of four animals goes well enough along a plain, the only way to get them down steep places, or over very rough ground, is to unfasten them, and to make a servant go to each mule's head. In this way, if the loads are properly packed upon Otago saddles, they will go anywhere; the mules can pick their way without being hurried, and the loads will not shift; whereas the government mules, being fastened three or four in a string, under the charge of a single driver, are continually coming to grief. The leading mule steps over stones or down steep places with comparative ease, and when on level ground steps boldly forward; while the unfortunate animals behind him, who are still on the difficult ground, are unable to pick their way, their heads are pulled into the air, they hang back and vainly resist, and either lie down at once, or are pulled off their legs. The present state of the Bombay saddles assists to aggravate the evil. The leather loops which were attached to them, and through which the ropes which fastened the baggage passed, are now in a majority of cases torn off, and the consequence is, that the load at once slips forwards or backwards immediately the animal gets upon an incline, and the saddle remains on the back, while the load rolls off. The mountain-side was thickly covered with shrubs; and as we went down in a long confused line, with the baggage-guard scattered at intervals along it, most of the men being incessantly employed in repacking the loads, with their arms piled near them while they did so, one could not but reflect that we shall have to travel in a very different fashion when we approach Magdala. Two or three hundred men, armed only with spears, concealed among the bushes, and rushing out at a given signal, could have annihilated the whole convoy before a bayonet could have been fixed or the slightest resistance offered. I believe that it is settled that we shall take no tents forward with us for the last three or four days' marches; and this, with the fact that a comparatively small number of mules will be required for the commissariat stores, will diminish our train to one-fourth of the present size. If Theodore has made up his mind to fight, there is little doubt that he will begin while we are in the passes. He has always been famous for his night-attacks, and we have been especially warned to beware of sudden attacks. The King of Tigre was very impressive on this score. Waldo, the other day, also warned us most earnestly to be upon our guard night and day. We had a turn-out of the troops this morning at Atzala. It took place at about ten in the morning, and was for a few minutes quite an exciting affair. With the exception only of Sir Charles Staveley and a few of his personal staff, no one knew whether it was a real alarm or not. We were now in the Gallas country, where we had been told to expect raids, and it was quite possible that the convoy, the rear of which was still mounting the hill, had been suddenly attacked. When, therefore, the first bugle sounded the alarm, and after a pause sounded again and again, quite a thrill ran through the camp. All the regimental bugles repeated the calls, and the camp presented the appearance of an ant-hive suddenly disturbed. The men tumbled out from their tents in hot haste, buttoning-up their tunics and buckling-up their belts; the cooks and butchers left the half-cut-up carcasses, to run to their tents for their arms and accoutrements; officers shouted for their swords; the men who were out for wood or water came scampering up; the mule-drivers rapidly drove in the animals which were grazing on the plains; the dhoolie-bearers mustered round the palkees; the grasscutters buckled on swords of various descriptions; and I observed my servant busily engaged in loading a great double-barrelled pistol. The result showed that an enemy must manage to creep up very close before being observed, to catch us unawares. In two minutes and a half from the first bugle, the 4th were drawn up in close order in front of their lines, and being joined by the Beloochees, marched off, throwing out skirmishers before them. In another five minutes the Mountain Artillery were in motion, and the 3d Native Cavalry, who had, when the alarm sounded, been in their native undress, had dressed, saddled, and were dashing across the plain. A little in rear of the infantry the dhoolie-bearers were staggering along with their palkees, and an apothecary was in full chase with an armful of splints and bandages. It is evident that we shall not be caught asleep. Alarms of this sort do good occasionally, but should not be too often repeated, or the men get so accustomed to the cry of "Wolf!" that they will not believe it when the real animal makes his appearance.

But I am leaving myself and my mules an unconscionable time upon the hill; scarcely, however, so long as I was there in reality, for it was getting dusk when I reached the foot, just three hours after my arrival at the top. There was no camp in sight, and, although we knew it was still six miles distant, we were ignorant of the direction in which it lay. Fortunately, none of the loads had shifted, and we were thus enabled to push past great numbers of animals who were standing with their loads upon the ground beside them. It was a very weary and unpleasant six-miles' march. There was no moon, and it soon became extremely dark; and as the way was a mere track, we were quite ignorant whether we were going in the right direction or not. Of course we followed mules in front of us, but there was no knowing whether they were going right—for a mule stopping for a minute, for a readjustment of the load, would lose sight of the one in advance, and would be just as likely as not to go in the wrong direction, and inevitably be followed by all in his rear. The way was across an undulating plain, with many deep nullahs covered with trees, and so dark that we could not see our horses' ears. There was very little shouting now; everyone rode or walked along in a sort of sulky silence; the pace was of the slowest, the mules being scarcely able to crawl along. We could not pick our way, for we could not see the ground. Some got off and led their horses, others trusted to their horses' eyes, and it was astonishing how well the animals picked their way; still there were some awkward falls. Even if one escaped these greater dangers, it was not pleasant to be caught by a bramble suddenly between the eyes, or to be nearly borne over the crupper of the horse by a stiff bough under the chin. At last, just when we had arrived at the conclusion that we must have missed our road, and that it would be better to draw off the way and pitch our tent until daybreak, we saw the camp-lights in the distance, and, after another mile's travelling, arrived here, as I began this letter by saying, at half-past nine o'clock.

Ashangi Lake, March 19th.

I finished my last letter on the night of my arrival at Mahkan, very tired, very hungry, and a good deal out of temper. We halted at Mahkan on the 17th, as the animals imperatively needed a day's rest. There can be no question that these very long marches are a mistake in every way. Many of the animals which started at seven in the morning did not get in until ten or eleven o'clock next day; and fatigue of this sort, together with an almost starvation diet, is too much for any animals. The number which actually died upon the road was very small—only three or four, I am told; but then the animals have had a rest at Antalo, and have still some little strength left. I have no hesitation, however, in saying that three or four such marches as this would find the great majority of the transport-train animals *hors de combat*. It is terribly fatiguing too for the troops. Nor is anything gained by it. The old proverb, "the more haste the less speed," is amply verified. We did fifteen miles, and then had to halt a day; whereas had we halted at a spring at the foot of the steep descent, six miles from Mahkan, the animals could have easily marched some miles beyond Mahkan on the following day. Fifteen miles over a flat country is one thing, fifteen miles over a succession of mountains, with a rifle, sixty rounds of ammunition, and etceteras, is quite another; and I sincerely trust that we shall not again attempt such a tremendous march as this.

The mule-train is at present all that can be desired. The number of animals attached to the advanced division is 8000, and comprises the Lahore mule-train, the Raul Pindee mule-train, and the A and D divisions of the transport-train. I have had occasion more than once to speak of the efficiency of the

Lahore and Pindee trains, which arrived from Bengal in the most perfect order, and which, being marched straight to Senafe, did not share in the general disruption at Zulla. The A division, under Captain Griffiths, I have also spoken of, as being in excellent condition. This is the division which went up with the exploring party to Senafe, and staying there, partially escaped the crash. The D division is commanded by Captain Twentyman; an officer whose energy and devotedness at Zulla during the worst times helped to pull the transport-train through its greatest difficulties, as I had the pleasure of testifying at the time. These four divisions are under the control of Captain Hand, of the Lahore mule-train, who has been appointed their director. He is an able and energetic officer, and his management of the train gives the highest satisfaction. The transport-train authorities at Zulla have nothing whatever to do with the advanced portion, which is under the sole orders of Captain Hand.

On the morning after our arrival at Mahkan the wing of the 33d was sent on to make the road, the head-quarter camp remaining with only the escort of the 2d Horse and 3d Cavalry. In the afternoon, however, a party of Beloochees and Punjaub Pioneers came in. During the day a man came in with one of the curious lozenge-shaped guitars I have already described, and kept up a monotonous chanting for some time. The words Magdala and Tèdros were the only words generally recognised; and it was supposed that he was singing some song he had composed in our honour. An interpreter, however, who happened to come up, undeceived us by explaining that the singer, relying upon our ignorance of the language, was reciting our certain defeat, and the vengeance that Theodore would take upon us. I have no fear of the man turning out a true prophet; but it is certain that the people of the country generally look upon our chance of victory over Theodore as being a very poor one indeed. Yesterday morning we started at eight o'clock on our march to this place, and, owing to the 33d having gone on, our baggage-train was much smaller, and the difficulties and delays proportionately less. We found, upon mounting the first hill, that we had come on an entirely new and agreeable phase of Abyssinian scenery. Instead of the bare hills and plains over which, interspersed with wooded valleys, we had journeyed since we entered Abyssinia, we were transported at one bound into the very heart of Switzerland. Everywhere to the very mountain-tops was a pine-forest. In some places the trees grew closely together, with a thick underwood, which shut-in the path on both sides, and through which the road had been partially cleared by the 33d. At other times the trees were more thinly scattered about, or stood in clumps, affording every variety of park-like scenery. It was a delightful ride for about six miles through these, the road being smooth and easy. At the end of that time our difficulties began, the way lying over and along steep and very rocky hills covered with forest and brushwood. The General had expected to have found the road to a certain extent cleared by the 33d, but owing to an error, for which Major Cooper was in no way to blame, they had scarcely begun their work when we passed, instead of having been engaged upon it for twenty-four hours. Their orders had been to encamp at a stream five miles on from Mahkan, and then to set to work upon the road; and as they had started twenty-four hours before ourselves, it was anticipated that the road would be perfectly practicable for mules by the next day. The 33d were, however, furnished with no guide, and the spring was not visible from the line of march; consequently they marched past it, and did not find out their error until they were miles ahead. Major Cooper then determined upon the best course to be pursued, namely, to march straight on to this station, to encamp there, and to march his men back at daybreak to work upon the road. They had done a good deal when we arrived; but of course the mules stopped their work for a time. In some places the track was very bad; and at one of these, a rocky wall along a ledge, on the face of which we had to pass, I found Sir Robert Napier himself engaged in planning another road to avoid this obstacle, which was dangerous in a high degree for loaded animals, as the projecting load nearly pushed each one over the edge. No accident, so far as I heard, occurred, and the delays were nothing like so long or tedious as those we had incurred on many previous occasions, while the delightful shade, the songs of innumerable birds, and the fresh odour of the pine-trees rendered these halts most enjoyable. At last we reached the summit of the last ascent, and below us, at a distance of five miles, lay Lake Ashangi, a pretty sheet of water of about three miles in diameter. Its shores are in some places quite flat, but in others hills come down with gradual slopes to its very edge. Looking at England for an illustration, I should say that, except in being smaller, it more resembles Ulleswater than any of our other north-country lakes.

Beyond the lake several mountain-ranges rise one beyond another, and offer no prospect of easy journeys for some time to come. Our camp is pitched half a mile from the lake upon ground which slopes gradually down to the water's edge, above the level of which we are probably elevated thirty feet. The lake and its shores swarm with ducks and geese. The latter are very tame, and walk about to graze in the most unconcerned manner. A great many have been shot, and are, although rather fishy, fair eating. The great difficulty attending the sport is the exceedingly boggy nature of the ground. The fissures spoken of by Mr. Munzinger, and which I mentioned in my last upon the authority of his letters, are simply nonsense. It is a large and in some places a dangerous bog; but it is simply and purely a bog, and nothing else. I was out yesterday with my gun, as were a dozen others, and although I went in above my boots, I came upon nothing really impassable, nor, with one exception, did I hear of any one else doing so. Captain Hogg, however, of the quartermaster's department, got upon a very bad part of the bog, and was some time finding his way out; indeed, he fell into one deep place, where he would unquestionably have lost his life had he not had a man with him, who was able to put the end of his gun within reach of Captain Hogg's hand, and so draw him out of the quagmire, into which he was sinking fast. All round the level shore of the lake, a belt of white mud of sixty or seventy yards wide extends. Upon this the game congregate, and are safe from the sportsmen, as the mud will not support a man's weight, and the dead birds could not be recovered. The geese in plumage more resemble ducks than geese, being dark brown and green, with a large white patch upon the under part of the wing, and which only shows during their flight. A good many escape, who would fall victims to large shot; but the amount of ammunition in camp is scanty, and the shot generally of small sizes, which merely rattle against a goose's feather at a distance of fifty yards.

To-day we have remained here quietly. Another durbar has taken place; the ambassador, or nuncio—the latter, I suppose, being the appropriate word—having come in from the chief Ulem of the Gallas tribes. This man has immense influence with the Gallas, who are Mahommedans; and it was therefore a matter of great importance to conciliate him as far as possible. I have already described two of these official receptions, and as this was precisely similar to those I have before written about, I need not enter into particulars. The only variety was, that the proceedings opened with a long letter from the Ulem to Sir Robert Napier. It was of a most friendly character, and expressed the priest's concurrence in the "belief which we hold in common, namely," he said, "the Old and New Testament, and the Koran." I was not aware that the Koran was an essential part of our creed, but I have learnt something from the Ulem's letter. Later on, too, he speaks of Mahomet as the only true mediator. These, however, were not, apparently, according to the Ulem's view, points of vital difference, and he accordingly states that he prays unceasingly in our behalf, which is, at any rate, kind on his part. He warned us very solemnly to be extremely watchful and ever upon our guard, and the general tone of his letter was anything but hopeful. He mentioned that it was the custom of the country to send presents to travellers, and that he therefore sent the chief a present, but that the greatest present he could give us would be his prayers. One thing is certain, if his prayers are not of vastly greater value than his other present, they will not be of any great worth, for the material present was a pot of honey, value one dollar. The chief of course replied civilly, expressed our toleration of all religions and opinions, and that we had many Mussulmans in our ranks, and stated our friendly feelings towards the people of the country. He wound up by giving presents of robes, &c., for the priests. These robes were put upon the ambassador, who is a son of the Ulem, and one of the most inane-looking young men I have seen in Abyssinia. His face, as he was being invested in the robes, was one of the most comic things I ever saw, and the officers present had the greatest difficulty in restraining their gravity. He looked exactly like a baboon affecting humility. Later in the afternoon another chief came in, preceded by tom-tom and flutes, and accompanied by a considerable body of warriors. A remarkable thing which I noticed then, and which I had not before seen, was that they carried headless lances, in token of amity.

We had rather a curious scene this afternoon. A native was detected in the act of thieving, and was sentenced by Colonel Fraser, who acts as provost-marshal, to two dozen lashes. His friends and relatives, however, made so great a howling that the Commander-in-chief came out of his tent to see what was the matter. Finding that the natives took the matter greatly to heart, he gave the man over to be punished by themselves; and after a palaver of an hour, he was sentenced to pay one quarter of the value of the article stolen, or to receive six blows with a stick. Mr. Speedy was about to remonstrate with them upon the insufficiency of the punishment, when the chief who had acted as judge drew him aside, and stated that in the course of the examination they had found that the offender was a Christian, whereas they were themselves Mussulmans; and that if they were to punish him as he deserved, it would cause a war. Throughout Abyssinia,—that is, as far as we have travelled,—even where Christians are in the majority, the Mahommedans look down upon them; and there is no doubt that in a moral point of view the Mahommedans are greatly the superior. Christianity certainly does not work well among natives. Both in India and here a Christian is by no means a man of high standing either in respectability or morality. It is singular that the abodes of the natives here are precisely similar to those at Zulla. There they were built of wattles, with conical thatched roofs. Since that time we have passed mud huts with flat roofs, stone huts with flat roofs, stone huts with thatched roofs, and now we have again come upon the Zulla type of cottages, wattled walls with conical thatched roofs. The villages are always perched upon eminences, and the houses are crowded together and surrounded by a thick fence of boughs, with the ends outwards like a military abattis. The natives are not quite so dark as the people of Tigre, and are not so well armed, for I have not seen any fire-arms among them. Sir Charles Staveley has, I hear, arrived at Mahkan, with the 4th, the 3d Native Cavalry, and Penn's battery. He, like ourselves, is engaged in road-making. The orders are, that the pioneer force are to make the road practicable for mules, and that General Staveley's force is to make it practicable for elephants. As elephants can go almost everywhere that mules are able to do, he will not be long delayed, and will probably arrive at Lât, which is two days' march forward, within a day or two of ourselves. It is probable that we shall halt two or three days there, to allow the force to concentrate. I hear that Twiss's Mountain Train and the Naval Rocket Brigade are only a march behind General Staveley, and will arrive with him at Lât. I have seen to-night that the 45th has also been ordered to come on at once, to form part of the first division. This order will not only give satisfaction to the regiment itself, but also to us all; for the 45th is said to be one of the best and most efficient regiments in India.

Lât, March 21st.

We had all looked forward to a halt at this place for at least two or three days. This hope, however, has not been realised; for we arrived this afternoon, and start again to-morrow morning, at which time our real hardships may be said to commence in earnest. But it is better, before I enter upon this, to relate our doings of the last two days.

Leaving our camp near Ashangi, the road ran on level ground parallel to the lake for a mile or so, and then, the mountains approaching to the edge of the water, we had to climb over the spur. The height was not very great, but it was one of the roughest, and certainly the steepest climb we have yet had. Once on the crest, the hill sloped gradually down, and we presently came upon the water again near the head of the lake. This spot was the next day the scene of a fatal accident. Two or three officers came down to shoot, and one of the birds fell into the water. One of their servants, who was a good swimmer, at once went in to fetch it out. It is probable that he was seized with cramp, for he sank suddenly. Captain Pottinger at once jumped in, and swam out to the spot, but was unable to see anything of him. Our camping-ground was about two miles distant from the head of the lake, upon flat ground. The distance from Ashangi was little over six miles.

We halted here the next day in order to let General Staveley's Brigade reach Ashangi. This they did upon the day after we had left it. There was considerable regret in camp to hear that General Staveley himself, who had been attacked at Atzala with acute rheumatism, was very much worse, and had been carried in a palkee. He had entirely lost the use of his limbs, and it was considered improbable that he would be able to come on farther with the army. This would be a very great loss for the expedition, and I sincerely hope that their apprehensions will not be verified.

The morning of our halt, a general order was promulgated which filled us with consternation. No baggage whatever is to be henceforward allowed either for men or officers. Soldiers are to carry their greatcoat, a blanket, and waterproof sheet, in addition to their rifle, ammunition, havresack, &c. This will bring the weight to be carried by each man up to fifty-five pounds; an overwhelming weight over such a tremendous country as that which we have to traverse, and beneath a tropical sun. I question very much whether the men will be able to stand it, and several of the medical staff to whom I have spoken are quite of that opinion. What the roads are likely to be, is manifest enough by a portion of the general order, which says that in future no mule is to carry over 100 pounds; and yet the authorities put more than half that weight upon a man's shoulders. It is not even as if the men had their knapsacks, in which the greatcoat, &c. could be packed, and carried with comparative ease; they will have to be slung over the shoulders by the coat-arms, and will distress the soldier far more than they would have done if carried in knapsacks. It was an extraordinary oversight leaving the knapsacks behind at Antalo; for it was evident even then that they would be required. Unmounted officers are to have a greatcoat, blanket, and waterproof-sheet carried for them, and mounted officers may carry what they can put upon their horses. No baggage-animals whatever are to go forward with luggage. The men are to be packed twenty in a bell tent, and twelve officers are to have the same accommodation. More than a fourth part of the soldiers are out on picket and guard every night; therefore the number of men in each tent will be practically about the same as the officers. Fancy twelve officers in a tent! They will be packed like herrings in a tub; and men are calculating to-day how many square inches of ground each will possess. Everyone takes it good-humouredly, and there is no grumbling whatever; but for all that, it is rather a serious business. If it were for two or three days, it would be all well enough; but Magdala is a considerable distance from here. The Quartermaster-general's department talk about a six days' march. Captain Speedy says that sixteen is very much nearer the mark; and as he has a knowledge of the country, while the Quartermaster's department have uniformly been wrong in their distances, it is safe to assume that it is a fifteen days' march; that is to say, even without allowing a day for the capture of Magdala, or for arranging matters there, we cannot be back to Lât under a month. There is some talk of the baggage coming up after us; but this will certainly not come to anything. I know that we have barely animals enough with us to carry our food, and every available mule in the rear is coming on with Staveley's Brigade. We may, then, calculate with tolerable certainty that we shall not get any of our baggage until we return to Lât, which, at the very earliest, will be a month hence, and not improbably twice that time. We are told that the cold at night is very great on ahead, and that the rains are heavy and frequent. It is therefore a very serious matter for men to start without a single change of clothes of any kind. Putting aside the rain, the men will suffer so greatly from the heat, and from the labour of climbing mountains with so heavy a load upon their backs, that it would be a most material matter for them to have at any rate a dry flannel-shirt to put on when the cold evening wind begins to blow. Time will show how the men stand it; but it is certainly a hazardous experiment.

This morning we started for this place. Lât has always been spoken of as a place where we should halt and form a dépôt, and we had therefore expected to have found a large village; but as far as I have seen, there is not a native hut in the neighbourhood. Upon leaving our last camping-ground, we ascended a lofty and steep hill, and then had to wind for a long distance upon a rocky ledge, where a false step would have been certain death. After several minor rises and descents, we came down to the valley in which the stream, near which we are encamped, runs. Although there are no villages in sight, there must be a considerable native population in the neighbourhood, for a large number of natives have come in with supplies. The officers of the transport-train are buying every sword and spear brought in, for the use of the muleteers; as, although Theodore is reported at Magdala, he might at any moment make a sudden march down with a few thousand men, and might be upon us before we knew that he was within fifty miles' distance. Should we be attacked in one of these gorges, or on a narrow ledge with a precipice below, scattered as we should necessarily be over an immense length of road, Theodore might, by a sudden attack upon our baggage, do such damage in a few minutes, that we might be obliged to retire to Antalo, to fetch up fresh supplies. There is no disguising the fact, that in making our rush from such a long distance we are running no inconsiderable risk.

Sir Robert Napier's original plan was to have formed a dépôt with five months' provisions at some place about half-way between Antalo and Magdala, and to have marched forward from that place with two months' provisions. Instead of this we are starting from Lât with only fifteen days' provisions, and there is no dépôt of any importance, nor will there be, nearer than Antalo itself. The whole of the available mules will accompany the advancing division, and we shall have to depend entirely for future supplies upon the native carriage. The stock of food we have with us will barely last us to Magdala; we know not whether we shall be able to purchase any flour on the way, or how we may fare for forage for our animals. Between Antalo and Magdala are many tribes and chiefs,—we have already passed Waldo Yasus and the Gallas,—and some of these, after we have passed, may take it into their heads to stop the native animals going up with stores; and the whole of the system upon which we have solely to depend would then break down, and our position would be as precarious a one as it is possible to imagine. It is indeed a tremendous risk to run; but then we are playing for a very high stake. We are running a race with the rains. If we were to stop here for a fortnight or three weeks, and to send the whole of the transport animals down to Antalo to fetch up more provisions, we should infallibly have to wait out here over the rainy season; and the difficulties of provisioning the force during that period, and the probable mortality which might ensue, would be so great that Sir Robert Napier no doubt considers himself justified in running a very considerable risk in order to reach the sea-coast before the rains. Of course the matter has been discussed and talked over in every light among the officers; and the general opinion is, that unless we obtain an unlooked-for supply, as we did at Antalo, somewhere between this and Magdala, our position will be a very critical one. With most other generals, men would, I think, be inclined to take rather a gloomy view of it; but everyone has such confidence in Sir Robert Napier that they are quite content to leave matters in his hands.

Dildee, March 24th.

I sent off a very hurriedly-written letter two days since from Lât. In these two days we have crossed thirty-one miles of as rough a country as the warmest admirer of the desolate and savage could wish to see. Around us, as far as the eye could reach, was stretched a perfect sea of mountains; and up and down these we have tumbled and stumbled—not a few horses getting tremendous falls—from morning until long after nightfall. It has been one long monotonous toil. Sometimes we climb upon smooth slippery rock; then we ascend steep paths covered with loose boulders of every size; then we are upon a narrow ledge on a mountain's face; then we are crashing through thick bushes. One can no longer keep count of the number of ravines we cross, for we climb a dozen hills a day. It would puzzle even the engineers of the Topographical Department to lay down this rugged and broken country in a map. It would be as easy to make a map of the Straits of Dover, and to draw each wave to its proper scale. The toil of the troops during these two days has been tremendous. The first day's march was thirteen miles; yesterday's was eighteen,—many say it was twenty; but I think a long eighteen was about the mark. Eighteen miles would be a long march in England, but here it is a tremendous journey. Each man is carrying with him ammunition, &c.—fifty-five pounds—more than half a mule-load. In addition to this, most of the troops are now upon baggage-guard, and have to assist in constantly adjusting loads and looking after the mules. Lastly, a fourth of the troops are out every night upon picket. I had occasion, in a letter written from Mahkan, to speak upon the cruel over-marching of men and animals; but that was nothing to these two days' marches. The country now is much rougher, the distances longer, and the men have in addition to carry their kits. The troops came in last night in a prostrate state; very many did not come in at all. I should say that not more than half the baggage arrived until this morning; and to add to the other disagreeables, we had a tremendous thunderstorm about eight o'clock, which wetted every soul, except the very few who had been fortunate enough to get up their tents, to the skin. The men have no change of clothes with them, and of course had to sleep in their wet clothes. Of those who were on the road when the rain began, some held on and came straggling in up to ten o'clock; the greater number, however, unrolled their blanket and waterproof-sheet, and lay down where they were for the night. I say fearlessly that such a march over such a country was never before made by similarly-weighted men. Of course we have to halt to-day, and then by to-night we shall have progressed a less distance towards Magdala than we should have done had we made three days' marches of, say, eleven miles each. Nor is there any reason why we should not have done so. We are fortunately now in a well-watered country. Good-sized streams run between each of the higher ranges, and we crossed four or five of them yesterday.

General Staveley, who I am glad to hear is better, is only one day in our rear. An officer has gone back this morning to direct him to halt to-night at the stream three and a half miles behind. The weather has been warmer for the last two days, and this has of course increased the labour of the soldiers. Had it not been for the frequent occurrence of water, I do not think that one quarter of the troops would have got in last night. Yesterday's camp was admirably chosen for defensive purposes, being surrounded on all sides by a deep nullah. To-day's camp is convenient, and is also defended on one side by a nullah, but has the disadvantage that the nullah is two hundred feet deep, and is extremely precipitous, the water being only accessible even on foot at two places, and consequently the difficulty of watering the animals is very great. The water, however, and indeed all that we have met with for the last day or two, is delicious. This is indeed a treat. Hitherto the water has been singularly nasty—thick and full of insects when stagnant, earthy and bad-tasting when running. Here it is fresh, clear, and pure. Rum is quite at a discount. The ravine through which the stream runs is very picturesque. The slope is steep, but well-wooded down to the bottom of the nullah; but the stream itself has cut a way from twenty to thirty feet wide through the solid rock at the bottom. The sides are as perpendicular as walls, and are in some places thirty feet deep. It is only, as I have said, at two points that we can get down to the water. This narrow gorge is overhung with trees, and in every cranny and on every tiny ledge grow lovely patches of green ferns. It requires no stretch of fancy to imagine oneself by the side of a pretty mountain-stream in Wales or Ireland. The vegetation is too bright and varied for a Highland stream. Nearly every officer in camp, and a good number of the men, have been down this morning for a bathe, which is doubly refreshing after the fatigue of yesterday and the paucity of our present washing appliances. The camp yesterday morning presented quite an unusual appearance. The head-quarter camp had shrivelled in dimensions from twenty tents down to four; and outside of them, soon after daybreak, the whole staff might be seen engaged in the various processes of washing and dressing. Twelve men may manage to sleep in a tent, but it is quite impossible that they can simultaneously dress there. Not, indeed, that any of the tents contained their full complement. Some had slung their blankets like hammocks upon the trees; others were content to roll themselves in their rugs, and sleep upon a waterproof-sheet under a bush; and besides this there was a hospital-tent, and as there are no sick, some of the officers were drafted off into this. Indeed, all might have been very much more comfortable, had those of their number who, like ourselves, have brought *tentes d'abri*, been allowed to carry them on their horses. I was very fortunate in getting into shelter before the storm came on last night. I had ridden on before my spare horse, which, with my tent and etceteras upon his back, was nearly at the rear of the column. I arrived here about half-past four, having been nearly nine hours upon the road; and I was fairly exhausted when I got in from fatigue and want of food. Fortunately, however, the natives had brought in bread for sale, and after eating some of this, and going down to the nullah for a bathe, I was quite restored again. I was not, however, comfortable in my mind; for the clouds had been banking-up fast, and the thunder had been almost incessant in the hills for the last two hours. I could see by the baggage which was coming in, that my animal could not, if he kept his place in the line, be in for hours, if at all. When I got up to the camp, I was delighted to see my little tent pitched. My companion, who had been behind me, had, finding that the road was badly blocked, got them along by other paths, fortunately without more damage than one of the horses falling over a precipice twelve or thirteen feet high, into some bushes, which broke the animal's fall. The horse was but little hurt; and with this slight mishap, which is nothing here, where horses and mules are constantly rolling over steep places, he had succeeded in getting into camp three or four hours before the animals could have possibly reached it, had they kept in their original place in the line; indeed it was most improbable that they could have got in last night at all. The lightning during the next half-hour was incessant, and before the dinner could be cooked, great drops began to patter down. We shouted to the servants to do the best they could for themselves with their blankets and waterproof-sheets, while we took refuge in our little tent, with an officer whose baggage, like that of the great majority, had not arrived. In a minute or two, it came down almost in a sheet. We lit our pipes, and consoled ourselves that if we had nothing to eat, we were no worse off than anyone else, whereas we were in shelter, while hardly another soul was so. While thus philosophising to our own contentment, the front of the tent was suddenly opened, and a hand was thrust in with a dish of cutlets, then plates and knives and forks. Our fellows had nobly stuck to their work, preferring to get drenched to the skin rather than that their masters should go without dinner. These Goa-men are certainly excellent servants. They are not physically strong: they are quiet, weakly-looking men, with little energy and no habitude to hardships. They make capital hotel-waiters, but could scarcely have been expected to have supported the fatigue of a campaign like this. They do so, however, and seem none the worse for it. Altogether they are worth any money upon an expedition of this sort, and are infinitely more serviceable than an English servant would be.

The storm ceased last night at about half-past ten. It is now thundering among the distant hills, and it is evident that we shall have, this afternoon, a repetition of last night's storm. It will, however, find us better prepared to withstand it. The natives are bringing in an abundance of goods of all kinds. Honey, grain, onions, goats, sheep, fowls, bread, and eggs. The fowls and eggs are the first we have seen since Attegrat. Prices rule about the same. Two little fowls, a dollar; twelve eggs—about half of which average bad—at the same price. A bottle of honey, a dollar, &c. Dear as things are, it is unnecessary to say that they are all eagerly bought up. We are accustomed to high prices now; and I heard a soldier, who did not get in until this morning, say that he paid a dollar in the night for a drink of water.

Of course we have now a constant succession of news from the front. It is very contradictory, but the general report is that Theodore is marching towards Dalanta, to attack us on our way. Some of the spies assert that two o'clock on Friday night is the hour fixed for our destruction. If Theodore does mean, as is likely enough, to make a night attack, I do not think he would be weak enough to let it be known many hours beforehand as to where it will take place. However, it is no use offering any speculation now upon events which we may see determined in two or three days, and the result of which will be known by telegraph long before this letter can reach London.

Santarai, March 29th.

We are beginning to believe Magdala to be a *fata morgana*, an *ignis fatuus*, which gets more and more distant the nearer we approach it. At Dildee we were told that it was only four marches distant. We have made three marches, and have sixty more miles to go; and yet Magdala is not more than twenty-five miles in a straight line, and is visible from a point four miles distant from this camp. It is found, however, that the country is perfectly impracticable, and that we must take a detour of sixty miles to get there. I can hardly imagine what this country in a direct line to Magdala can be like, for we have passed over hundreds of miles which no one would have imagined it possible for an army with its baggage-animals to surmount. We have scaled mountains and descended precipices; we have wound along the face of deep ravines, where a false step was death; we are familiar with smooth slippery rock and with loose boulders; and after this expedition it can hardly be said that any country is impracticable for an army determined to advance. I hear, however, that between this and Magdala there are perpendicular precipices running like walls for miles, places which could scarcely be scaled by experienced cragsmen, much less by loaded mules. We must therefore make a detour. It is tiresome, for everyone is burning with impatience to be at Magdala, and to solve the long-debated problems—will Theodore fight? will he fight in the open, or defend Magdala? or will he hand over the captives with an apology? and shall we be content to receive one? I believe that I can answer the last question with certainty. We shall not. If Theodore sends in the captives we shall receive them, but shall certainly exact retribution from him. We shall either take him prisoner or compel him to fly. If we obtain the prisoners unhurt, we shall still take Magdala. If he escape to the mountains with a few adherents, we shall, in that case, be content to retire, and to leave the task of hunting him down to his numerous enemies; but if he murder the prisoners we shall ourselves remain here until he is captured. I think I may positively state that this, or something very like it, is the tenor of the instructions given to Sir Robert Napier by the Government; and I think that they will be heartily approved by all, except by those negrophilists who deny that a black man can do wrong. It would be impossible to allow Theodore to go unpunished; indeed, it would be offering a premium to all savage potentates in future time to make prisoners of any English travellers who may fall into their hands.

I now return to Dildee, from which place I last wrote, while we were halting in consequence of the tremendous march of the preceding day. Upon the evening of the day upon which we halted we heard that General Staveley had arrived with the force under his command at a stream five miles in our rear, and had there halted. He had with him the 4th, a wing of the 33d, six companies of the Punjaub Pioneers, Twiss's Battery, and the

Naval Rocket Train. It was decided that the wing of the 33d, who were with us, should halt for a day, and should come on as a complete regiment, and that the 4th, which is numerically much weaker than the 33d, should push on with the advance. The next day's march was short, but severe, as we had to climb a mountain 3000 feet above our camping-ground. It was hard work, but was got over much more speedily than usual, as the train was much smaller, owing to our diminished numbers; and we had consequently fewer of the tedious blocks so trying to both man and beast. The road was in most places pretty good; but was dangerous for a long distance where it wound along the face of a deep ravine. The country here must be either much more densely populated, or the people much more industrious than in most of the districts over which we have passed; for there were patches of cultivation to the very top of the mountain, which, where we crossed it, was about 11,000 feet above the sea. The mountain side was bare of trees, or even bushes; but, curiously enough, very near the summit were large quantities of small palm-trees, with thick straight stems, three or four feet high, and clustered heads of spreading leaves. Several Indian officers agreed with me in considering them to be a species of palm, but we had no botanist amongst us, and it seemed most unlikely that even dwarf palm-trees should be growing in such a lofty and exposed position. I have only before seen palm-trees twice in Abyssinia, once at Goun Gonna, where two or three grew near the church, and in a valley between Attegrat and Antalo.

Arrived at the top of the pass, we found ourselves at the head of a deep ravine, on the side of which, a quarter of a mile from the summit, it was decided that the camp should be pitched. A more uncomfortable place for a camp could hardly be imagined. The ground was ploughed, and was extremely sloping. The supply of water was deficient, and was four or five hundred feet below us, and the wind swept over the top of the pass with piercing force. However, there was no help for it. The 4th had started four miles behind us, and there was no ground even so good as that selected for another seven miles. Immediately on our arrival, and before the tents were pitched, a tremendous shower came on, and everyone got drenched before the baggage-animals arrived with the tents. The black earth turned, as if by magic, into slimy clay, and our position was the reverse of agreeable. Far worse, however, was the condition of the 4th, which, having halted at Dildee for two hours, did not arrive until between eight and nine in the evening, wetted of course to the skin. We now felt bitterly the inconvenience of not having even one change of clothes with us. It could, however, have hardly been foreseen that, after having had only two or three showers since we arrived in Abyssinia, we were to be exposed to heavy rains regularly every day, which has, with one exception, been the case for the last week. As it is, it is impossible to say how long we shall be in our present state of only having the clothes we stand in. It is a week since we left our little all behind us at Lât. We are still a week's march from Magdala, and may calculate on being fully a month without our baggage. Officers have all managed somehow to bring on a second shirt and pair of stockings; but the soldiers have no change of any kind. For them, and indeed for the officers, to be wetted through day after day, and to have no dry clothes to put on, and this at an altitude of 11,000 feet above the sea, and when the cold at night is more pierceing than anything I ever experienced, is trying in the extreme, and a great many are already complaining of rheumatic pains. That night at the top of the hill was the most unpleasant that officers or men have passed since their arrival in the country: wet through, cold, and lying upon ground so steep that we kept perpetually sliding down off our waterproof sheet. As to lying in the orthodox fashion, side by side, with all the heels close to the pole, like the spokes of a wheel, the thing was simply impossible. In many of the tents the men's feet would have been a yard higher than their heads. However, there were few grumblings at the discomfort; but I can answer that I for one was greatly pleased when I saw daylight break, to get up from my uncomfortable sliding couch. We were ordered to start at eight, but the men's things were still so wet that the march was postponed for two hours, to allow the blankets and greatcoats to be dried in the wind and sun.

Our next march was again only seven miles to a place called Muja, not that there was a village of any kind there, or indeed at eighteen out of twenty places we have stopped at. To suppose that the natives have a name for every field is absurd. Two speculations have been started as to how the quartermaster-general's department always obtain a name for our camping-ground—the one is that they say something to a native, and the first word he utters they put down at once for the station; the other is that they draw a certain number of vowels and consonants from a bag, drop them on the ground, and see what word they form. It is certain that scarcely a name corresponds with those set down in maps, and instead of calling these flats and plains by any name the first native may tell them, it would be much more sensible, and would render it much more easy for an English reader to follow our course, if our quartermasters were to take some good map, and fix upon the name which most nearly corresponds with the position of our camps.

The seven-miles road down to Muja was not difficult, but was one of the most dangerous we have passed over. The path for the whole distance wound along on the face of a deep ravine. It was often little more than a foot wide, and was formed sometimes upon rock, and sometimes on black earth, which had been dried hard by the wind and sun before we passed along it, but which if wet would have been perfectly impassable. Had a storm come on when we were upon it, we must have stopped to unload the animals. As it was, only one stumbled and went over the edge, and was of course killed.

We have had a good many casualties lately among the animals. The Scinde Horse, too, have lost several horses, but this is hardly surprising from the way in which they ride them. A Scinde horseman, and I believe most of the native cavalry, have an idea that it shows good horsemanship to ride a horse up and down very steep places. It would be a great saving of horseflesh if an order were issued that all native cavalry should dismount and lead their horses up, if not down also, long or steep hills. Our camping-ground at Muja was flat and turfy, but it had the disadvantage of being a great height above water. Sir Robert Napier himself upon his arrival rode a couple of miles farther in search of some site more convenient for watering the animals, but he was unsuccessful in doing so. The camping-ground had also the disadvantage of a very great scarcity of wood.

Our view from Muja was very striking. Six miles in front, and a thousand feet below us, lay the valley of the Tacazze. Beyond arose a straight line of mountains, more steep and formidable than anything we have hitherto seen. The slope at their feet was comparatively easy, but it increased rapidly, and a wall of perpendicular rock of upwards of a hundred feet high ran along the crests without the slightest apparent break. The range looked like a mighty natural barrier to our further progress into Abyssinia. However, we knew that the exploring-party was upon the plateau on the summit, having gone up by the native road. Our order for the morrow was, that we were to march early down to the Tacazze; that we were to encamp in the valley, and that the troops were to set to work to make the road up the ghaut practicable for our ascent upon the following day. At eight o'clock in the evening, however, Captain Fawcett, of the quartermaster's department, rode into camp with a letter from Colonel Phayre, evidently written in great consternation of mind, and saying that Mr. Munzinger, who is with Gobayze's army, was missing, and had no doubt fallen into Theodore's hands—that Theodore himself, with his army, had crossed the Bachelo river, and was advancing to attack us; and urging that more troops should be sent on.

Of course there was great excitement in the camp at this news. We were only thirty-five miles in a straight line from Magdala, only twenty-three from the Bachelo, and as Theodore, with his lightly-weighted natives would march nearly straight, it was probable that we should be attacked on the next night. In another hour an order was issued, which showed that Sir Robert Napier, as well as ourselves, looked upon this information as most important. The column was only to halt for two or three hours at the Tacazze, while a strong working-party made the road to some extent passable. We were then to march up it, and to encamp upon the plateau for the night.

It was evident that the Commander-in-chief felt the importance of gaining the summit of the precipitous range opposite before Theodore got to its top to prevent our so doing. All the evening our talk was of Sniders and night-attacks, and every *pro* and *con* was warmly discussed. At seven the troops started, and in two hours and a half reached the Tacazze. The Tacazze is here an insignificant stream, very inferior to many of those we have previously crossed. Indeed, it is more a succession of pools than a stream, and yet as one crossed it, one could not forget that this was one of the fountain-heads of the mighty Nile—that it was this little streamlet, which, swollen by a thousand tributaries, rushes every July into the main river, raising its level many feet, and fertilising all Egypt with the rich Abyssinian soil it carries down.

We went on half-a-mile farther across the valley to a point where the commissariat had collected a dépôt of grain. Here the mules were unloaded, fed and watered, and the troops had breakfast, while strong fatigue-parties of the Beloochees, Punjaubees, and 4th went up the hill to work upon the road, under the direction of Captains Goodfellow and Lemessurier of the Engineers. In three hours afterwards the signallers on the top of the hill waved us word that the road was passable, and we started for a climb of a clear two thousand five hundred feet. It was hard work, but the road was surprisingly free from difficulties or dangers until we reached within two or three hundred feet of the top. Then there were some exceedingly nasty bits, but upon the whole it was nothing like what we had anticipated, and not to be compared to many places we have before passed.

As we reached the top, Colonel Cameron called upon the 4th for three cheers, telling them that thrashing Theodore would be nothing to the task of climbing that hill. The men responded heartily but feebly; breath, not inclination, being wanting. They then marched cheerily on across a plateau level for another mile, in high spirits at the brush they were looking forward to with Theodore. We soon found, as I had imagined that we should do, that this anticipation was destined for the present to be disappointed.

Munzinger was not missing, and never had been. He had gone out for a ride, and his servant said, on being questioned, that he did not know where he was. Theodore had not crossed, and apparently had not the least idea of crossing the Bachelo, but was still making every effort to get his guns into Magdala.

We had no sooner reached the plateau than we became conscious of a very great change in the temperature. The wind blew bitterly cold, and not a single tree or even bush of the smallest size was visible for the purposes of firewood. There were numerous native cattle grazing on the hill-sides, and the men at once set to work to pick up dried cow-dung, which the natives habitually use for fuel; others busied themselves in cutting peat; and the fires were soon lighted under the cooking-pots. At six o'clock we had our usual heavy rain, lasting for two hours; but fortunately before it set in the tents were safely pitched. Only, therefore, the men on duty got wet. The night was most piercingly cold. To say that ice formed upon water gives no idea whatever of the cold. A strong March east wind blew with a force which penetrated to the very bones. I can safely say that never in my life did I feel the cold so much as I have the two last nights. The troops, especially the natives, of course feel it still more severely. Rheumatic pains are beginning to be generally felt, and a week of this work will fill the hospital-tents. The cold will tell more severely when the stock of rum is exhausted. Each regiment brought up some with their fifteen days' supplies, and this is not yet exhausted; but the commissariat supply is finished, and we have had none now for four days. The sugar has been also exhausted, and the tea was running very short. I am happy to say, however, that a fresh supply has arrived to-day; for cold water only in such a climate as this would be the reverse of cheering.

It was arranged that we should halt here for two days, to allow General Staveley to come up with the force under him. Yesterday, early, news was brought in to the Chief that the uncle of Wagshum Gobayze was coming in to pay a visit, and Major Grant and Captain Moore went out to meet him. The Adjutant-general carelessly omitted to notify the pickets of the coming of the envoy; and accordingly, when the outlying sentry of the 4th regiment saw a body of 700 or 800 horsemen advancing, he naturally supposed that it was the enemy. He very properly called out the picket, who loaded their Sniders, and went out in skirmishing order to meet the enemy. In another quarter of a minute they would have opened fire, when an officer of the 4th came running up and stopped them. Had he been a minute later the consequences would have been most disastrous. Every shot would have told upon the dense body of horsemen, and the twenty men, in the minute or two which must have elapsed before the cavalry could have reached them, would have done terrible execution; and even had the cavalry charged, would, by falling into a small square, not improbably have defended themselves against the whole force. But the lives so sacrificed would have been only the beginning of misfortunes. Nothing would ever have convinced Gobayze that the affair was the result of a mistake, and we should have had him for our foe as well as Theodore. And with Wagshum's army hovering around us, cutting off our baggage-train and attacking small parties, our position would be indeed a precarious one.

Wagshum Gobayze's uncle arrived with his body of cavalry at the other side of the little stream which borders our camp, and here halted for a few minutes. The troops were in the mean time paraded in front of their respective lines. Gobayze's troops, of whom there were 700 or 800 present, drew up in a long line and dismounted, every man sitting down in front of his horse. They were by far the most formidable body we have seen since our arrival in this country. They were really cavalry, and rode small but very strong and serviceable horses. They were armed with shield and spear. I do not of course mean that these troops could stand for a moment against a charge of regular cavalry. It is probable that a hundred of the Scinde Horse or of the 3d Cavalry would scatter them like chaff; but for rough work, for dashing down a mountain side and attacking a convoy, they would be most formidable enemies. Their horses are all unshod, are marvellously surefooted, and will go at a gallop over places where an English horse could scarcely walk. We were greatly surprised at the sight of this body of cavalry, for heretofore we had not seen an animal which could even by courtesy be called a horse since we landed in Abyssinia.

Leaving the main body of the force behind, the envoy advanced, escorted by the 3d Cavalry, who had gone out to meet him, and attended only by a dozen or so of his personal followers. As he passed through the lines the regiments saluted and the bands played. The envoy was an intelligent-looking man, dressed in a crimson-silk dressing-gown, brocaded with yellow; over this he wore the universal Abyssinian white-cloth wrapping, and had a white turban upon his head. By his side rode the officers who had gone out to meet him and Mr. Munzinger. The envoy could not be received in a public durbar, as the previous ambassadors have been, for Sir Robert Napier has now only a small tent of some eight to ten feet square. I am unable to say, therefore, what took place at the interview, except that the envoy expressed very considerable dread of Theodore, who, he said, had 10,000 men, and would unquestionably fight us at Magdala.

At the conclusion of the interview the envoy was presented with a horse and a double-barrelled gun. While the interview was going on we amused ourselves by inspecting the envoy's shield, which was carried by an attendant, and was a very magnificent affair indeed. The shield itself was of course of rhinoceros hide, and upon it was a piece of lion's skin, with numerous raised bosses of gilt-filigree work, which appeared to me to be of Indian workmanship. It was one of the ten royal shields, all precisely similar, which exist in Abyssinia. The attendants were mostly fine, well-built fellows, as were the general body of cavalry, and of superior physique to any men we had hitherto seen. I should mention that all the horses have a strap going from the forehead down to the nose, upon which are two or more round plates of metal with a sharp spike in them, exactly resembling, but smaller, those worn upon the foreheads of the horses of the knights of old. The 4th, the Scinde Horse, and a body of 3d Native Cavalry, were drawn up in front of the tent, and saluted as the envoy left. There is no doubt that Theodore will be no despicable foe, and the further we go the more evident this becomes. Gobayze's army is said to be 20,000 strong; and if, as I understand, those we saw to-day were a fair sample of them, they would be certainly formidable antagonists. And yet Gobayze has been watching Theodore for months, and did not dare to attack him, even when encumbered by his artillery and baggage. Gobayze indeed confesses that his army would have no chance with that of Theodore. The army of the latter, then, when garrisoning a position of such immense natural strength as that of Magdala, will be formidable even to an army of 4000 British troops. There can be no doubt that we shall capture the place; but the British public must not be surprised if we do not do it directly we arrive.

Sir Charles Staveley arrived to-day with his force, which slept last night at a halting-place at the foot of the ghaut. I am glad to say that the general has so far recovered from his attack of rheumatism as to be able to sit on his horse for a portion of the journey. He brought with him the whole of the 33d, six companies of the Punjaub Pioneers, Twiss's steel battery, the 3d Native Cavalry, and the Naval Rocket Brigade. The 45th regiment, the 3d Dragoon Guards, and the second wing of the Beloochees are all coming up by forced marches, and, as well as the elephants with G 14 Battery, will arrive here in three days. This afternoon the Naval Brigade went out to exhibit rocket practice. There was not room in the valley for the practice, and they therefore went up on to a hill, and fired at another hill about 2000 yards distant. There are twelve mules, each with a tube, and there is a supply of ninety rockets to each tube: there are four men to each tube, beside the man who leads the mule. At the word "unload!" the tubes, which are about three feet in length, are quickly taken off the mules and arranged in line. Each tube is provided with a sort of stand, with a marked elevator, by which it can be adjusted to any required angle. The order at first was to fire at ten degrees of elevation; and upon the word "fire!" being given, one after another of the rockets (which have no stick) rushed from the tube, and buzzed through the air to the top of the opposite hill. Three rockets were fired to this elevation, and then three from an elevation of five degrees. A very strong wind was blowing, and it was difficult therefore to form any opinion of the accuracy of aim attainable. The bolts as they shot through the air certainly did not appear to swerve in the slightest from their original line; and there is no doubt that this novel instrument of war will strike terror into the hearts of the garrison of Magdala.

Scindee, April 5th.

When I wrote from Santarai we were twenty-five miles in a direct line from Magdala. After marching thirty-five miles we are at exactly the same distance. In fact, we have marched along the base of a triangle, of which Magdala forms the apex. We have been obliged to do this to arrive at the one practicable point for crossing the tremendous ravine of the Djedda. For the whole of this distance we have marched along a nearly level plateau ten thousand feet above the sea. The sun by day has been exceedingly hot, the wind at night piercingly cold, and we have had heavy thunderstorms of an afternoon. The extremes of temperature are very great, and it is indeed surprising that the troops preserve their health as they do. I have seen the thermometer register 145° at eleven o'clock, and go down to 19° at night. The plateau land has been bare and monotonous in the extreme, not a single shrub, however small, breaks the view, and the only variety whatever has been, that whereas in most places the soil is a black friable loam, at others it is so covered with stones of all sizes that the soil itself is scarcely visible, and travelling is difficult and painful in the extreme. Our first march was twelve miles in length to Gazoo, which is the name of a stream running for nearly the whole distance parallel to our line of march. At Gazoo, the very serious news reached us that the arrangements for the native transport had broken down, and that no supplies were on their way up. This was what I had, when we started from Lât for our rush forward, foreseen was exceedingly likely to happen, and our position at once became a very precarious one. We had only six days' provision remaining. Magdala was five days' march distant. It was now certain that no fresh supplies could possibly arrive until long after those we have with us are exhausted. It is hardly probable that we shall find any provisions upon our way, for to-morrow we shall come upon Theodore's track, and it is said that he has burnt and plundered the whole country in the neighbourhood of his line of route. It is very doubtful whether we shall obtain enough food for our animals; even now, when in a cultivated country which has not been ravaged, forage is very scarce, and the animals are upon the very shortest allowance which will keep life together. The prospect, therefore, was gloomy indeed, and there was a rumour that the Chief had made up his mind to halt, and to send the whole of the animals back to bring up provisions. This idea, however, if it was ever entertained, was abandoned; those energetic officers, Major Grant and Captain Moore, were sent back to endeavour to arrange the hitch in the native carriage; the ration of biscuit was reduced from a pound to half-a-pound per diem, and the army moved on. Fortunately news came up that the natives were bringing in a thousand pounds of flour a-day to the commissariat station which had been established at the Tacazze, and with these and our half-rations we might hold on for some time.

The next day's march was sixteen miles, to Ad Gazoo, through a country precisely similar in character to that passed on the preceding day, except that it was more cultivated. The villages, indeed, were everywhere scattered, and although small were snug and comfortable-looking, the little clusters of eight or ten huts, with their high conical thatched roofs, looking very like snug English homesteads with their rickyards. Here, as indeed through the whole of the latter part of our journey, the people came out to gaze on the passing army of white strangers. Picturesque groups they formed as they squatted by the wayside. In the centre would probably be the priest, and next to him the patriarch and the chief of the village. Round them would sit the other men, and behind these the women and girls would stand, the latter chattering and laughing among themselves, or to the younger men, who stood beside them. Here, too, would be the mothers, some with their little fat babies in their arms, some with two or three children hanging round them, and peeping bashfully out at the strange white men. Some of the women would generally have brought goats, or a pot of honey, or a jar of milk or ghee, or a bag of grain to sell, but they soon forgot to offer them in their surprise at the strange attires and beautiful horses of the strangers.

From Ad Gazoo we yesterday moved our camp to this place, a distance of only two miles, Sir Charles Staveley bringing up his division to the camp we had left, so that the whole force is now well together in case of an attack. An affair took place yesterday evening, the consequences of which might have been very serious. Ashasta, Gobayze's uncle, who visited us at Santarai, again came into camp with a couple of hundred followers. Care had been taken this time to prevent the possibility of his being fired into by the pickets, and when his visit was over he was escorted by an officer beyond the lines. After he had left us, he went to a village not far distant, where he billeted half of his men. With the remainder he started for another village; but upon his way he passed close to an outlying picket of General Staveley's brigade, consisting of a corporal and four men of the 3d Native Infantry. These men of course knew nothing of his having come from our camp, and shouted to the party to keep their distance. The natives, who, as I have before said, have a strong impression that we cannot fight, replied by derisive cries and by brandishing their lances. The corporal, naturally supposing that it was a party of Theodore's cavalry, ordered one of his men to fire, which was answered by a couple of shots on the part of the natives. The corporal then gave the word to the others to fire, and then to charge, and the little party, sword in hand, went gallantly at the numerous party of their supposed enemy. Ashasta, seeing that it was a mistake, ordered his men to retreat, which they did, pursued by the picket, who came up with some of the hindmost of the party. They pursued for some distance, and then halted. Two of the natives were killed in the affair, one with a bullet, one by a sword-thrust, and two others were wounded. At the sound of the firing Staveley's brigade was called out under arms, and considerable excitement prevailed for some time. Late in the evening, when the matter was understood, M. Munzinger went out to explain to Ashasta how it had happened; and as the men killed were not chiefs, and human life does not go for much in Abyssinia, our apologies were accepted, and Ashasta came into camp again to-day. Thus what might have been a very serious business is happily arranged. The men upon picket are in no way to blame; in fact, they behaved with great gallantry, and must have opened the eyes of the natives to the fact that we can fight when we like. Technically, they were somewhat to blame in charging, as the rule is that a picket should never advance, but should fire and hold its ground when possible, or retire upon its supports if threatened by an overwhelming force.

The Naval Rocket Brigade now form a portion of this camp. They are an admirable body of men, and do great credit to Captain Fellowes, their commanding officer. They support the fatigues and hardships with the good-temper peculiar to naval men. They march, contrary to what might have been expected, even better than the soldiers, and never fall out, even on the most fatiguing journeys. They are a great amusement to the troops, and their admonitions to their mules, which they persist in treating as ships, are irresistibly comic. I saw a sailor the other day who was leading a mule, while a comrade walked behind it. A stoppage occurred, but he went right on into the midst of a number of soldiers.

"Hallo, Jack!" they said good-humouredly, "where are you coming?"

"Coming?" Jack said, "I ain't coming anywhere. I am only towing the craft; it's the chap behind does the steering."

It is always so with them. The head-rope is always either the "tow-rope" or "the painter." They starboard or port their helm, "tack through a crowd," or "wear the ship round" in a most amusing way. They have of course shore-titles for the occasion, but do not always answer to them.

The other day I heard an officer call out, "Sergeant-major!"

No answer.

"Sergeant-major!" This time louder.

Still no reply.

A third and still louder hail produced no response.

"Boatswain, where the devil are you?"

"Ay, ay, sir!" was the instant answer from the man, who was standing close by, but who had quite forgotten his new rank of sergeant-major.

Of an evening, if we have a halt, Jack sometimes dances. The band of the Punjaubees—between whom and the sailors there is a great friendship, although of course they do not understand a word of each other's language—comes over to the sailors' camp, and plays dance-music; and half-a-dozen couples of sailors stand up and execute quadrilles, waltzes, and polkas.

The scene is a very amusing one. The Punjaubees do not stand, but sit in a circle, and play away with the greatest gravity; very well they play too, for they are beyond all comparison the best band out here. The sailors dance without the least idea that there is anything comic in the business; while round stand a crowd of amused soldiers and of astonished natives of the country, to whom the whole performance is a profound mystery.

The Punjaub Pioneers still maintain the high opinion they have earned by their hard work. They are indeed a splendid regiment, and reflect the greatest credit upon Major Chamberlain, their popular commanding-officer. Major Chamberlain's case is a particularly hard one. He was promoted to the rank of major during the mutinies, and was subsequently, for his great services, recommended no less than three times for his colonelcy. The Indian Government, however, refused, on account of his recent promotion. Eleven years have since elapsed, and that objection must long ere this be done away with; and yet Major Chamberlain is only Major Chamberlain still. It is to be hoped that at the end of this campaign a tardy recognition will be made of his services.

It was Major Chamberlain and his Punjaubees who found water at a short distance from Zulla. He asserted, and very rightly, that as there was water at Koomaylo, it must find its way down to the sea somehow, and so he set his men to work to dig. Down he went steadily, amidst the laughter and chaff of his friends in the Engineers. Still he persevered, and at nearly sixty feet from the surface he struck water. An abundant supply is now obtainable from this well, and by this service alone he has amply earned his promotion.

The difficulties of writing since we left Lât have been greater than ever, and the manual operation of inditing an epistle is a most serious business. Of course there is nothing resembling a chair or a table,—not even a box. The only way to write is lying upon the ground, and putting one's paper upon one's pillow. Now my pillow is not a comfortable one for sleeping upon, much less for writing. It is composed of a revolver, a box of cartridges, a telescope, a bag of dollars, a packet of candles, a powder-flask, a bag of bullets, a comb, a pair of stockings, and a flannel-shirt,—in fact, all my worldly belongings. A most useful kit, no doubt, but uncomfortable as a pillow, inconvenient as a writing-table. However, one gets accustomed to anything; and if this campaign lasts another month or two, we shall not improbably have learnt to dispense with much more important articles than tables and chairs; for we have only the clothes we stand in, and these are already giving unmistakable signs of approaching dissolution.

Dalanta, April 5th.

We are now getting to names which are somewhat familiar to us. The river Djedda, which the troops crossed yesterday, and the plain of Dalanta, where we are encamped to-day, were both mentioned frequently in the letters from the captives. The river Djedda was the place where Theodore was detained so long making a practicable road for his guns, and where he was represented as encouraging his men at their task by working with his own hands. Dalanta was the province or tract which was spoken of as in rebellion against him for a considerable time previously, but which submitted as soon as he had crossed the Djedda.

After I had sent off my letter of the 3d, intelligence arrived that Theodore had broken up his camp before Magdala, and was moving to attack us. I need hardly say that the news was untrue. The Chief, however, was bound to act upon it, and consequently we were ordered to march at seven; and instead of halting, as previously intended, upon the edge of the ravine of the Djedda, we were to cross and encamp on the other side, so as to avoid the possibility of having to take such a strong position. Colonel Milward, who had marched the evening before with the Punjaubees, and two companies of the 4th, was ordered to cross early, and General Staveley was to bring up his force to the edge of the ravine. We started punctually at the time ordered, and marched across a precisely similar country to that we had traversed for the few previous days. Some miles before we reached the edge of the Djedda the whole aspect was changed. The yellow stubble and hay, which had before stretched away upon both sides, was all burnt, and the ground was covered only with a black ash. The flocks and herds which had dotted the country were gone, and scarcely a human being was to be seen over the black expanse. The snug homesteads and villages had disappeared, and in their places were bare walls and heaps of stones. I rode up to one of these. On the floor lay the half-charred thatch of the roof; among it were portions of broken pots and baking effects. Here was a long round stone, which was used as a rolling-pin to make the flat bread; there was a large vessel of baked earth and cow-dung which had once held flour or milk. A rat scuttled away as I looked in. There was not a living soul in what had once been a large village. This was indeed the desolation of war. Presently we saw rising, apparently a few feet above the plain, at a distance of five or six miles, a long perpendicular wall of rock. This, we knew, was the upper edge of the opposite side of the Djedda. The ground then sank a little in front of us, and, riding along the slight depression, we suddenly turned a corner, and below us lay the wonderful gorge of the Djedda. Its width from edge to edge was four or five miles, its depth to the stream 3800 feet. It was a wonderful ravine. As far as eye could see either way, the upper part upon sides appeared like two perpendicular walls of perhaps a third of its total depth. Then, on either side, was a plain or shoulder of from a mile to a mile and a half in width, with a gradual slope towards the stream. The lower portion was again extremely steep, but still with a gradual descent, and not mere walls of rock like the upper edges. It was easy to imagine the whole process of the formation of this gorge. Originally it must have been an arm of the sea; a gulf of five miles across, and with perpendicular cliffs upon either side, and its depth the level of the broad shoulders. Then the land rose, and a great river ran through the centre of what was now a noble valley, gradually eating its way down until its bed attained its present enormous depth. It was this ravine which had been the cause of the immense detour we have had to make. Forty miles back, at Santarai, we were said to be as close to Magdala as we were when we stood prepared to descend into the Djedda. But the perpendicular walls barred our progress, and we have marched along nearly parallel to its course until we have reached the one spot where a break in its iron walls allow of our descent. By this route Theodore marched, and when we saw the road he had made for us, we felt for the first time since our arrival really grateful to the Abyssinian tyrant.

It is really a wonderful road, almost as good as could have been made by our own engineers; the only difference being that they would have thrown a layer of earth over the loose stones to bind them together, and to afford a firm and level surface. The road is really constructed with great engineering skill. Blasting-tools have been freely used wherever the rock required it. Every wind and turn, every shoulder and slope, has been taken advantage of in order to make zigzags, and render the descent more gradual. It is true that in places it is fearfully steep—an incline of one and a quarter to one—which, to convey the idea more popularly, is about the slope of the bank of a railway-cutting. The leaving the road in its present state, with loose stones, may have been done with an object, for upon a solid road of this angle it would have been next to impossible to have kept heavy cannon on wheels from running down, whereas upon a very loose and heavy road the matter was comparatively easy. The length of the descent is four miles and a half, that of the ascent three miles and a half. Two miles and a half of the former, and a mile and a half of the latter, are across and partially along the shoulders, where the slope was very slight. In consequence, it may be said that actually three thousand feet of depth were on either side attained in two miles, which would give an average incline of one in three. The road is from twenty to thirty feet in width; generally it is made through basalt, which, in cooling, had crystallised, so that its surface resembles a mosaic pavement, and this readily breaks up. Parts, however, are cut through a hard stone, and portions through a conglomerate, which must have tried to the utmost the tools and patience of Theodore's army. How he achieved the task with the means at his disposal I am at a loss to understand; and the road has certainly raised Theodore very many degrees in the estimation of our men. Upon every level space in the camping-ground of his army, there are their fireplaces, and innumerable little bowers of five feet high and little more in diameter, in which his troops curled themselves up when their day's work was over. It was a long and very weary descent. Going down a steep place is comparatively easy when one carries no load; but when one has over fifty pounds upon the back it is extremely trying. At last we reached the bottom, a stony waste of a quarter of a mile wide, with a few large trees growing upon what in the rainy season are, no doubt, islands. The bed of the stream is perfectly dry, except that here and there, at intervals of a quarter of a mile or so, were pools of water, very soft and unpleasant to the taste, and full of tadpoles. The troops when they arrived here were a good deal done up, having already marched thirteen miles, and it was hoped that the Chief would order a halt for the night. He, however, considered it essential that the plateau should be gained that evening, and Milward's corps, whose rearguard left the river as we descended to it, supported. The troops were ordered to halt and rest until four o'clock, and to have their dinners, and the mules were to be unloaded, fed, and watered.

It was three o'clock before the baggage began to arrive in the valley, and it was evident that it would not be all down until dark, and that much of it could not reach the plateau above that night. Three of us, therefore, resolved upon sleeping where we were, and upon going on at daybreak. We accordingly pitched our tents under a tree, saw our horses picketed and fed, and dinner in course of preparation, and then went out for a walk to explore the valley. The temperature was very many degrees warmer than upon the plateau above, and the flora was more than proportionately luxuriant. Here I find, among hundreds of other plants of whose names and properties I am unfortunately ignorant, the wild verbena and heliotrope, also the cucumber.

Unfortunately the cucumbers had only just begun to form, and were scarcely as large as gherkins, or we might have had an unexpected addition to our fare. I also found quantities of the rare palm-fern growing in crevices of the rocks. It was altogether a splendid field for a botanist, and I think it a great pity that a learned botanist did not accompany the expedition instead of a geographer, who, although a most distinguished savant, can but tell the world nearly the same particulars of the narrow strip of country through which we are travelling as must occur to any ordinary observer. Had this gentleman merely taken advantage of the protection given by our presence in the country to travel generally through it, he might have no doubt added largely to our store of information; but keeping to the line of route followed by the army, he can, with the exception of ascertaining the precise heights over which we travel, tell us really next to nothing. I believe, however, that this staying with the army is in no degree the fault of the gentleman in question, but of the military authorities, who here appear to have the idea that a civilian is a sort of grown-up baby, who must be kept strictly under their own eyes, or else that he will infallibly get into mischief, and either come to harm himself, or else be the cause of that dreadful and mysterious thing—complications. Had King Kassa, at the time he visited us, been applied to by the Commander-in-chief, he would, no doubt, have afforded every facility to the geographer and archæologist to have wandered as they pleased among his dominions, and the latter especially might have visited the interesting cities of Adowa and Axum, and made discoveries of an important and interesting nature, instead of wasting his time on the summit of the bleak Abyssinian mountains.

We enjoyed our little picnic amazingly. It was such a relief to get for once out of the routine of camp, with its sentries, and its countersigns, and bugle-calls, and mules, and to lie outside our tent and enjoy the warm evening air, which we had not been able to do since we left Zulla, where there was only sand to lie on. At eight o'clock, however, the rain came on and drove us in, with the pleasant knowledge that we had chosen well in stopping, for the last of the baggage was not down the hill until past six; and although they at once started upon their weary climb, it was impossible that they could reach the camp before morning. Our camp was presently increased in size by a dozen commissariat coolies, who were driving several hundred sheep and some oxen, and who did not get to the river until nearly eight o'clock. Jackals and hyænas were very numerous, so we piled together a good fire to keep them off our horses, and then lay down to sleep with our rifles and revolvers within reach, for it was of course just possible, although not—as some of the members of the staff to whom we had mentioned our intention to stay considered likely—probable, that some of Theodore's cavalry might come along down the valley upon the look-out for stragglers. We came up at daybreak next morning, and after a cup of sugarless tea, started for camp. It was a very severe climb, and at the shoulder we came up to many of the mules which had been unable to get up the night before. The road which Theodore has cut enables us to see very clearly the formation of the valley, and I have not the least question that coal would be found there. I do not mention this as a commercial, but as a scientific, fact; for, commercially, coal here would be of no more value than stones. But of the fact itself I have no question. The character of the formation, the stone, the bands of fireclay, and of black friable shale, are very distinct, and there is in my mind no doubt whatever of the existence of coal. On the way we passed several dead mules and horses, and there can be no question that the journey was a most cruel one. This extreme fatigue may not cripple a man at the time, he may be ready for duty the next morning; but it must tell, and tell severely upon his constitution, and there are not a few men here who will feel the effects of Mahkan, Dildee, and Dalanta, to the end of their lives. The camp is situated upon a dead-level about a mile from the top of the ascent. I find upon inquiry that the troops in general got in at nine o'clock—of course wet through—but that very many of them, and a great deal of baggage, did not come in until this morning. There were rumours of an attack, Rassam having sent in a letter warning the Chief to be particularly on his guard against night attacks. The men, therefore, went to sleep in their boots, with their rifles by their sides. No attack took place. The same precaution is used to-night. We find, as I expected, that very little is brought in by the natives. The horses and mules to-day only get two pounds of grain each. We are still upon half-rations of flour, which, by this means, and with what is bought at Tacazze and upon the way will, I hope, enable us to hold on until supplies arrive. Nothing positive has yet been heard of the native carriage. Sir Robert Napier has been out all day making a long reconnoissance. From one point which he attained the tents of Theodore's army upon the plain in front of Magdala were clearly visible. The party did not return until dark, and I have heard no particulars. Theodore is known, however, to be still there, and his efforts are directed to fortifying the hill which defends Magdala. He has several guns in position on the summit, and I apprehend that we shall have to capture it before we assault Magdala. It is not known yet whether we advance to-morrow or not, but it is believed that we shall start late, and make a short march, and that Sir Charles Staveley, who is encamped to-night at the bottom of the Djedda ravine, will come up to our present camp. It is a tremendously wet night.

Dalanta, April 7th.

We have had many surprises since we arrived in the country, but none greater, and certainly none more satisfactory, than that which we have here experienced. The letters from the captives had informed us that Theodore had burnt everything upon the plain of Dalanta; and we had in consequence imagined that we should be able to obtain nothing whatever either for ourselves or animals, and that the prospect of the latter especially was gloomy in the extreme, for we had not any corn whatever remaining for them. Captain Speedy, however, rode out to see the chief of Dalanta, with whom he had an acquaintance when residing in the country. He returned in the afternoon with the tidings that the chief had promised at least 100,000 lbs. of grain in two days. It is evident that he is a man of his word, for we have had a market to-day which has surpassed anything we have seen in the country except at Antalo. There is a crowd of people with grain, bread, fowls, &c. &c., and the four or five commissariat Parsees cannot pay out the dollars for the bucket-loads of grain half as fast as the natives bring them in. It is indeed quite a scramble among these latter.

This unexpected influx of grain, &c., may be said to be the turning-point which secures the success of our expedition. Had we found no grain here we must have lost all the transport-animals, as these have already been on very short commons for some days. The supplies for the men too were running extremely short, and if Magdala holds out for a week our position would have been most unpleasant; now we are safe. We have abundant grain for the animals for another week, and we are told that supplies will continue to come in in any quantities. Very large quantities of bread too have been purchased, and both officers and men have laid in a stock of fowls, eggs, &c. All anxiety is at an end. We have fairly overcome now all the difficulties of the country, and of supplies. Theodore and his men are, in comparison, contemptible foes.

Staveley's brigade came up yesterday, and are encamped at a spot about two miles beyond us. Now that supplies are coming in in abundance, and a day is no longer of vital consequence, we shall, I believe, wait for another day or two to allow the wing of the 45th, the second wing of the Beloochees, and the 3d Dragoon Guards, to come up.

Yesterday almost every officer in camp went to the edge of the ravine to have a look at Magdala. It is a ride of a little over two miles, and the ravine goes down in an almost unbroken precipice of 500 or 600 feet from the upper edge. The view is one of the finest, if not the very finest, we have had in Abyssinia. It is grand in the extreme. At our feet was the perpendicular precipice, then a short shoulder, and then another sharp fall down to the Bachelo, which is 3900 feet below us. This side of the ravine is very similar, but steeper, to that of the Djedda. Upon the other side, however, the character is altogether different. In place of a corresponding ascent, as at the Djedda, the ground rises in a succession of billows one behind another, higher and higher, to the foot of some very lofty mountains, which form the background forty miles away. Such an extraordinary sea of hills I never saw. It was most magnificent, and stretched away east and west as far as the eye could reach. Above all this Magdala rose like a great ship out of the surrounding billows. There was no mistaking it, with its precipitous sides, its frowning aspect, and the cluster of tents clearly discernible upon its summit. As the crow flies it was about eight miles distant.

I will endeavour to give as clear a description of it as possible, in order that our future operations may be readily understood. From the bed of the Bachelo the ground rises in a mass of rounded hills, with somewhat flat tops; down through these, deep ravines convey the streams from the distant hills into the Bachelo. One of these ravines comes down nearly direct from Magdala, and it is up this that the road goes, until it gets within about two miles of Magdala, when it leaves the ravine and goes up on to the flat hill-tops from the midst of which Magdala rises. Magdala, from here, appears like a three-topped mountain with almost perpendicular sides. Two of the summits, which together resemble a saddle with high flat peaks, face this way. The hill to the right is Fahla; that on the left, which is some hundred feet higher, is Salamgi. The road winds up the face of Fahla to the saddle between the two, and it is evident that Fahla will be the first position to be attacked. There are apparently very few huts upon Fahla. The road, we hear, after reaching the top of the saddle, turns to the left, and crosses over Salamgi. Salamgi is tremendously strong; it is a series of natural scarps, of great height; and upon the terrace formed by these scarps a great portion of Theodore's force is encamped. Salamgi, if well defended, even by savages, will be a most formidable position to assault. The third top of this singular fortress is Magdala itself. This, like Fahla, has a flat top, which is completely covered with large huts. We see only the top of Magdala, over the saddle between Salamgi and Fahla. It is apparently lower than Salamgi, but higher than Fahla. It is, we hear, connected with Salamgi by a flat shoulder. It appears to be about a mile distant from the summit of this mountain, and when, therefore, we have taken Salamgi, our light guns will not be of much utility in bombarding Magdala at so great a distance.

I have now given an idea of the scene in which the great drama, which will commence to-morrow or next day, will be played. My next letter will, at any rate, give you the opening scene, and possibly even the entire drama.

Before Magdala, April 11th.

Although it was evident when I last wrote to you that the last act of our long drama was approaching, I certainly did not imagine that my next letter would convey the tidings that all was over—that the captives were free, their prison captured, their oppressor punished, and general triumph amidst a blaze of blue fire. But so it is; for although Magdala has not yet fallen, it will undoubtedly do so before the post closes, and a more gratifying termination to our expedition than has eventuated could not have been desired by the most sanguine. I had better continue my letter in a narrative form from the date when I last wrote—for if I describe the final events first it would deprive the rest of the matter of all interest.

I wrote last on the evening of the 7th from Dalanta. The following day brought in largely-increased supplies, and the market was completely thronged with the country people. In the three days we were there we purchased over 100,000 lbs. of grain, besides quantities of bread, &c. &c., and nowhere, even at Antalo, did supplies flow in with such rapidity as at this place, where we expected to find a desert.

On the afternoon of the 8th the wing of the 45th marched into camp, having done the distance from Scindee. The authorities had thoughtfully sent down mules to the Djedda river to carry up their coats and blankets, and the men consequently arrived comparatively fresh. The sailors of the Naval Brigade turned out as they came into camp, and saluted them with three hearty cheers. The 45th are a remarkably fine body of men.

Thus reinforced Sir Robert Napier determined to move forward and to encamp before Magdala, even if he decided upon delaying the assault until the other wing of the Beloochees and the 3d Dragoon Guards joined us. The order was accordingly issued for a march the next day to the edge of the Bachelo ravine, to which the second brigade, which were now two miles ahead of us, were also to proceed. We started at ten o'clock, and were soon upon our camping-ground, which was only five miles distant. Here the second brigade joined us, and together we formed a larger camp than any we have had since our landing at Zulla. From the front of the camp we had an excellent view of Magdala, which stood up, with Salamgi and Fahla, a thousand feet above the surrounding hills. We could now see that the ridge connecting Salamgi with Fahla was longer than it had appeared from our previous point of view, the distance from one end to the other of the saddle being apparently over half a mile.

The first brigade was ordered to advance at daybreak. The Commander-in-chief and his head-quarters were to move with the second brigade at ten o'clock, so as to allow the baggage of the first brigade to get first to the bottom of the ravine. The first brigade were to march to within two or three miles of Magdala. The second were to encamp upon the river, and to march on early the next morning. There was then not the slightest intention on the part of Sir Robert Napier that any attack should take place, and indeed, as I have before said, it was considered very probable that we should await the arrival of the troops hurrying up from behind before any assault was made upon Magdala. However, I determined to go on early, as it was quite possible that something would take place, and I had afterwards good reason to congratulate myself upon having so done, as several others who had not started until ten o'clock lost the exciting scene at the end of the day.

Sir Charles Staveley was in command of the advance, and Colonel Phayre, as quartermaster-general of the army, went on in front with six companies of the Bombay and Madras Sappers to prepare the road, should it be necessary.

At half-past five the next morning (Good Friday) we were in motion, and at once entered upon the steep descent to the Bachelo. It is a ravine of about the same depth as the Djedda, namely, 3800 feet, and the road, as made by Theodore, is a wonderfully good one. It is shorter, but at the same time scarcely so precipitous as parts of that down to the Djedda, and can hardly have presented quite so many difficulties, that is, there were fewer places where the basalt had to be cut through with blasting-tools. Still, it was a fatiguing descent to the Bachelo, and the sun, when it rose, came down with tremendous power. The men had had but a scanty supply of water the night before, and hardly any before starting; they therefore looked forward eagerly for the welcome stream at the bottom. It turned out, however, a disappointment, for although there was an abundance of water, the river being eighty yards wide, and nearly waist-deep, the water was of a consistency and colour which would have rendered it perfectly undrinkable except to men suffering from great thirst. I do not think I ever saw such muddy water in a stream. It was the colour of coffee with milk in it, and perfectly opaque with mud. It looked like nothing so much as the water in a dirty puddle in a London street, just as it has been churned up by the wheels of a passing omnibus. However, there was no help for it, and, dirty as it was, everyone had a drink, and the soldiers filled their canteens, for it was probable that no more water would be obtainable during the day.

From the Bachelo a broad ravine with a flat bottom ran nearly straight to Salamgi, and along this Theodore's road was made. It was believed, however, that guns had been laid to command this road, and it was not improbable that Theodore might make a sudden attack. It was therefore determined that the mountain guns, rocket trains, and baggage should proceed by this road, preceded by the six hundred Sappers and Miners; and that the infantry should at once climb the hills to its right, and should march along them, so as to clear them of any possible enemy. To cross the river the men had to wade, the first time that they have had to do so since they landed. Some wisely took off their trousers, others thinking vainly that the water would not reach above their knees, merely rolled their trousers up, and, of course, got thoroughly wet. Most of them took off shoes and stockings, but many stopped in the middle and put their boots on again, for the stones were so extremely sharp that wet shoes were preferable to cut feet. At last the troops were across, and after a short halt moved forward, the Sappers having gone on an hour previously with Colonel Phayre. After proceeding up the valley we prepared to climb the hill. On crossing it the 4th formed the advance, the men loading before they started, as it was impossible that we could tell when we might be attacked. Sir Charles Staveley, with General Schneider, the able and popular officer commanding the first brigade, with their staffs followed; and after them came the 4th—the little party of Engineers under Major Pritchard, the Beloochees, the Punjaubees, and two companies of the 10th Native Infantry; also a squadron of the 3d Native Cavalry, the only cavalry we had with us. We have had some stiff climbing since we entered Abyssinia, but this altogether surpassed any of our previous experience. In fact, when we got near the summit of the first range, we came to a spot which was almost impassable even for infantry, and quite so for the horses of the staff. Two or three officers endeavoured to drag their horses up, but the animals, although pretty well accustomed by this time to stiff places, were quite unable to get up, and one or two tumbled backwards and were nearly killed. The infantry therefore clambered up to the top; but we had to wait where we were for half-an-hour, until the Punjaub Pioneers cleared a sort of track up which we were able to scramble. When on the first level we had a halt for half-an-hour, for the troops were all very much exhausted by their climb, under one of the hottest suns I ever felt. They were now, too, beginning to suffer much from thirst, and the muddy water in the skins was drunk most eagerly. It tasted muddy, but was not otherwise bad; but we had to shut our eyes to drink it. While we were waiting here a messenger arrived from Colonel Phayre, saying that he held the head of the valley with the Sappers and Miners, and that the road was quite practicable. Sir Charles Staveley at once sent off an aide-de-camp to Sir Robert Napier, saying that the baggage and guns, which were waiting at the river for the receipt of this intelligence, might move forward in safety. We then marched four miles farther up a succession of rises to the place where it was hoped from the native accounts that we should find water; but there was only one small pool of very dirty water, with which, however, three or four skins were filled. The disappointment of the men, who were now suffering severely, was very great, but there was no help for it. Here, however, we met with a surprise, which to the commanding-officers quite dispelled any thought of thirst or discomfort; for here, to the astonishment and dismay of Sir Charles Staveley, he found Colonel Phayre and the 800 Sappers and Miners, who were supposed to be holding the head of the valley below us. This was now, we knew, crowded with our artillery, ammunition-baggage and supplies. This valley, as I before stated, ran straight to Magdala, and of course was visible for its whole length to the garrison of that fortress.

The whole of the baggage was therefore open to an attack from Magdala, and we upon the hill-top were powerless to give them the slightest assistance. Had Theodore made an attack at this period, it is not too much to say that the whole of our guns, ammunition, and stores must have fallen into his hands, for their whole guard was only eighty or a hundred men of the 4th scattered over a long line. What Colonel Phayre meant, or how he accounted for this extraordinary conduct, I know not; but a more stupendous blunder never was made, and had we had the most contemptible European force to deal with instead of savages, we must have sustained a crushing disaster.

General Staveley at once sent off an officer to acquaint Sir Robert Napier with the state of affairs, and then ordered the troops to advance at once.

Another couple of miles brought us to our camping-ground, which lay a little behind the crest of a hill, and was not visible from Magdala. Here the tired troops threw themselves down, while the General advanced with his staff to the edge of the rising ground. As the scene before it was destined, although we were at the time ignorant of it, to become our battle-field, I will endeavour to give as accurate a description of it as possible, in order that the fight may be better understood.

We stood on the edge of a sort of plateau. At our feet was a small ravine or valley, dividing us from another plateau, which extended to the foot of Fahla and Salamgi. This plateau was a hundred feet or so below the spot upon which we stood, and would have been completely commanded by our guns. This plateau was bounded both to the right and left by ravines, the one to the left being the head of the valley in which was our baggage. The little valley which divided us from the plateau widened out to the left, the spot where it fell into the main valley being half a mile distant; and here we could see the spot where our baggage would arrive when it had climbed up from the valley beneath.

Sir Charles Staveley at once despatched the Punjaub Pioneers to this point; that done, there was nothing for it but to wait the event; and this waiting was painful in the extreme.

It was now half-past three. Everyone was devoured with a burning thirst, which the scanty draught of mud seemed to excite rather than allay. Any money would have been cheerfully given for a drink of pure water. A storm was seen coming up, but it unfortunately did not pass over us; we got, however, the tail of the shower, and by spreading out my waterproof-sheet, I caught nearly half a pint, which I shall long remember as one of the most refreshing draughts I ever tasted.

In the mean time Sir Robert Napier had arrived with his staff, and it was evident, by the anxious care with which he reconnoitred the hill before us, and the head of the valley, that he considered our position to be a critical one. We could see with our glasses half-a-dozen guns in line on the flat top of Fahla, and as many more upon Salamgi, and presently we saw two artillerymen go from gun to gun, and load them in succession. Still all was quiet; but it was a time of most anxious suspense, for we knew that from the fortress they could see our long line of animals winding up the valley, and that the head of the train must be fast approaching. Presently the Naval Rocket Brigade, which was in front of the baggage, emerged upon the flat below us and joined the Punjaubees; and almost at the same moment a dozen voices proclaimed, "A large force is coming down the road on the brow of the fortress."

Every glass was turned there, and a large body of horse and foot-men were seen hurrying down pell-mell, and without any order or regularity. At first there was a divided opinion as to whether this was a peaceful embassy or an attack; but all doubt was put an end to in another minute by the booming of a gun from Fahla, and by a thirty-two pound shot striking the ground at a few yards from the body of Punjaubees. It was war, then, and a general burst of cheering broke from the officers who were clustered round the General. Theodore actually meant to fight, and not only that, but to fight in the open.

Still our position was a most serious one. The second brigade was miles behind, the baggage undefended except by the Punjaubees, and it was easy enough for the enemy to make a circuit down the ravine and to avoid them. Sir Robert Napier instantly despatched an aide-de-camp to Major Chamberlain, commanding the Pioneers, to order him to take up a position on elevated ground to his left, where he could the better protect the baggage, and to order the Naval Brigade to hurry up the valley to the commanding spur upon which we were standing. Aide-de-camp after aide-de-camp was sent back to bring up the infantry. It was a most exciting five minutes. The enemy were coming down with very great rapidity. They had already descended the road from the fortress, and were scattered over the plain; the principal body moving towards the valley in which was our baggage, the rest advancing in scattered groups, while the guns upon Fahla kept up a steady fire upon the Punjaubees. A prettier sight is seldom presented in warfare than that of the advance of the enemy. Some were in groups, some in twos and threes. Here and there galloped chiefs in their scarlet-cloth robes. Many of the foot-men, too, were in scarlet or silk. They kept at a run, and the whole advanced across the plain with incredible and alarming rapidity, for it was for some time doubtful whether they would not reach the brow of the little valley,—along which the Rocket Train was still coming in a long single file,—before the infantry could arrive to check them; and in that case there can be no doubt that the sailors would have suffered severely. The road, or rather path from the valley, up to the spur upon which we stood, was steep and very difficult, and considerable delay occurred in getting the animals up. After a few minutes, which seemed ages, the infantry came up at the double; all their fatigue and thirst vanished as if by magic at the thought of a fight. The 4th, who were only about 300 strong—the remainder being with the baggage—were ordered to go on in skirmishing order; they were followed by the little party of Engineers, then came the Beloochees, and after them the two companies of the 10th N.I. and the Sappers and Miners. Just as the head of the infantry went down into the valley, the leading mules reached the top of the crest by our side, and in less than a minute the first rocket whizzed out on the plain.

It was our first answer to the fire which the guns of the fortress had kept up, and was greeted with a general cheer. As rocket after rocket rushed out in rapid succession, the natives paused for a minute, astonished at these novel missiles, and then, their chiefs urging them forward, they again advanced. They were now not more than five hundred yards from ourselves, a hundred from the edge of the little ravine up the side of which the skirmishers of the 4th were rapidly climbing. With my glass I could distinguish every feature, and as we looked at them coming forward at a run, with their bright-coloured floating robes, their animated gestures, their shields and spears, one could not help feeling pity for them, ruffians and cut-throats as most of them undoubtedly were, to think what a terrible reception they were about to meet with. In another minute the line of skirmishers had breasted the slope, and opened a tremendous fire with their Sniders upon the enemy. The latter, taken completely by surprise, paused, discharged their firearms, and then retreated, slowly and doggedly, but increasing in speed as they felt how hopeless was the struggle against antagonists who could pour in ten shots to their one. Indeed, at this point they were outnumbered even by the 4th alone, for they were in no regular order, but in groups and knots scattered over the whole plain. The 4th advanced rapidly, driving their antagonists before them, and followed by the native regiments. So fast was the advance that numbers of the enemy could not regain the road to the fortress, but were driven away to the right, off the plateau, on to the side of a ravine, from which the rockets again drove them, still further to the right, and away from Magdala. The 4th and other regiments formed up at a few hundred yards from the foot of the ascent to the fortress, and for half-an-hour maintained an animated fire against the riflemen who lined the path, and kept up a brisk return from small rifle-pits and the shelter of stones and rocks. All this time the guns upon Fahla and some of those upon Salamgi, kept up a constant fire upon an advancing line; but the aim was very bad, and most of the shot went over our heads. Much more alarming were our own rockets, some of which came in very unpleasant proximity to us. Presently, to our great relief, the sailors joined us, and soon drove the enemy's riflemen up the hill, after which they threw a few salvos of rockets with admirable aim up at the guns a thousand feet above us, doing, as it afterwards turned out, considerable damage, and nearly killing Theodore himself, who was superintending the working of the gun by his German prisoners. In the mean time a much more serious contest was taking place upon our left. The main body of the enemy had taken this direction to attack the baggage, and advanced directly towards the Punjaub Pioneers, who were defending the head of the road. Fortunately Colonel Penn's mountain train of steel guns, which were following the naval train, now arrived at the top of the road, instantly unloaded, and took their places by the side of the Punjaubees. When the enemy were within three hundred yards the steel guns opened with shell, the Punjaubees poured in their fire and speedily stopped the advance of the head of the column. The greater part of the natives then went down the ravine to the left, along which they proceeded to the attack of the baggage, in the main valley of which this ravine was a branch. The baggage-guard, composed of a detachment of the 4th, scattered along the long line, had already been warned by the guns of the fortress that an attack was impending, and Captain Aberdie, of the transport train, gallopping down, brought them word of the advancing body of the enemy. The various officers upon duty instantly collected their men. Captain Roberts was in command, and was well seconded by Lieutenants Irving, Sweeny, and Durrant of the 4th, and by the officers of the transport train.

As the enemy poured down the ravine they were received by a withering fire from the deadly Snider. A portion of the Punjaubees came down the ravine and took them in flank, and some of the guns of Penn's battery, getting upon a projecting spur, scattered death everywhere amongst them. From the extreme rapidity of the fire of the Snider, the firing at this time in different parts of the field was as heavy and continuous as that of a general action between two large armies. The Punjaubees behaved with great gallantry and charged with the bayonet, doing great execution. The natives, who had fought with great pluck, now attempted to escape up the opposite side of the ravine, but great numbers were shot down as they did so, their white dresses offering a plain mark to our riflemen; at last, however, the remnant gained the opposite bank, and fled across the country to our left, their retreat to Magdala being cut off. The action, from the first to the last gun, lasted an hour and a half. It was, as far as our part of the fray was concerned, a mere skirmish. We had not a single man killed, and only about thirty wounded, most of them slightly. Captain Roberts, however, was hit in the elbow-joint with a ball, and will, it is feared, lose his arm. On the other hand, to the enemy this is a decisive and crushing defeat. Upwards of five thousand of Theodore's bravest soldiers sallied out; scarcely as many hundreds returned. Three hundred and eighty bodies were counted the next morning, and many were believed to have been carried off in the night. Very many fell on the slope of the hill, and away in the ravines to our right and left, where our burying-parties could not find them. Certainly five hundred were killed, probably twice as many were wounded, and of these numbers have only crawled away to die. It was a terrible slaughter, and could hardly be called a fight, between disciplined bodies of men splendidly armed, and scattered parties of savages scarcely armed at all. Much as the troops wish for an opportunity of distinguishing themselves, I have heard a general hope expressed that we shall not have to storm the place, for there is but little credit to be gained over these savages, and the butchery would be very great. The natives are, however, undoubtedly brave, and behaved really very gallantly. Not a single shield, gun, or spear has been picked up except by the side of the dead. The living, even the wounded, retreated; they did not fly. There was no *sauve qui peut*, no throwing away of arms, as there would have been under similar desperate circumstances by European troops. As the troops returned to the rear we passed many sad spectacles. In one hollow a dozen bodies lay in various positions. Some had died instantaneously, shot through the head; others had fallen mortally wounded, and several of these had drawn their robes over their faces, and died like Stoics. Some were only severely wounded, and these had endeavoured to crawl into bushes, and there lay uttering low moans. Their gaudy silk bodices, the white robes with scarlet ends which had flaunted so gaily but two hours since, now lay dabbled with blood, and dank with the heavy rains which had been pitilessly coming down for the last hour.

I have omitted to mention that a tremendous thunderstorm had come on while the engagement was at its height, and the deep roar of the thunder had for a time completely drowned the heavy rattle of musketry, the crack of the steel guns, and the boom of the heavy cannon upon Fahla. Once, when the storm was at its height, the sun had shone brightly out through a rift of the thunder-clouds, and a magnificent rainbow shone over the field upon which the combatants were still fiercely contending. Only twice was the voice of man heard loudly during the fight. The first was a great cheer from the natives upon the hill, and which we could only conjecture was occasioned by the return unharmed of some favourite chief. The other was the cheer which the whole British force gave as the enemy finally retired up into their strongholds. Thus terminated, soon after six o'clock, one of the most decided and bloody skirmishes which, perhaps, ever occurred. It will be, moreover, memorable as being the first encounter in which British troops ever used breech-loading rifles. Tremendous as was the fire, and great as was the slaughter, I am of opinion, and in this many of the military men agree with me, that the number of the enemy killed would have been at least as great had the troops been armed with the Enfield. The fire was a great deal too rapid. Men loaded and fired as if they were making a trial of rapidity of fire, and I saw several instances in which only two or three natives fell among a group, the whole of which would have been mown down had the men taken any aim whatever. At the end of an hour there was scarcely a cartridge left of the ninety rounds which each man carried into action, and the greater portion of them were fired away in the first quarter of an hour. The baggage-guard used up all their stock, and were supplied with fresh ammunition from the reserve which they guarded. Against close bodies of men the breech-loader will do wonders. In the gorges, where the natives were clustered thickly together, it literally mowed them down. Upon the open not one shot in a hundred told. In a great battle the ammunition, at this rate of expenditure, would be finished in an hour. From what I saw of the fighting, I am convinced that troops should, if possible, load at the muzzle when acting as skirmishers, and at the breech only when in close conflict against large bodies of cavalry or infantry. It is all very well to order men to fire slowly, a soldier's natural eagerness when he sees his enemy opposite to him will impel him to load and fire as quickly as possible. He cannot help it, nor can he carry more than sixty rounds of ammunition, which will not last him twenty minutes. It certainly appears to me that a soldier's rifle should combine breech- and muzzle-loading, and that he should only use the former method when specially ordered by his commanding officer.

The troops retired amidst a heavy rain, and were marched back to the camp they had left to fetch their greatcoats and blankets, which had been left behind when they advanced to the fight. Then they returned to the ground held by the Punjaubees, and took their station for the night, as they here guarded the top of the road, at which the baggage was now arriving, it having been kept back during the fight. It was perfectly dark before we reached our camping-ground, and as this was in many places covered with thorns and bushes, which in the darkness were quite invisible, very considerable confusion prevailed. Now that the excitement was over, everyone was again tormented with thirst, but it was felt less than it would otherwise have been, owing to the thorough soaking which every man had got. Of course there was no getting at the baggage, which remained on a flat behind us, and everyone wrapped himself in his wet blanket and lay down to snatch a little sleep if he could, and to forget hunger and thirst for a while. As we had marched before daybreak, and went into action long before any of the baggage-animals came up, no one had taken food for the whole of the long and fatiguing day. Very strong bodies of troops were thrown out as pickets, and the whole were got up and under arms at two in the morning, lest Theodore should renew his attack before daybreak. There was now news that there was water to be had in a ravine to our left, and the bheesties were sent down with the water-skins, and numbers of the soldiers also went down with their canteens. The water was worse than any I ever drank before, and ever think to drink again. Numbers of animals, mules or cattle, had been slaughtered there; it appeared, in fact, to have been a camp of Theodore's army. The stench was abominable, and the water was nearly as much tainted as the atmosphere. The liquid mud we had drank the day before was, in comparison, a healthy and agreeable fluid. However, there was no help for it, and few, if any, refused the noxious fluid. This climate must certainly be an extraordinarily healthy one; for, in spite of hardship and privation, of wet, exposure, bad water, and want of stimulants, the health of the troops has been unexceptionally good. Only once, at Gazoo, have we had threatenings of dysentery, and this passed away as soon as we moved forward. I question if we had a single man in hospital upon the day of the fight, which is certainly most providential, considering the extreme paucity of medical comforts, and the very few dhoolies available for the sick and wounded. Before daybreak we again started—as the place upon which we were encamped was within range of the enemy's guns—and marched back to this, the camping-ground of the preceding afternoon.

The 2d brigade arrived soon after daylight, and took up their camp a little in the rear of the position in which we had passed the night. Our baggage came on with us, and we had now the satisfaction of being in our tents again, and of getting what we greatly needed—food. After breakfast I rode over to the camp of the 2d brigade, and then, leaving my horse, went down into the ravine, where fatigue-parties were engaged in the work of burial. The scene was very shocking. In one or two narrow gorges in which they had been pent up, fifty or sixty dead bodies lay almost piled together. Very ghastly were their wounds. Here was a man nearly blown to pieces with a shell; near him another the upper part of whose head had been taken off by a rocket; then again, one who lay as if in a peaceful sleep, shot through the heart; next to him one less fortunate, who, by the nature of his wound, must have lingered in agony for hours through the long night before death brought a welcome relief. Two of them only still lived, and these were carried into camp; but their wounds were of so desperate a nature that it was probable they could not live many hours. Strangely enough, there were no wounds of a trifling nature. All who had not been mortally wounded had either managed to crawl away, or had been removed by their friends. With a very few exceptions it was a charnel-place of dead, whose gaudy silk and coloured robes were in ghastly contrast with their stiffened and contorted attitudes. Among the few survivors was the Commander-in-chief of Theodore's army, who was carried to the camp. He, like the others we were able to succour, expressed his gratitude for our kindness, and said the affair had been a complete surprise to them. They saw what was apparently a train of baggage without any protection whatever coming up the valley; and they had not noticed our small body of infantry on the brow. They sallied out therefore, anticipating little or no resistance. It certainly speaks well for the courage of the natives, that, taken by surprise, as they must have been, by our infantry, with the rockets and shells, they should yet have fought as bravely and well as they did. There can be no doubt that, had not the fight been brought on so suddenly as it was, and had the 2d brigade been at hand, we should have gone straight up upon the heels of the fugitives, and captured the place then and there. As it was, although it might have been done, the troops were too tired and exhausted to have put them at such an arduous task; for Theodore would, no doubt, have fought with desperation, and we should have lost many men before we could have surmounted the hill. I say this, because it is the opinion of many that we might have taken the place at once, had we chosen to go on.

Altogether it was a wonderful success, especially considering that we fought under the disadvantage of a surprise, and without the slightest previous plan or preparation. It is only fortunate that we had to deal with Theodore and Abyssinians, and not with regular troops.

Theodore was general enough to perceive and to take advantage of Colonel Phayre's egregious blunder; but his troops were not good enough to carry out his intentions. As to Colonel Phayre, it is not probable that we shall hear any more of him while the expedition lasts; for Sir Robert Napier's long-suffering patience for once broke down, and he opened his mind to Colonel Phayre in a way which that officer will not forget for the rest of his life.

Before I left camp for my ride to the ravine, an event of great interest occurred, but which I deferred mentioning in its place, as I wished to complete my description of the battle and field without a break. At half-past seven, just as I was at breakfast, I heard a great cheering and hurrahing, and found that Lieutenant Prideaux and Mr. Flad had come in with proposals from Theodore. This was a great relief to us all, as there was considerable fear that Theodore, in a fit of rage at his defeat the day before, might have put all the captives to death. This, however, was not the case. The prisoners had indeed passed an unenviable afternoon while the battle was going on; but Prideaux and Blanc consoled each other, as they heard the heavy firing of our rifles, that at least, if they were to die that night, they were to some extent avenged beforehand. These two gentlemen have throughout written in a spirit of pluck and resignation which does them every honour.

Theodore had come in after the engagement in a rather philosophical mood, and said, "My people have been out to fight yours. I thought that I was a great man, and knew how to fight. I find I know nothing. My best soldiers have been killed; the rest are scattered. I will give in. Go you into camp and make terms for me."

And so the two captives came into camp. Both looked well and hearty, and acknowledged that, as far as eating and drinking go, they have been far better off than we are ourselves. Indeed, with the exception of captivity and light chains, the captives do not appear to have been ill-treated for many months. They have their separate houses, their servants, and anything they could buy with the supplies of money sent to them.

A horrible business took place in Magdala on the very day before our arrival. Theodore had all the European captives out, and before their eyes put to death three hundred and forty prisoners, many of whom he had kept in chains for years. Among them were men, women, and little children. They were brought out chained, and thrown down on the ground, their heads fastened down to their feet. Among this defenceless and pitiable group the brutal tyrant went with his sword and slashed right and left until he had killed a score or so. Then, getting tired, he called out six of his musketeers, who continued to fire among the wretched crowd until all were despatched. Their bodies were then thrown over a precipice.

There is a general feeling of surprise expressed in camp that the Englishmen who were witnesses of this horrible spectacle, and who were themselves unfettered, did not make a rush upon the monster and cut him down then and there. They could hardly have increased their own danger, for they tell us that they expected that they themselves would be put to death after the murder of the native prisoners. Besides, in the presence of so dreadful a butchery as this must have been, a man does not calculate—he feels; and the impulse to rush with a scream upon the drunken tyrant and to kill him would, one would think, have been overpowering.

The captives describe the usual mode of execution, by cutting-off the hands and feet, as being a refinement of cruelty. A slight gash is made round the member, and it is then wrenched-off by main force, the arteries being so much twisted that very little loss of blood takes place. The wretched beings are then left to die; and some of them linger for many days, and then expire of thirst more than of their wounds, it being death to administer either food or water to them.

We can feel no pity for this inhuman monster; and should he resist, there is every hope that he will be killed in the fight. Sir Robert Napier declined to grant any conditions whatever, demanding an instant surrender of the whole of the prisoners and of the fortress, promising only that Theodore and his family should be honourably treated. With this answer the two captives returned, but came back again at three o'clock with a message from Theodore, begging that better terms might be offered him. Sir Robert Napier was most reluctantly obliged to refuse, and the captives again returned amidst the sorrowful anticipations of the camp. At half-past six, to the great joy of all, Mr. Flad came in with the news that the captives would all be in in an hour; and at seven the whole of them came in safe and sound, with the exception of Mrs. Flad and her children. She, being unable to walk, had been left behind by the carelessness or haste of Rassam, to whom the business had been intrusted by Theodore. This person, Rassam, is very unpopular among the rest of the prisoners; the only person who seems to have liked him being Theodore himself, to whom his demeanour, so different from that of Prideaux and Blanc, had to a certain extent ingratiated him. I trust that to-morrow will see Mrs. Flad and her children safe in the camp, and then one of the objects of our expedition will have been completely and satisfactorily attained. Theodore has until mid-day to surrender Magdala; and if he does not do so, we shall storm it to-morrow night or next day. Some more scaling-ladders are in process of preparation, the materials being the long bamboo dhoolie-poles for the sides, and the handles of pickaxes for the rungs. The ladders are about five feet wide and twenty long.

I close this letter now; but anticipate that my next, describing the fall of Magdala, will be in time for the same post by which this reaches England.

April 12th.

Contrary to expectation, the day has passed-off without event. One reason for this was, that Mrs. Flad and her children were still in Theodore's hands, as also were some of the European workmen. At two o'clock, however, they came in; and we have now the whole of the captives safe in our hands. We have quite a native camp within our own, indeed, so large is the number of their attendants and following. The principal English prisoners have done very well with the money constantly supplied to them; but many of the German workmen have a miserably pinched and starved appearance. There are several half-castes among the party that have come in; their fathers being English or other Europeans who have resided in Abyssinia, their mothers natives. The natives who have come in have an idea that wearing a piece of red cloth round the head is a sign of friendliness to us, and they therefore are generally so adorned. The released captives start to-morrow for England. Theodore this morning sent down a thousand cattle and five hundred sheep as a propitiatory offering; but Sir Robert Napier refused to receive them, and has sent-in a renewed demand for the surrender of the fortress. It has been all day thought that the assault would take place to-night, or rather at daybreak to-morrow. No orders have, however, yet been issued, and it is now believed that the attack will take place to-morrow, in which case it is doubtful whether any description of the affair will reach you, as I had hoped, by this mail.

Ten o'clock P.M.

I have just received certain information that the attack is postponed. Sir Robert Napier, one of the kindest-hearted of men, has sent-off a letter this evening to Theodore, urging him to surrender, with a promise that his life shall be spared, and the lives of all his men. He has pointed out to him that his men cannot possibly resist our superior weapons; that cannon greatly superior to those we used in the fight of Good Friday have now arrived, and also the rest of our forces; so that our success is certain. He has therefore implored him to surrender, and to save any further effusion of blood, if not for his own sake, at any rate for that of the women and children, of whom alone it is said that there are 7000 in the fortress. I most earnestly trust that Theodore will consent to the appeal. Of course, the effusion of blood is to him, who only three days ago murdered 350 men, a matter of small moment. Still his own courage is failing. He yesterday, when he heard of the terms demanded, pretended to attempt to commit suicide, and fired a revolver close to his head; but the ball only grazed his neck. This, however, shows that his courage is failing: a brave man will never commit suicide; still less will he, if driven by desperation to the act, inflict only a slight wound upon himself. It is evident that he is now afraid; and I trust that to save his own miserable life he will surrender, and so save the butchery that must ensue if we storm Magdala.

To-day being Easter Sunday, we had, as usual, a church-parade, and our chaplain read the thanksgiving for our success, in which I am sure all will heartily join.

Before Magdala, April 14th.

When I closed my letter of the 12th, I mentioned that Sir Robert Napier had written to Theodore, urging him most strongly to surrender, as he had no possibility of a successful resistance; and the destruction of life, if we were to open fire upon Magdala, would be terrible.

On the next morning several of the principal chiefs came into camp, and said that they could not fight against our troops, and would therefore surrender. They held, with their people, Fahla and Salamgi, and would hand-over these fortresses to us, on condition that themselves and their families were allowed to depart with their property unharmed. With them came Samuel, a man who has been frequently mentioned in connection with the prisoners, both in their own letters and in Dr. Beke's work. This man exercised a strongly prejudicial influence at the early period of their captivity, but has since shown them kindness. Having been one of Theodore's principal advisers, one could hardly have expected to see him deserting his master in his adversity. Samuel is a strongly-built man, with remarkably intelligent features, and rather grizzly iron-gray hair, which he wears in its natural state, and not plaited and grease-bedaubed in the Abyssinian fashion. Sir Robert Napier accepted the surrender, and gave permission for the departure of their families and effects. Captain Speedy was ordered to return with them, with fifty of the 3d Native Cavalry, under Colonel Locke. Orders had been previously given for the whole of the troops to parade on the flat in front of the fortress. In half an hour after the departure of the cavalry, the troops were formed up, and made an imposing show, the first we have had since we landed. Hitherto the brigades have been separated, and so large a portion of them have been scattered along the line of baggage, that we have never had an opportunity of seeing our real force. We could now see that it was a very formidable body. The 33d were drawn up 750 strong; the 4th, 450; the 45th, 400. We had now the whole of the Beloochees, their left wing having arrived during the night, and the whole of the Punjaubees. We had two companies of the 10th Native Infantry, and six companies of Sappers and Miners—altogether a very complete body of infantry. We had Murray's Armstrong battery, two seven-inch mortars, Penn's Mountain Train of steel guns, Twiss's Mountain Train, and the Naval Rocket Brigade—a very respectable corps of artillery. In cavalry alone we were wanting, having only the fifty troopers of the 3d Native Cavalry, who had come as the Commander-in-chief's escort, and who had now just reached the top of the crest of Fahla. The rest of the cavalry—namely, the 3d Dragoons, 3d and 12th Native Cavalry and Scinde Horse—had been sent round into the valley to cut off Theodore's retreat. General Staveley was, of course, in command of the division. We moved forward, headed by the 33d, to whom, as having—of the European regiments—borne the brunt of the advance work throughout, was now assigned the honour of first entering and of placing the British flag upon Magdala. They were followed by the 45th, Murray's and Twiss's battery, and the rest of the second brigade, which had not had an opportunity of taking part in the action on Good Friday. Then came the 4th and the rest of the 1st brigade, with the exception of the troops who were left behind to take care of the camp. Major Baigrie, as quartermaster-general of the 1st division, rode in advance.

As the long line wound up the steep ascent in Fahla the effect was very pretty, and elicited several remarks that this was our Easter-Monday review. On the way up we met a large number of men, women, and children upon their way down. Once upon the shoulder which connects Fahla and Salamgi, we found ourselves in the midst of a surprising scene. A perfect exodus was in progress. Many thousands of men, women, and children were crowded everywhere, mixed up with oxen, sheep, and donkeys. The women, children, and donkeys were laden with the scanty possessions of the inhabitants. Skins of grain and flour, gourds and jars of water and ghee, blankets for coverings and tents—these were their sole belongings. It was a Babel of noises. The women screamed their long, quavering cry of admiration and welcome; men shouted to each other from rock to rock; mothers who had lost their children screamed for them, and the children wailed back in return; sheep and goats bleated, and donkeys and mules brayed. It was an astonishing scene. All seemed extremely glad to see us, and to be relieved from the state of fear and starvation in which they had existed; men, women, and children bent until their foreheads touched the ground in token of submission. The men who bore no arms carried burdens, as did the women; but the warriors only carried their arms. The number of gaudy dresses among the latter was surprising, and their effect was very gay and picturesque. Shirts of red, blue, or purple brocade, with yellow flowers, and loose trousers of the same material, but of a different hue, were the prevailing fashion with the chiefs. These were distinguished from the soldiers by having silver ornaments upon their shields. At present all retained their arms; but the 10th Native Infantry had been left at the foot of the hill with orders to disarm them as they came down the road. All along our march over Salamgi this extraordinary scene continued; and we saw more people than we have seen during the whole time we have been in Abyssinia. The general opinion is, that there could not have been less than thirty thousand people congregated here; and I believe that this computation is rather under than over the mark.

There was a universal feeling of thankfulness that we had not been obliged to bombard the place, as the slaughter among this defenceless crowd of people would have been terrible. Wherever was a level piece of ground, there their habitations were clustered. They were mere temporary abodes—a framework of sticks, covered with coarse grass, placed regularly and thickly, so as to turn the rain. They were about the size and shape of ordinary haycocks, and show that the people must sleep, as they sit, curled almost into a ball.

From the shoulder we climbed up the very winding road on the face of the natural scarps to Salamgi. The natural strength of these positions is astounding. Fahla is tremendously strong; but yet it is as nothing to Salamgi, which commands it. Colonel Milward, who commands the artillery, remarked to me that in the hands of European troops it would be not only impregnable, but perfectly unattackable. Gibraltar from the land side is considered impregnable; but Gibraltar is absolutely nothing to this group of fortresses. After capturing Fahla and Salamgi—if such a thing were possible—an attacking force would still have Magdala to deal with; and Magdala rises from the end of the flat shoulder which connects it with Salamgi in an unbroken wall, except at the one point where a precipitous road leads up to the gate. It is 2500 yards from the top of Salamgi to Magdala, and even the heaviest artillery could do nothing against the wall of rock. We may well congratulate ourselves that Theodore sent his army to attack our baggage; for had they remained and defended the place, provided as they were with forty cannon, our loss would have been very heavy; and even with our superior weapons it is a question whether we could have succeeded, the road in many cases winding along the face of a precipice, which a few men from above merely rolling down stones could have cleared. When we had reached the brow of Salamgi—a still higher scarp of which rose two hundred feet above us—Major Baigrie halted for orders, and I rode on with two or three others to the little body of the 3d Native Cavalry, who were half a mile further on, at the edge of the flat between Salamgi and Magdala.

I should say that early in the morning we had received news that Theodore had left in the night with a small body of his adherents, and intended to gain the camp of the Queen of the Gallas, and to throw himself upon her hospitality, the Gallas being wandering tribes, who, like the Arabs, would protect their bitterest enemy if he reached their tents and claimed hospitality. When we were nearly at the top of the hill, we had received a message from the cavalry, saying that there was a rumour that Theodore had returned, and had committed suicide.

When we reached the cavalry, however, we found a state of some excitement prevailing: some eight or ten horsemen, among whom Captain Speedy had recognised Theodore himself, having just galloped up brandishing spears and discharging their muskets in defiance. Colonel Locke could not, of course, charge without orders; and, indeed, it would have been most imprudent to do so, as the whole of the shoulder, a quarter of a mile wide, and six or seven hundred yards to the fort of Magdala, were covered with the little huts, behind and in which any number of men might be concealed. Colonel Locke then threw-out a few of his men as skirmishers. The horsemen continued to gallop about, sometimes approaching to within three hundred yards, sometimes dashing across the plateau as if they meditated a descent into the valley far below by one of the winding paths which led down. To prevent this, Colonel Locke called to five or six soldiers of the 33d, and two or three artillerymen, who had somehow got separated from their corps and had come down towards us, to take up a position to command the path, and to open fire if the horsemen attempted to go down it.

At the same time we saw upon the top of Salamgi, behind us, a company of the 33d, who had gone up there to plant the colours. Colonel Locke had the advance blown, and signalled to them to come down to command the opposite side of the shoulder, in case the horsemen might attempt to descend into the valley by any path which might exist upon that side. The horsemen again moved in and discharged their rifles at us; and the cavalry keeping their places, our little party of 33d answered with their Sniders. As they did so, they moved forward, and in another hundred yards we came upon no less than twenty cannon, which Theodore had, no doubt, intended to have moved across into Magdala, but had had no time to accomplish. These were, of course, taken possession of; and, as an officer remarked with a laugh to me, it is probably the first time that twenty guns were ever captured in the face of an enemy by six men of the line, two artillerymen, three or four officers, and the press. In the tumbrils of the guns were their ammunition; and Lieutenant Nolan, of the Artillery, assisted by two artillerymen, Captain Speedy, and the civilians, at once proceeded to load them, and opened fire with ball upon the foot-men, a hundred or so of whom we could now see clustered at the foot of the road up to Magdala; the 33d men keeping up a fire upon the horsemen and a few foot-men running over the plains, and who occasionally answered; and the company of the 33d, who had now come down nearly to the foot of the slope behind us, also opening fire. It was one of the funniest scenes I ever saw. There was Magdala at 500 yards' distance, with its garrison keeping up a scattered fire at us, none of the bullets, however, reaching so far; there were a few shots from behind the little haycock huts; there was Theodore himself galloping about with half a dozen of his chiefs—picturesque figures in their bright-coloured robes; and there was our little party waging a war upon them, with not another soldier in sight, or, indeed, within half a mile of us. This lasted for ten minutes or so; and then an officer rode up to order the infantry to retire into the slope, but to keep the guns under their fire. The cavalry had previously been ordered to retire. In another quarter of an hour Penn's battery came down to us and opened fire, and the steel shells soon drove the enemy up the road into the fortress. For a quarter of an hour they continued their fire; and, when they had once got the range, every shell burst close to the gateway, through which the road passed. Then there came an order to cease firing; and Murray's guns, which had taken up their position upon the top of Salamgi, Twiss's battery more to the right, and the Naval Rocket Brigade, took up the fire. For nearly two hours, with occasional intervals, these guns and Twiss's battery kept up their fire. While this was going on, we discovered in a small tent, a hundred yards or so in our front, the Frenchman Bardel, who is sick with a fever, and was at once carried to the rear. We had, too, plenty of time to examine the guns. Some were of English, some of Indian manufacture: all were of brass, and varied in size from a fourteen-pounder downwards. There were two or three small mortars among them. This was evidently the arsenal, for here were tools and instruments of all descriptions—files, hammers, anvils, &c. There were bags of charcoal and a forge; and here were many hundreds of balls, varying in size from grape-shot to immense stone balls for the giant mortar, which shattered to pieces the other day at the first attempt to fire it.

At this time we made a discovery which quite destroyed the feeling of pity which the gallantry of Theodore in exposing himself to our fire had excited. The Beloochees had joined us, and were posted near the edge of a precipice to our right. Their attention being attracted by an overpowering stench, they looked over the edge of the rock; and there, fifty feet below, was one of the most horrifying sights which was ever beheld: there, in a great pile, lay the bodies of the three hundred and fifty prisoners whom Theodore had murdered last Thursday, and whom he had then thrown over the edge of the precipice. There they lay—men, women, and little children—

in a putrefying mass. It was a most ghastly sight, and recalled to our minds the horrible cruelty of the tyrant, and quite destroyed the effect which his bravery had produced.

At last, at half-past three, the troops came down and took their places; and at a quarter to four the whole of the guns and rockets opened a tremendous fire to cover the advance; and the 33d, preceded by a small band of Engineers and Sappers under Major Pritchard, and followed by the 45th, advanced to the assault, the 4th and the rest of the first brigade retaining their places as a reserve. When within three hundred yards of the rock, the 33d formed line and opened fire at the gateway and high hedge which bordered the summit of the precipice—the most tremendous fire I ever heard. Even the thunder—which was, as during the fight of Good Friday, roaring overhead—was lost in the roar of the seven hundred Snider rifles, and which was re-echoed by the rocks in their front. Under cover of this tremendous fire the Engineers and the leading company advanced up the path. When they were half-way up, the troops ceased firing, and the storming-party scrambled up at a run. All this time answering flashes had come back from a high wall which extended for some feet at the side of the gateway, and from behind the houses and rocks near it. When the Engineers, headed by Major Pritchard, reached the gateway, several shots were fired through loopholes in the wall, and two or three men staggered back wounded, Major Pritchard himself receiving two very slight flesh-wounds in the arm. The men immediately put their rifles through the holes, and kept up a constant fire, so as to clear-away their enemies from behind it.

Then there was a pause, which for a time no one understood; but at last a soldier forced his way down the crowded path with the astounding intelligence that the Engineers, who had headed the storming-party for the purpose of blowing the gate in, had actually forgotten to take any powder with them! Neither had they crowbars, axes, or scaling-ladders. General Staveley at once despatched an officer to bring up powder from the artillery-wagons.

The 45th opened fire to prevent the enemy's skirmishers doing damage; and a few pioneers of the 45th were sent up with axes to force open the gate. In the mean time, however, the men of the 33d, upon the road leading up to the gate, discovered a spot half-way up, by which they were able to scramble up to the left, and, getting through the hedge, they quickly cleared away the defenders of the gate. A large portion of the regiment entered at this spot, the gate not being fairly opened for a quarter of an hour after the storming-party arrived at it; for when it was broken down, it was found that the gate-house was filled with very large stones; and therefore, had powder been at hand, and the gate been blown in, a considerable time must have elapsed before the party could have entered. Behind the gateway were a cluster of huts, many of whose inhabitants still remained in them in spite of the heavy fire which had for two hours been kept up. Behind them was a natural scarp of twenty-five or thirty feet high, with a flight of steps wide enough only for a single man to ascend at a time. At the top of this was another gate, which had been blown open by the rifles of the 33d. I entered with the rear of the regiment; but all was by that time over. By the first gateway were six or seven bodies, and two or three men by the second. Beyond this was the level plateau, thickly scattered with the native huts of their ordinary construction—not the haycock-fabrics which had covered the other hills and plateau. At a hundred yards from the gate lay the body of Theodore himself, pierced with three balls, one of which, it is said, he fired with his own hand. He was of middle height and very thin, and the expression of his face in death was mild rather than the reverse. He had thrown-off the rich robe in which he had ridden over the plain, and was in an ordinary chief's red-and-white cloth.

The fighting was now over. A hundred men or so had escaped down a path upon the other side of the fortress, and the rest of the defenders had fled into their houses, and emerged as peaceable inhabitants without their weapons. Nothing could be more admirable than the behaviour of the 33d. I did not see a single instance of a man either of this or of the regiment which followed attempting to take a single ornament or other article from the person of any of the natives. These latter thronged out of their houses, bearing their household goods, and salaaming to the ground, as they made their way towards the gate of the fort. I went into several of the abandoned huts; they contained nothing but rubbish. A few goats and cattle stood in the enclosures, and bags of grain were in plenty. The poor people had been well content to escape with their lives, and with what they could carry away on their own shoulders and those of their pack-animals.

I presently met an affecting procession. These were the native prisoners. Laden with heavy feet-chains were at least a hundred poor wretches who had lingered for years in the tyrant's clutches. Many of them were unable to walk, and were carried along by their friends. We pitied them vastly more than we have done the prisoners sent in to us, who, with commodious tents, numbers of servants, and plentiful supplies of money and food, have had a far better time of it than these poor wretches of natives. They endeavoured in every way to express their joy and thankfulness. They bent to the ground, they cried, they clapped their hands; and the women—at least such as were not chained—danced, and set-up their shrill cry of welcome. Very kind were the soldiers to them, and not a few gave-up their search for odd articles of plunder to set-to with hammer and chisel to remove their chains. There were some hundreds of huts upon the flat plateau, but not one of them bore any signs of the bombardment; and fortunately the great distance at which the guns were fired had saved the inhabitants from the injury which they must otherwise have suffered from the needless bombardment. A few people had been wounded when the 33d had first entered, but their number was very small; and it seems incredible that out of so large a population only some ten or fifteen, and these the defenders of the gate, were killed.

The huts were all of the same size and description—stone walls with conical roofs, and no light except that which entered by the door. The King himself lived in a tent. His wife, or I should rather say wives, lived in a house precisely similar in shape, but larger than the other tents. One or two of these poor women were among the wounded, having rushed wildly about the place before the firing ceased, and being struck by stray bullets. It is extremely satisfactory to know that no lives, with the exception of those of the actual fighting-men, were sacrificed.

We have no killed, but have ten or fifteen wounded, most of them very slightly. One of the Punjaubees who was wounded in the fight three days before has since died. The loot obtained by the soldiers was generally of the most trifling description. Pieces of the hangings of the King's tent, bits of tawdry brocade, and such-like, are the general total. A very few got some gold crosses, and other more valuable articles. A general order has been issued, ordering all valuable spoil to be returned; but I do not imagine that the amount returned will be large. All the spoil taken, with the arms, &c., will be sold by auction in a day or two, and the result at once divided. It is known that considerable sums in dollars and gold have been buried, and a search is being instituted for them, but without, I imagine, much chance of success. In my wanderings I came upon a large hut, which turned out to be the royal cellar. Here the natives were serving-out "tedge"—which I have already described as a drink resembling small-beer and lemonade mixed, with a very strong musty flavour—to soldiers. There were at least a hundred large jars filled with the liquid, which the soldiers call beer, and which, thirsty as the men were, was very refreshing. It was now nearly six o'clock, and the soldiers had had nothing to eat or drink since early morning. I should say that every soldier in the force supped that night upon fowl. Their value here, except when offered to us for sale, is merely nominal, and none of the people took the trouble to take them away; consequently they were running about in hundreds, and gave rise to many animated chases.

Magdala itself is about half a mile long by a quarter of a mile wide, its narrow end joining the shoulder to Salamgi, and as this end is rather narrow, it touches the shoulder only for about fifty or sixty yards. At this point I should say that the plateau of the fortress is 200 feet above the shoulder. Upon its other side it would be 1200 feet sheer down. The 33d planted their colours upon the highest spot, and General Napier when he entered addressed a few words to the men, saying, "that they had made the attack in gallant style." Of course, as it turned out, the danger was slight; but this does not detract from the way in which the regiment went up to the assault; as, for anything they could tell, there might have been hundreds of men concealed in the huts immediately behind the gate.

The two most valuable articles of booty which were known to have been obtained were purchased by Mr. Holmes, of the British Museum, for the nation, of the soldiers by whom they were taken. The one was, one of the royal shields of Abyssinia, one of which I described as having been borne by Gobayze's uncle when he visited our camp. The other is a gold chalice, probably four or five centuries old. It has the inscription in Amharic, of which the following is the translation: "The chalice of King Adam-Squad, called Gazor, the son of Queen Brhan, Moquera. Presented to Kwoskwan Sanctuary (Gondar). May my body and soul be purified! Weight 25 wohkits of pure gold, and value 500 dollars. Made by Waldo Giergis." The name of the maker would seem to testify that he was either the son of an Italian, or an Italian who had adopted an Abyssinian first name. As these acquisitions are made for the nation, Sir Robert has decided that they are not to be given up. He has also directed that Mr. Holmes may select such other articles as may be suited to the Museum before the auction takes place.

The second brigade passed the night in Magdala, and still remain there; the first brigade returned to camp, which they did not reach until a very late hour. The aspect of the hill of Salamgi, and of the plains below it, was very striking, as I rode through it at night. The great emigrant population had encamped there, and their innumerable fires had a very pretty effect. During the night a very scandalous act of theft and sacrilege took place. The coffin of the late Abuna, a high priest, was broken open; his body was torn almost to pieces, and a cross, set with precious stones of the value of some thousands of pounds, was stolen. It is quite certain that this act was not perpetrated by our soldiers, as they of course knew nothing either of the Abuna or his cross. Suspicion generally points to some of the late prisoners, who knew, what was, it appears, a matter of notoriety, that the Abuna had purchased this extremely valuable ornament to be buried with it.

The expedition is now at an end. Its objects are most successfully attained, and the interest and excitement are over. We have now only our long and weary march back again. The day upon which we turn our faces homeward is not yet settled; the 20th is at present named. We shall probably halt at Dalanta for a day or two, and there it is said that Gobayze will visit the Chief, and that we shall have a grand parade.

The opinion which the natives will entertain of us upon our homeward march will be singularly different from those with which they regarded us upon our advance. Then they looked upon us as mere traders, prepared to buy, but incompetent to fight for our countrymen in chains; now they will regard us as the conquerors of the hitherto invincible Theodore, and as braves, therefore, of the most distinguished order.

Before Magdala, April 16th.

My letter describing the fall of Magdala was only written two days ago, and I have but few scraps of intelligence to add. These, however, I shall now send, in hopes that they may arrive by the same mail which conveyed my last. We have had only two excitements here; the one the perquisition—indeed, by the way it was conducted, I may call it inquisition—for loot; the other, the constant plunder by those arrant thieves, the Gallas. The first orders with respect to plunder were reasonable and sensible enough. They were, that all articles of intrinsic value, or which might be nationally interesting, were to be given up. This no one objected to. It was only fair that all booty collected of any value should be fairly divided for the benefit of the force in general. The next order, however, was simply ridiculous, and caused naturally a good deal of grumbling. It was ordered that every article taken, of whatever value or description, should be returned. Now, the men had possessed themselves of all sorts of small mementoes of the capture of Magdala. Spears and glass beads, books and scraps of dresses, empty gourds and powder-horns, all sorts of little objects in fact, the united intrinsic value of which would not be twenty dollars, but which were valuable mementoes to the three or four thousand men who had picked them up—all these were now to be given up; and so strict was the search, that I saw even the men's havresacks examined to see that they had hidden nothing. The pile of objects collected was of the most miscellaneous description, and looked like the contents of a pawnbroker's shop in the neighbourhood of Whitechapel.

These things were valuable to the men, as having been collected by them in Magdala; but they will fetch nothing whatever when sold. It is a very great pity that the original order was not adhered to, as the men would have all acquiesced cheerfully enough in the summons that articles of intrinsic value should be delivered up. As it is, the whole value of the plunder will not exceed ten thousand dollars in value, and, indeed, I question if it will approach that sum. The principal articles of value, with the exception of some crosses, are of English manufacture, double-barrelled guns, &c.; in fact, the presents which the English Government sent out by Rassam. A medical court have examined Theodore's body, and have come to the conclusion that he died by his own hand. Mr. Holmes, of the British Museum, has taken an exceedingly good likeness of the dead monarch; indeed, I do not know that I ever saw a more striking resemblance. The Engineers have also taken a photograph of him.

The Gallas have been extremely troublesome for the last three days. The unfortunate fugitives from Magdala are encamped at the foot of the hill, and are gradually moving-off to their respective homes. Round their camp, and round the unfortunates upon their march, the Gallas swarm in great numbers, robbing, driving-off their cattle and donkeys, carrying-off their women and children into captivity, and wounding, and sometimes killing, all who oppose them. Sometimes, too, they attempt to rob our mules and stores. We do all we can to protect the defenceless people, and detachments are constantly going out to drive the robbers off. The infantry, the rocket-train, and the guns have several times had to fire, and several of the plunderers have been killed. Eighteen are at present prisoners in our camp, some of whom were concerned in the murder of one of the Abyssinians. The night before last they made an attack upon some of the mules with the baggage of the 33d, near Magdala, but were beaten off with the loss of several men. Now that we have got Magdala, our difficulty is to dispose of it, and it is this only which is keeping us waiting here. Magdala is, as I have already said, an almost impregnable place, even in the hands of these savages. North and west of them the people are Christians. Whether their Christianity, or the Christianity of any savage people, does them any good whatever, or makes them the least more moral or better than their neighbours, it is needless now to inquire. At any rate they are a settled people, living by the culture of their land. To the east of these agricultural people are the Gallas, nomadic Mussulmans, whose hand is against every man's, who live by robbery and violence, and who are slavers and man-stealers of the worst kind. Against them Magdala stands as a bulwark. It is on the road between their country and Abyssinia proper, and the garrison can always fall upon their rear in case of an attempted foray. It was therefore desirable that it should be intrusted to some power strong enough to hold in check this nation of robbers. Theodore's son, who, with his wives, has fallen into our hands, is too young to be thought of, and there remains only Gobayze, and his rival Menilek. Menilek in the early days of the expedition was heard a good deal of. General Merewether was always writing about him and his army of forty thousand men, and his great friendship; but, like most of the gallant general's promised lands, Menilek's assistance turned out a myth, and we have never heard of him since we came within a hundred miles of Magdala. Gobayze, on the other hand, has at any rate turned out to be a real personage. He has never, it is true, done the slightest thing to assist us in any way; still his uncle paid us a visit, and nearly got shot, so that we may presume that this uncle really has a nephew called Gobayze. Gobayze has been written to, to come and take possession of Magdala, but he has not arrived; but this morning his uncle has again appeared upon the scene, and, I understand, declines, in the name of his relative, to have anything to say to Magdala. Magdala, in fact, except as a stronghold to retreat to as a last resource, is absolutely valueless. It is too far removed from the main portion of Abyssinia to be of any strategical importance, and it would require a couple of thousand men to garrison it, and who would have to be supplied with provisions from a considerable distance. Gobayze wants all his available force for the struggle he will be engaged in with Menilek as soon as we leave the country, and he does not at all care about detaching two thousand men to an extreme corner of his dominions, where they could in no way affect the issue of the war. He may change his mind; but if he should not do so, we shall in a couple of days start upon our backward course, and abandon Magdala to the first comer. The Abyssinians complain bitterly of our mode of fighting. With them an engagement is a species of duel. Both sides charge simultaneously, discharge their pieces, and retreat to load, repeating the manœuvre until one side or the other has had enough of it. They object, therefore, excessively to our continuous advance and fire, without any pause to reload. It is to this unseemly practice that they attribute their defeat.

The whole army are looking forward with the greatest eagerness for the order to retire. Existence here is not a pleasant one. The weather in the day is dry, hot, but not unpleasant; in the afternoon we have always heavy rains, and cold at night. Our variety of provisions is not great. We have plenty of meat, and little flour; no rum, no tea, no sugar, no vegetables. By the way, the commissariat actually managed to supply the extraordinarily liberal allowance of one dram of rum per man to the force on the day after the capture of Magdala. But our great want is water. We are literally without water. A mile and a half off is a limited quantity, but it is very limited indeed, and stinks abominably; so bad is it, that it is difficult to distinguish what one is drinking, even if one is fortunate enough to procure tea or coffee; and even of this there is not sufficient for drinking purposes alone, and a man enters another tent and asks as eagerly for a cup of water as if it were the choicest of drinks. Washing is altogether out of the question; and the animals have to be taken down to the muddy Bachelo, fifteen hundred feet below us, and six miles distant, for their daily draught. Decidedly the sooner we are out of this the better. At present the 18th is the happy day decided upon; and I earnestly hope that nothing will occur to postpone our departure. Some of the troops will certainly start to-day or to-morrow.

Antalo, May 1st.

There are few things of less interest than the closing chapter of a campaign. The excitement and anxiety, the success and triumph, are over; the curtain has fallen upon the play, and we have only to put on our wraps and go home. Even by the present date the telegraph has told England of the success with which the expedition has been crowned. When he has once read the details, the English reader will, after the first little burst of natural pride and satisfaction, sit himself down with a slight sigh to count the cost, and then endeavour, as far as possible, to forget the unpleasant subject. I feel that the heading of my letter, "The Abyssinian Expedition," will no longer be an attractive one. Epilogues are gone out of fashion, and are only retained as a relic of the past at the annual play of the Westminster boys. I should imagine that at the end of a modern play very few people would sit-out an epilogue; and in the same way, I anticipate that very few readers will care for hearing any more about the barren and mountainous country in which it has been our lot to sojourn for the last six months. I should imagine that they must be nearly as weary of the subject as we are ourselves. Never certainly in my experience have special correspondents had so hard or so ungrateful a task as that which has devolved upon us here. The country through which the army has marched has been barren and mountainous in the extreme. The actual events have been few and far between. There has been no opportunity for generalship or strategical movement. It has been one long, slow, monotonous march, accompanied with more or less hardship to all concerned. It has presented no points of comparison with the shifting scenes and exciting phases of a European campaign. It is only by its results, and by the remembrance of the hostile criticisms and lugubrious prophecies with which it was assailed in its early days, that we ourselves can judge of the difficulty of the task accomplished, and of the way in which the world will view it. It has to us been simply a monotony of hard work and hard living. Until the last week of our march we had no excitement whatever to enliven it; and, as far as the incidents of the campaign have been concerned, there has been but little to recompense the British taxpayer for his outlay. In other respects there is no doubt that, worthless as were the set of people as a whole in whose favour this costly expedition has been undertaken, the money has been well spent. In no other way, with so comparatively small an outlay, could Great Britain have recovered the prestige which years of peace had undoubtedly much impaired both in Europe and the East. England has shown that she can go to war really for an idea; that she can embark in a war so difficult, hazardous, and costly, that no other European Power would have undertaken it under similar circumstances, and this, without the smallest idea of material advantage to herself. England had, *pace* our French critics, no possible benefit to derive from the conquest or occupation of Abyssinia. With Aden and Perim in our power, the Red Sea is virtually an English lake, and the possession of Abyssinia, hundreds of miles from the port of Annesley Bay, which in itself is quite out of the track of vessels between Suez and Aden, would be a source of weakness rather than of additional strength. The war was undertaken purely from a generous national impulse, aggravated by the feeling that the captivity of our unfortunate countrymen was due to no fault of their own, but attributable to the gross blundering of the men to whom the foreign affairs of the nation were unfortunately intrusted. Our success has been astonishing even to ourselves, and has been providentially accomplished in the face of blunders and mistakes which would have ruined any other expedition.

In my last letter I stated that Gobayze had declined to accept the charge of Magdala. It was consequently determined to burn it; and on the 18th ultimo fire was applied, and in a very short time the whole of the thatched tents were in a blaze. The wind was blowing freshly at the time, and in a few minutes the whole of the plateau of Magdala was covered with a fierce blaze, which told to the surrounding country for miles that the last act of atonement was being inflicted. Had the scene taken place at night, it would have been grand in the extreme; but even in broad day the effect of the sheet of flame, unclouded as it was by smoke—for the dry roofs burned like tinder—was very fine. Imagine a gigantic farmyard of three-quarters of a mile long by nearly half a mile wide, and containing above 300 hayricks, in a blaze; and the effect of burning Magdala may be readily conceived. Simultaneously with the conflagration the gates were blown up and the pieces of ordnance burst; and then the troops who had been told-off for the task retired from the scene of their signal success to join their comrades, and march the next day for the sea-shore. I started for Dalanta the day before the departure of the troops, and was very glad that I did so, as I thereby avoided the tremendous confusion of the baggage, part of which was nearly thirty hours upon the road, and witnessed one of the most extraordinary scenes I ever beheld. At the Bachelo river I came upon the van of the principal column of the fugitives from Magdala, who had encamped upon the previous night by the stream. Here the number of empty gourds, cooking-vessels, and rubbish of all kinds, showed that, scanty as their baggage was, it was already too great for their means of transport. A mile farther I came upon their rear. As far as the eye could reach up the winding path to the summit of the gorge, they swarmed in a thick gray multitude. Thirty thousand human beings, men, women, and children, besides innumerable animals of all kinds. Never, probably, since the great Exodus from Egypt, was so strange a sight witnessed. All were laden; for once, the men had to share the labours of their wives and families; and indeed I may say that the males of this portion of Abyssinia are less lazy, and more willing to bear their share of the family-labours, than were the men of Tigre, who, as I before mentioned, never condescend to assist their wives in any way. The men carried bags of grain—which, by the way, the men always carry on one shoulder, and not upon their backs as the women do; the women were similarly burdened, and in addition had gourds of water and ghee, with a child or two clinging round their necks. The children, too, carried their share of the household goods, all but the very little ones; and these, little, naked, pot-bellied things, trotted along holding by their mothers' skirts. A few, who in the crowd and confusion had lost their friends, sat down and cried pitifully; but as a general thing they kept steadily up the steep ascent, which was trying enough to men, to say nothing of these poor little mites. Although an involuntary exodus, it did not appear to me to cause any pain or regret to anyone. Neither upon this occasion nor upon the day when they quitted Magdala did I see a tear shed, or witness any demonstrations of grief. Now, the Abyssinians are an extremely demonstrative people, and weep and wail copiously and obstreperously over the smallest fancied grievance; consequently, I cannot but think that the great proportion of the people were glad to leave Magdala, and to return to their respective countries. All pressed steadily forward; there was no halting, no delay, scarce a pause to take breath; for on their rear and flank, and sometimes in their very midst, were the robber Gallas plundering all whom they came across. I spoke of the Gallas in my last. Since that time they have become even more bold and troublesome, and not a few have fallen in skirmishes with our troops. Soon after we had joined the body of fugitives, I heard screams and cries in front, and riding-in at a gallop with my friend, we came upon a number of natives in a state of great excitement, the women crying and wringing their hands. They pointed to a ravine, and made us understand that the Gallas were there. Riding up to it, we came upon a party of eight or ten men with spears and shields driving off a couple of dozen oxen they had just stolen. Before they could recover from their surprise we were in their midst, and our revolvers soon sent them flying up the hill with two or three of their number wounded. We drove back the cattle, and were received with acclamations by the unfortunate but miserably cowardly natives, who could only with stones have kept their assailants at a distance, had they had the pluck of so many sheep. A few hundred yards further on we came upon another party of Gallas actively engaged in looting; and at the sight of us with our rifles and revolvers in hand, most of them fled; but we captured two of the robbers, who saw that throwing themselves upon their faces was the only chance of escape from being shot. We tied their hands behind them, and handed them over to our syces, who drove them before them until the end of the day, when we delivered them over to Colonel Graves of the 3d Cavalry, who was in command at Dalanta, and had the satisfaction of seeing them get two dozen lashes each, well laid on. After this skirmish, seeing numbers of Gallas hanging about, we constituted ourselves a sort of rearguard to the native column, and my double-barrelled rifle soon drove them to a distance, the long range at which it sent balls into groups waiting for an opportunity of attack evidently astonishing them greatly, and causing them to scatter in the greatest haste. I think it a question whether the Gallas or the Abyssinians are the greatest cowards. Two or three officers coming up later upon the same day had skirmishes with them, and three or four of the Gallas were killed. The natives encamped upon the plains of Dalanta, their black blanket-tents extending over a great extent of ground. The next day they crossed the Djedda, and after mounting to the table-land beyond, were safe from the attacks of the Gallas, and were able to pursue their way to Gondar, and the other places to which they belonged, in quiet.

On the 20th the whole of the troops were at Dalanta, and a grand parade took place. The troops marched past, and were then formed into hollow square, and the following order of the day was read to them:

"Soldiers of the Army of Abyssinia,

"The Queen and the people of England intrusted to you a very arduous and difficult expedition—to release our countrymen from a long and painful captivity, and to vindicate the honour of our country, which had been outraged by Theodore, King of Abyssinia.

"I congratulate you, with all my heart, for the noble way in which you have fulfilled the commands of our Sovereign. You have crossed many steep and precipitous ranges of mountains, more than ten thousand feet in altitude, where your supplies could not keep pace with you. When you arrived within reach of your enemy, though with scanty food, and some of you for many hours without food or water, in four days you have passed the formidable chasm of Bachelo and defeated the army of Theodore, which poured down upon you from their lofty fortress in full confidence of victory. A host of many thousands have laid down their arms at your feet.

"You have captured and destroyed upwards of thirty pieces of artillery, many of great weight and efficiency, with ample stores of ammunition. You have stormed the almost-inaccessible fortress of Magdala, defended by Theodore with the desperate remnant of his chiefs and followers. After you forced the entrance, Theodore, who never showed mercy, distrusted the offers of mercy which had been held out to him, and died by his own hands. You have released not only the British captives, but those of other friendly nations. You have unloosed the chains of more than ninety of the principal chiefs of the Abyssinians.

"Magdala, on which so many victims have been slaughtered, has been committed to the flames, and remains only a scorched rock.

"Our complete and rapid success is due—first, to the mercy of God, whose hand I feel assured has been over us in a just cause. Secondly, to the high spirit with which you have been inspired. Indian soldiers have forgotten their prejudices of race and creed to keep pace with their European comrades.

"Never has an army entered on a war with more honourable feelings than yours; this has carried you through many fatigues and difficulties. You have been only eager for the moment when you could close with your enemy. The remembrance of your privations will pass away quickly, but your gallant exploit will live in history. The Queen and the people of England will appreciate your services. On my part, as your commander, I thank you for your devotion to your duty, and the good discipline you have maintained; not a single complaint has been made against a soldier of fields injured or villages wilfully molested, in property or person.

"We must not forget what we owe to our comrades who have been labouring for us in the sultry climate of Zulla and the Pass of Koomaylo, or in the monotony of the posts which maintained our communications; each and all would have given all they possessed to be with us, and they deserve our gratitude.

"I shall watch over your safety to the moment of your embarkation, and to the end of my life remember with pride that I have commanded you.

(Signed) R. Napier, Lieut.-general,
Commander-in-chief.

(Signed) M. Dillon, Lieut.-colonel,
Military Secretary."

The proclamation, if a little grandiose in style, is true to the letter. The men have endured privation and toil such as seldom falls to a soldier's lot, with a good feeling and cheerfulness which has been literally beyond praise. The only occasions throughout this expedition upon which I have heard grumbling has been when the troops have been told by the quartermaster's department that they were to march a certain distance, and when the march turned out to be half as far again. But this grumbling was not against the distance or the toil, great as both were; it was against the incapacity which had inflicted an unnecessary toil upon them. At any necessary privation, at picket-duty in wet clothes after a hard day's march, at hunger and thirst, fatigue-duty, wet and cold, I never heard them grumble; and I feel assured that, as the general order says, the people of England will appreciate their toils and services. In one point at least they may be to some extent rewarded. Their pay here is exactly the same as they would have drawn in India; they have no field or other extra allowance whatever. Had the war taken place in India, the army would, most unquestionably, be granted a year's "batta," as a reward for their suffering and toil. In the present case the English Government holds the purse-strings, but I trust that this well-earned extra pay will be granted. It would form a comparatively small item in the expenses of the expedition, and the boon would be an act of graceful recognition on the part of the nation to the men who have borne its flag so successfully under the most arduous and trying circumstances.

After the reading of the general order, Sir Robert Napier handed over the rescued prisoners to the representatives of the Governments to which they belonged; and the general feeling of every one was, that we wished these officers joy of them, for a more unpromising-looking set could hardly be found anywhere else outside the walls of a prison. Sir Robert Napier, in handing these prisoners over, thanked the foreign officers for having accompanied the expedition, and for having shared in its toils and hardships. The ceremony over, the last act of the Magdala drama may be considered to have terminated, and the army on the next day marched for the coast, the second brigade leading, and the first following a day in their rear. The interest of the campaign being now over, I determined to come on at full speed, instead of travelling at the necessary slow pace of the army with all its encumbrances of material and baggage. It is, too, vastly more pleasant to travel alone, the journeys are performed in two-thirds of the time, and without the dust, noise, and endless delays which take place in the baggage-train. At the end of the journey the change is still more advantageous: one selects the site for one's tent near the little commissariat stations, but far enough off to be quiet; and here, free from the neighing and fighting of horses and mules, the challenge of the sentries, the chattering of the native troops, who frequently talk until past midnight, and the incessant noise of coughing and groaning, and other unpleasant noises in which a Hindoo delights when he is not quite well, we pass the night in tranquillity. The hyenas and jackals are, it is true, a little troublesome, and howl and cry incessantly about the canvas of our tent; but the noise of a hyena is as music compared to the coughing and groaning of a sick Hindoo; and so we do not grumble. We have a party of four, making, with our ten servants, syces, and mule-drivers, a pretty strong party; no undesirable thing, as the country is extremely disturbed all the way down. Convoys are constantly attacked, and the muleteers murdered; indeed, scarce a day passes without an outrage of this kind. It is, perhaps, worst between Lât and Atzala; but beyond Antalo, and down even in the Sooro Pass, murders are almost daily events. The killing is not all on one side, for numbers of the natives have been shot by the guards of the convoys which they have attacked. The evil increases every day, and the Commander-in-chief has just issued a proclamation to the natives, which is to be translated into Amharic and circulated through the country, warning the people that the scouts have orders to fire upon any armed party they may meet, who do not, upon being called upon to do so, at once retire and leave the path clear. The fact is, that, except at this point, we have not enough troops in the country to furnish guards of sufficient strength to protect the convoys. A great many very wise people have talked about our force being too large. At the present moment it is actually insufficient for our needs, insufficient to protect our convoys even against the comparatively few robbers and brigands who now infest the line. A convoy of a thousand animals extends over a very long tract of country; three or four miles at the least. What can a dozen or so guards do to protect it? An instance occurred to-day within three miles of this place. A convoy of a thousand camels were coming along; the guards were scattered over its length; and a man in the middle of the convoy was murdered by three or four Abyssinians, whom the soldiers, who had gone on, had noticed sitting quietly on some rocks at a few yards from the line of march. The soldiers behind heard a cry, and rode up, only in time to find the muleteer lying dead, and his murderers escaped. When the robbers are in force, and attempt to plunder openly, they are invariably beaten.

The other day Lieutenant Holt was in command of a train with treasure for Ashangi, having a guard of ten Sepoys. He was attacked by a band of fifty or sixty men, who came up twice to the assault, but were driven off, leaving three of their number dead upon the ground. These cases are not exceptional; they are of daily occurrence, and are rapidly upon the increase. It is greatly to be regretted; but it was to be foreseen from the course of conduct pursued in the first instance towards men caught robbing in the Sooro Pass. I predicted at the time of my first visit to Senafe, early in December last, what must be the inevitable result of the course pursued to the men caught pillaging. They were kept in the guard-house for a day or two, fed better than they had ever before been in their lives, and then dismissed to steal again, and to encourage their companions in stealing, believing that we were too weak and too pusillanimous to dare to punish them. And so it has been ever since. In the eyes of our political officers a native could do no harm. Any punishment which has been inflicted upon them has been given by regimental officers, or officers of the transport-train, who have caught them robbing. And even this moderate quota of justice was rendered at the peril of the judges. Lieutenant Story, 26th regiment, a most energetic officer of the transport-train—to give one example out of a score—found that at one of the stations the natives who were anxious to come in to sell grass and grain were driven away by two chiefs, who openly beat and ill-treated those who persisted in endeavouring to sell to us. The result was, that the natives kept away, and only a few ventured in at night to sell their stores. Lieutenant Story found that his mules were starving, and very properly caught the two chiefs, and gave them half-a-dozen each. The chiefs reported the case; the mild "politicals" as usual had their way; and Lieutenant Story was summarily removed from the transport-train.

I mentioned in a former letter the case of the mule-driver who wrested the musket from a man who was attempting to rob the mules, and shot him with his own weapon, and who was rewarded for his gallantry by having a dozen lashes. I could fill a column with similar instances. Had we had the good fortune to have had a man of decision and energy as our political officer instead of Colonel Merewether, all this would have been avoided.

The first man caught with arms in his hands attacking and plundering our convoys should have been tried and shot; it is what he would have received at the hands of the native chiefs; and it would have put a stop to the brigandage. Instead of which, the policy—if such pottering can be termed policy—has been to encourage them, by every means in our power, to plunder our convoys and murder our drivers and men. A stern policy with savages is, in the end, infinitely the more merciful one. A couple of lives at first would have saved fifty, which have already on both sides been sacrificed, and a hundred more, which will be probably lost before we are out of the country. Sir R. Napier, now that he has taken the reins into his own hands, is fully alive to the error that has been committed, and to the absolute necessity of showing no more leniency to the robber-bands which begin to swarm around us. It is most unfortunate that the early stages of our intercourse with the natives had not been intrusted to a man of firmness and sound sense. With the repeated caution of the officers at the various stations in our ears, and with the accounts we received at almost every halting-place of some attack and murder in the neighbourhood within a day or two of our arrival, it may be imagined that we took every precaution. Our servants were all armed with spears, our mules were kept in close file, and two of us rode in front, two in the rear of our party, with our rifles cocked, and our revolvers ready to hand. As we anticipated, we were not attacked; for, as a general rule, the cowardly robbers, however numerous, will not attack when they see a prospect of a stout resistance. Our precautions were not, however, in vain; for we knew that at least in one case we should have been attacked had we not been so palpably upon our guard. On the brow of the hill above Atzala we passed without seeing a single native; but looking back after we had gone three or four hundred yards, we saw a party of fifty or sixty men armed with spears and shields, get up from among some bushes and rocks by the roadside and make off. There is no doubt that, had we not been prepared, we should have been attacked, and probably murdered. For the remainder of our journey there is little danger. The looting, indeed, continues all down the line; but the country is open and bare, and the natives would never dream of attacking in the open.

I have very great regret in announcing the death from dysentery of Lieutenant Morgan, of the Royal Engineers. He died at the front, and the news of the sad event probably reached England by the last mail; but I did not hear of it at Antalo until after I had despatched my last letter. He was at the head of the signalling-department, and was one of the most energetic and unwearied of officers. I never, indeed, met a man more devoted to his work; and had he lived, he would have become most distinguished in his profession. Sir Robert Napier, who thoroughly appreciated his efforts, has issued the following general order: "The Commander-in-chief has received with great regret the report of the death of Lieutenant Morgan, R.E., in charge of the signallers of the 10th Company, R.E. Sir Robert Napier had constant opportunities of observing the unflagging zeal and energy of this young officer, and the cheerful alacrity with which he embraced every opportunity to render his special work useful to the forces. Lieutenant Morgan set a bright example to those under his command; and by his premature loss, owing to prolonged exposure and fatigue, her Majesty's service and the corps of Royal Engineers are deprived of a most promising officer."

Not often does it fall to the lot of a subaltern to win such high and well-merited praise from his commander-in-chief; but poor Morgan was one in a thousand. His death unquestionably was the result of his hard work and exposure. He was one of those to whom his duty, however severe, was a pleasure. Although he could have ridden, had he chosen to do so, he marched at the head of his little body of men, lightening their labours by some cheerful remark; and when arrived at camp, and when other men's work was over, he would perhaps be sent off to arrange for signalling orders to the brigade in the rear, a duty which would occupy the entire night. He would be off with a cheerful alacrity which I never saw ruffled. He was quiet and unaffected in manner, and was one of those men who are most liked by those who best know them. It is with sincere regret that I write this brief notice of his untimely death.

Respecting the country, I have little to tell that is not already known to English readers. After the tremendous gorges of the Djedda and Bachelo, which are now ascertained to be 3900 feet in depth, the hills upon this side of the Tacazze, which had appeared so formidable when we before crossed them, are mere trifles. The roads, too, were much better than when we went up, the second brigade and Sappers and Miners having done a good deal of work upon them to render them practicable for elephants. The rain which has fallen lately has done a good deal to brighten-up the country; not upon the bare hill-sides—there all is brown and burnt-up as before—but in the bottom of the valleys and upon the hill-sides, where streamlets have poured down during the rains, the bright green of the young grass affords a pleasant relief to the eye. The crops, too, look bright and well; and it is a curious circumstance, that here there appears to be no fixed time for harvest. It is no unusual thing to see three adjoining patches of cultivated land—the one having barley in full ear, the second having the crop only a few inches above the ground, and the third undergoing the operation of the plough.

The army is now about seven days in my rear, as I travel very much faster than they do. Every available mule is being sent up to meet them, to carry down stores and baggage; and there is rum and all other comforts for them at the principal stations upon their way. The native carriage is at work bringing down the spare supplies; and if there are but sufficient of them employed, the stores will soon cease to trouble us; for the natives are such arrant thieves, that between this and Atzala, only two days' march, bags of rice and flour which started weighing 75 lb. arrive weighing only 40 lb., 30 lb., and sometimes only 25 lb. The word Habesh, which is their own general name for the people of Abyssinia, means a mixture; and I can hardly imagine a worse mixture than it is, for they appear to have inherited all the vices and none of the virtues of the numerous races of whom they are composed.

Beyond this I need write no more; but I cannot close my journal of the Abyssinian expedition without expressing my gratitude for the very great and uniform kindness with which I have been treated by the Commander-in-chief, and by the greater portion of his staff. I would particularly mention Colonel Dillon, the Military Secretary; one of the most able and certainly the most popular officer upon the staff, and whose kindness and attention to us has been unbounded. He has been always ready to afford us any information in his power, and to assist us in all those little difficulties with which a civilian travelling with an army is unavoidably beset.

The Abyssinian expedition may now be said to be over, and has been a more perfect and extraordinary success than the most sanguine could have predicted. It would, in the face of the terrible forebodings which were launched when it was first set about, have seemed an almost impossibility that we could have journeyed here, defeated and almost annihilated Theodore's army, obtained the whole of the prisoners, stormed Magdala— incomparably the strongest fortress in the world—and killed Theodore, and returned before the rains, with the loss of only one man dead from his wounds, and two or three from sickness; a loss infinitely less than would have taken place in the ordinary course of nature among so large a body of men. And yet this apparent impossibility has been, by the special providence of God, achieved; for that He has specially blessed our efforts, it would be the height of scepticism to doubt. We have passed through fatigues and hardships which one would have thought must have told upon the strongest constitution. We have had wet day after day, with bitterly cold winds, and no change even of underclothing for a month; we have had no tobacco or stimulants to enable the system to resist this wet and cold; and yet the hospitals are empty, and the health of the troops perfect. We have defeated a large and hitherto invincible army, and taken the strongest fortress in the world, with the loss of one man. We have accomplished a march through a country of fabulous difficulties, destitute of roads and almost destitute of food, and with our difficulties of transport vastly aggravated by the untrustworthy reports of those sent on before, and by the consequent breakdown of our baggage-train, from disease, thirst, and overwork; and yet we shall leave the country before the rains.

Humanly, too much credit can scarcely be given to Sir Robert Napier. He has had to overcome innumerable difficulties, which I have from time to time alluded to; but he has met them all admirably. As is often the case with successful commanders, he is immensely popular. The extreme kindness and thoughtfulness of his manner to all make him greatly beloved, and I believe that the men would have done anything for him.

Upon the whole, England may well be proud of the campaign,—proud of her General, and of the gallant and hardy army, whose endurance and labour carried it out successfully. It has not numerically been a great campaign; but by our success under innumerable difficulties, England has gained a prestige which, putting aside the proper objects of the campaign, is cheaply attained at the cost, and which is the more gratifying inasmuch as that England, although she has always risen under difficulties, and has come triumphantly out of great wars, has yet notoriously failed in her "little wars."

Footnotes

1. It was not for some months after this date that the transport officers were allowed to move their camp to a more habitable spot.

2. This regimental arrangement was carried out during the latter part of the march to Magdala, and was found to answer extremely well.

3. My anticipations with regard to the railway were more than realised; for the last two miles of the railway to Koomaylo were not made at the termination of the expedition, and the portion which was completed was, without exception, the roughest, most shaky, and most dangerous piece of railway ever laid down. It is to be hoped that upon any future occasion a contractor will be employed instead of an engineer officer, who cannot have either the requisite knowledge or experience.